THE DISCARDED ONES

THE
DISCARDED ONES

A NOVEL BASED ON A TRUE STORY

JAMES TIPPER

A Waxlight Press Book

LOS ANGELES

Library of Congress Registration # TXu 1-806-561
ISBN-13: 978-0-9882433-0-9   ISBN-10: 0-98-824330-X

Text set in Constantia

To Tiffany

When I was an empty shell, you were the pearl.

Note from the author:

I am glad to say this book has reached you in a form that is consistent with its purpose. Allow me to explain: Usually by the time you, the reader, are holding this book in your hands, it will already have been overthought by many others besides me, all trying in turn to guess what you want as a reader and to alter the story accordingly. I don't blame them really. After all, it's a competitive world out there.

However, this story is a true one, and no matter how much some may want to err on the side of caution, no matter how great the temptation to add just a little more of this or have less of that, I feel that you would sense such meddling. Somehow you'd know it in your bones. I'd rather you know that you just read something that actually happened, faithfully recreated to unfold just like it would as if *you* were the one being thrown to the wolves. In the end, I trust you will sense the authenticity and the fact that no unnecessary embellishment took place; and that, dear reader, is the very thing that will get under your skin long after you are done reading this book.

After all, I consider this to be a horror novel regardless of how it is eventually marketed. No, there are no axe murderers. There is no blood. Sometimes, the things that haunt us the most are simply the things that we can never forget, or never forgive. For me, the first real horror I ever experienced in my life was being utterly helpless and alone in the world.

The hero of this book is a teenager. There are some who worry that you may not relate to a young hero with such fears because you may be older and beyond that. If that's the case, then you are far better off than I am. We have *all* been discarded and we may be so again-usually by those we least suspect. Until then, as long as we still have faith that we are still capable of great acts of courage from time to time, there is nothing to do but stay on this dark and winding road, gripping the hands of those who bless us by traveling at our sides.

Thank you for coming along,

James Tipper
Los Angeles, CA
October, 2011

You may tie my hands with chains and my feet with shackles,
and put me in the dark prison,
but you shall not enslave my thinking,
for it is free, like the breeze in the spacious sky.

- KHALIL GIBRAN

Prologue

"You're not our father!" Charlie screams at his bedroom door.

As soon as he says the words, he wishes he hadn't. He was inviting the devil back into his sanctuary. The door had already been slammed shut and he was safely on the other side, in the dark.

Leave it alone, warns his mind. It's suicide.

Still, something inside him, something he cannot control roils in defiance, demanding release. More words gather in his mouth, pushing on his clenched teeth with the pressure of a fire hose.

"I hate you!" he screams again.

He cocks a fist and slams it into his bedroom door. The thin wood of the hollow-core collapses and swallows his hand. The poster of Farrah Fawcett on the back of the door humors him with a wide grin, the pearl of her teeth barely visible in the gloom, only now there is a gaping wound beneath her breasts. Charlie stares in disbelief at the hole in her belly. He removes his trembling fist from the door, his knuckles flecked with paint. He flexes his fingers and stares at them. He has gone too far. Again.

Now, footsteps are pounding up the stairs and they are coming fast. Charlie steps away from the door. His breath chugs through his hot lungs, blood pulses through his neck. He snaps shut his open mouth and holds his breath

Like a backdraft explosion the bedroom door slams open. The jaundiced, overhead bulb in the hall lights his stepfather from behind with a halo of pale fire.

"What the hell is your problem," says Kurt.

Charlie winces, but the silhouette only stands in the doorway, stands leaning on the jam, motionless. There is something at the end of Kurt's limp arm, undoubtedly a beer bottle. Any moment now the bottle will fly at Charlie's head, he is sure of it. Any moment now...

Charlie sucks in a shuddering breath. The air thickens to hot syrup and time slows. Neither man nor boy move. Charlie's eyes twitch wildly in their sockets, watching the shadow man, waiting. He hears his little brother whimpering in the adjoining bedroom, through the thin wall.

Charlie finds the breath to speak: "Leave my brother alone."

To his ears, his voice sounds far away, like a stranger's voice, weird and thin. He tries to control the rage and fear twisting his face, but he cannot. He tries to stand his ground, but his feet step back.

Suddenly, Kurt's hand springs upward. The bottle Kurt was holding flies past Charlie, inches from his head, and crashes into the wall behind the boy.

Then, to Charlie's confusion and horror, another jarring sound, far worse than glass shattering against plaster, fills his darkened room and stipples him with icy goose flesh.

Kurt is laughing. The shadowy figure in the doorway has thrown back his head and is laughing.

PART ONE

A STORM IN THE EYES

June, 1983

Somewhere in the mountains of California

Chapter 1

A green road sign flashes by the window of Kurt's truck where Charlie sits in the passenger seat, his nose almost touching the cool glass. His gaze is fixed on the blur of conifers and rocky slopes whipping past his unblinking and narrowed pale blue eyes, eyes that are glazed with focus. His jaw is set and his lips are pressed into a thin, bloodless line.

Inside him, pressure is building; he can actually feel it in his chest. It could just be the increasing altitude, but he suspects it is really the harbinger of an entirely new kind of misery, the kind that will leave another scar. He wipes his swollen eyes peevishly with the back of his shirtsleeve.

"6000 feet" the road sign had read.

The aftermath of his expulsion from yet another school had been bad, no doubt about it, and for a time he didn't think things could get any worse. That was before "The Committee" had met.

"The Committee" was all about Charlie, but it would not have him as a member. No, only his mother and Kurt comprised "The Committee" and its decision was that Charlie had to go, and "The Committee's" decisions were always final.

He had never left home before, not like this. Granted, life at home had not been all that great lately, but it was all he had ever known. There was a time when they were a team: Charlie, his mother and his brother. Nothing could come between them, but now with each passing mile they are getting further apart.

As he stares at the passing wilderness outside the truck's window, he can think only of...

His little brother peeks his head into Charlie's darkened room: "Are you all right?"

"Yeah..."

"I think it's okay now. I just heard Mom pull up."

"Doesn't matter," Charlie says. "She's no help anymore. She's always on his side. Anyway, I think he's calmed down for the night."

"Can I help you pack?" says Brandon, staring at the dusty orange suitcase yawning empty on Charlie's trundle bed.

"No...no, I'll do it."

Now that his brother is in his room, the gloom seems inappropriate somehow and Charlie turns on his desk lamp. Brandon blinks against the light. The boy is 10, and although he stopped sucking his thumb long ago, he still bites its nail. His eyes are puffy and his light-brown, bowl-cut hair is a tangle of worry. The room isn't big, but Charlie thinks his brother looks small standing in the middle of it, small and lost.

"Kurt was bad tonight," says Brandon softly. Charlie crosses to him and pulls Brandon onto the edge of the bed and they sit.

"No big deal," Charlie says. "As long as we stick together we're going to be fine."

"But you're leaving," says Brandon, bleakly.

The words sting, and the pressure of charged silence pushes on them both.

"Yeah...but, not for long," Charlie manages a smile. "Just for the summer."

"I guess," Brandon says, staring at his curling toes. "I'll miss you though..."

"You want to get a bite to eat? I think we're almost there," Kurt said, flicking his eyes briefly to Charlie who started, peeling from his reverie. These were the first words in more than an hour to interrupt the labored hum of the truck's motor as it climbed the mountain.

"I'm not very hungry," Charlie muttered taking an absent swipe at his leaking nose with his beleaguered shirtsleeve.

"You could use some meat on those bones, sport," his stepfather joshed, jabbing a calloused finger between two of Charlie's ribs.

Charlie flinched. Now that he was 14 years old, he had hoped he would start to bulk up a bit, gain some weight. But, it hadn't happened yet. He brushed Kurt's hand aside with a wan smile and an expulsion of breath from his nose, which lately, had replaced his genuine laugh. He ran his thin fingers through his tangle of blonde hair and looked at his stepfather squarely for the first time in countless miles of nauseatingly twisting road.

"Mom said if I was good here I could..."

"I know what your mother said, Charlie," Kurt interrupted, "but first things first. Let's cross that bridge when we come to it. You may really like it at this place. You can make lots of new friends...it will be good for you," he recited with a betraying lack of conviction.

Charlie slumped and turned his attention once again to his window, to his tear-streaked reflection flickering in the glass.

Another green road sign streaked by the truck:

ELEVATION 6500

This followed closely by a listing white snow-measuring stick stuck in the shoulder of the road, a band of bright orange paint blazing three-quarters of the way up its length. Another sign came into view, this one much larger:

WELCOME TO BEAR CREEK
POP 4124

The highway shoulder widened and gave way to gravel driveways and weather-beaten A-frame cabins. A "Reagan/Bush in '84" sign passed the window, nailed to a tree. The woods were getting taller and thicker.

The truck was now in shadow and it was oddly quiet inside. Charlie knew why. Kurt was done softening the blows. He was all business now and in the home stretch of his plan to rid his household of the boy who would never accept him. Kurt had won. There was no longer a need to sell Charlie on anything, to get Charlie packed and into the car, to appease him with forced harmony to make the all day drive bearable.

Still, the truck climbed. Charlie wrapped his fingers around a spent can of Coke and slowly crushed it, relishing the popping of the aluminum.

Fortified briefly, he steeled himself and looked at Kurt. "Summer will be over before you know it. It always goes so fast."

Kurt said nothing. His mustache twitched.

Charlie continued: "I'm sure Brandon will be stoked to get the bathroom all to himself all summer. I bet Mom won't miss my AC/DC in the morning either." He paused, appraising Kurt with a sidelong glance. "I like the woods anyway. Maybe this place will be..."

"Shit..." Kurt slammed on the brakes. The Samsonite suitcase in the fluted bed of the pickup slid on its hard shell with a gritty whisper towards the cab where it thumped to a halt just behind Charlie's back.

"Too much yakkin'," Kurt hissed, "missed the damn turnoff."

The truck spun around spraying gravel from the back wheels, Kurt turning the wheel with hard slaps of his palms. The luggage roared to the back of the pickup's bed and slammed against the tailgate.

A road sign swerved into view:

SCHOOL ROAD

The Coke in Charlie's stomach felt like battery acid now. He visibly deflated, setting his face back to expressionless stone.

The corner of School Road had what looked like an elementary school to the left and a massive shed to the right that boasted of "seasoned firewood, aromatic fruitwood" with some scrawled prices on a small, makeshift billboard. The way narrowed as the dirt shoulders thinned and the trees crept closer to the road. The towering pine sentinels lining both sides of the lanes seemed to lean in, casting even deeper shadows on the gray asphalt. Bits of grand houses peeked through the occasional break in the forest. These dwellings were unlike the cabins in town. The wood that comprised their expansive decks and porches looked new and golden.

They had driven about a mile from the highway when Charlie became aware of the blood rushing through his ears. His heart pounded. The sense that they were getting close was palpable as if they were approaching a radioactive area charged with some new kind of energy that constricted your spit glands and twisted your bowels right through your clammy skin. He wished he could tell himself that this summer was going to be spent toasting marshmallows and singing "John Jacob Jingleheimer Schmidt" like he did when he was young, but he knew damn well this place was for kids in trouble.

Bad kids.

The dappled light from the forest's canopy shone on the brochure, face up on the dash. The glossy cover cast a reflection in the windshield, flickering with the passing treetops. "Solutions for Troubled Teens" it read. "Positive Behavior Change". "Saving Lives and Creating Hope Since 1968".

They have solutions for me? Charlie thought. Changes? My behavior will be changed? This is utter bullshit. This is not good, not good at all.

He squirmed beneath his seatbelt. He tried swallowing the lump in his throat but it wouldn't budge.

The road had seemingly reached a dead end at a weather-beaten wooden sign emblazoned with lemon-yellow letters:

PONDEROSA ACADEMY
PRIVATE PROPERTY

A small arrow indicated a left-hand decline in the road obscured by a thick copse of whitethorn and scrub oak. Kurt pumped the brake and coaxed the truck around the abrupt corner and down the slight hill. A flare of sun hit the windshield, obscuring the way ahead and illuminating the dusty gore on the glass. Kurt yanked down his sun visor. Charlie squinted, but could see nothing. The keys tinkled from where they hung in the ignition.

Kurt's eyes glittered as he turned to Charlie, "We're here, sport."

Chapter 2

A man stood at the far edge of the parking lot, hands clasped behind his back, waiting. Beyond the man stretched a large kidney-shaped lawn spotted with clusters of buttercups and heather. The man's auburn hair was feathered, parted in the middle, and glowed like dying embers under the soft mountain sun of early June. As Charlie walked towards him, a radiant smile spread across the man's face.

Charlie approached slowly, the bulk of the dusty orange suitcase hanging from his thin arm. The man offered a meaty hand; the wrist, ringed with a tank watch, flashed.

Glancing back over his shoulder, Charlie watched Kurt's pickup make short work of the broad parking lot and mount the small hill back to the road. The truck disappeared. Charlie turned his head back to the man, slowly accepting the extended hand.

"My name is Michael DiFranco," the man said, gripping Charlie's fingers with no pump of the arm as if out of respect for some assumed frailty. "I am one of the family heads here. Let's get you checked in. You can leave your suitcase here."

Two small modular buildings sat across the lawn in the shadow of a steep hill terraced with broad stone walls. One of the buildings did not betray its purpose, but the other structure had a porch with three steps and a wooden sign that read:

ADMINISTRATION

From this building, a pair of stout women emerged and came towards Charlie and Michael, the wooden soles of their shoes clomping and scraping along the cement path that snaked across the lawn. They offered Charlie dour smiles, muttered a terse welcome, seized the suitcase and briskly retraced their steps.

"We will get it to you in a bit," assured Michael. "This way, please. How was the trip? I understand you came all the way from…"

Charlie's ears had not popped from the ascent. He felt disoriented. The man's words seemed to be coming from far away, as if from within a diver's mask at the bottom of a swamp. The man's pleasantries continued but Charlie could not concentrate on the words or comprehend their meaning. The drive had been long, exhausting. He was left with a numb beehive for a head. He stretched his jaw. The mountain air was dry, thin and still.

They were walking now and Charlie followed behind as if in a dream. He noticed that the footpath was bordered on both sides with white stones, all of them almost identical, all of them meticulously-placed, and all of them wiped free of dirt. Charlie turned his attention back to the man's shiny loafers until they brought him to the wooden steps of the squat building that had just recently swallowed the women bearing his suitcase. They entered.

A secretary with her hair in a bun sat at a desk across the small room and absently played with her lower lip while reading a manila file. She didn't seem to notice them. Above her a wall clock ticked solemnly. To the left of her was a small reception area where a tall boy, around Charlie's age, stood silently in a shadow. He had a high forehead and bright, brown eyes beneath his close-cropped dark hair. He wore a white T-shirt tucked into a pair of blue jeans.

One of the bad kids, Charlie thought.

"Vince, this is our new student," Michael said. "Charlie Hoff, this is Vince Russo, your big brother. He will show you around and get you all set up. I'm sure you will have some questions for him."

"Hi," said Vince, stepping forward with an eager extension of his hand.

"Hi," muttered Charlie and took the hand slowly, aware of the film of perspiration that covered his own like a moist glove.

Michael clapped his hands at his chest and sucked air through his teeth. "Well," he exclaimed resolutely, "first things first. This way, please."

Charlie flicked his eyes to Vince who quickly nodded reassurance. He followed Michael past the secretary down a narrow hall lined with little rooms of file cabinets, laminated furniture, and quietly engaged adults. In fact, Charlie thought the place was far too quiet, as if it was quiet just for him, as if everyone were straining to keep some secret.

He pushed the thought from his mind, concentrating on following the boy and the man down the hall, a hall lit by dingy fluorescent overhead panel lights. The corridor ended at a square room where two black molded plastic chairs with chrome legs sat on either side of a small table.

"There is a bathroom, there," Michael said cocking a thumb towards the left wall. "Please remove your clothes. You can keep your underpants on. When you are ready just hand them to me through the crack in the door."

Charlie froze.

He glanced down at his clothes. He was wearing an open long-sleeved shirt over an official Oakland Raiders jersey, Levis, and Adidas high-tops. There was nothing wrong with them that he could see. He met the man's eyes, a flush rising to his face with the heat of sunburn.

"We have some more acceptable clothes for you that your parents sent," Michael DiFranco said, the perpetual smile unfaltering. "We don't allow clothing with logos or pants with holes in them."

Charlie glanced down again at his jeans. There was a small tear in the knee. Gaping, he looked at the other boy, Vince, but his face was free of expression.

"What you wear is an extension of how you feel inside," continued Michael. "Logos create an image and we don't want such distractions here; we want nothing that will remind you or others of their lives outside this environment."

This couldn't be right, it couldn't, Charlie thought, studying the man carefully, but he saw nothing but the same carefree smile spread across his face. Charlie was disarmed, confused. Did he really have to take off his clothes? His heart raced, demanding a revolt, but the insubordinate response that played at his lips could not manage to sound and was swallowed with an audible click. He kept his eyes locked on Michael anyway, hoping he was conveying enough incredulity in his expression to alter the request.

Michael only gestured to the bathroom door with his eyes as the smile on the man's face thawed, but it only thawed to placidity free of indulgence.

Charlie thought back to the brochure on the dashboard of Kurt's truck: "Solutions", "Change".

So this was it. He had hours to concoct dreadful situations in his imagination on the drive here, to brace for the unknown, to hammer new armor. But, he wasn't as prepared as he'd thought. He took a deep breath. The man didn't like his clothes. Fine. He could handle this if it was to be the worst violation of his rights, although he seriously doubted that it was to end with his clothes.

He disrobed and after a few minutes opened the bathroom door a crack and wiggled the pile of clothes clutched in his hand. They were taken, and Charlie gripped the air for the replacements, which soon lit upon his palm in a neatly-folded pile. Charlie yanked the clothes through the crack and glared at them suspiciously. He held a pair of new jeans, size "28 waist 33 length"--right on the money. Under the jeans was a size medium striped shirt of brown, gold, and white with Mervyns' tags still hanging from it, his mother's favorite bargain haunt.

Weird.

They sent these and didn't pack them? Isn't that what the man--Michael--said? "Your parents sent some clothes"? When? Why did they send clothes? New clothes he had never seen before? It made no sense. None of this made sense.

A rapping of knuckles on the bathroom door interrupted his thoughts.

"How you doing in there, Charlie?" came Michael's muffled voice. Charlie opened the door tentatively and slowly stepped out.

"Much better," said Michael.

"Can I have my wallet?" Charlie asked, with what he hoped would be assertiveness. His voice, however, sounded thin and childish to his ears. He was shaken, off his game. Disappointed in himself, he let his eyes fall submissively to his shoes.

"We will keep it safe for you," Michael said. "You will have no need for it here. The secretary has made a note that you had ten dollars and she will keep it for you until you leave."

Why couldn't he have his wallet? The vinyl Ocean Pacific wallet was the last gift his grandfather ever gave Charlie before he died. The grass on Papa Pete's grave had not even grown in yet. The wallet was his last connection to the only father figure he had ever known, the only man who ever gave a damn about him.

There wasn't much in it, only a transit pass and a public library card--pristine from lack of use--and the key to his bike lock. The Velcro closure made a pleasantly unsettling tearing sound whenever he had to produce money. It was his first real wallet and he loved it. Now, "they" had it. He was pretty sure they would take what they wanted until he could just get to a phone and talk some sense into his mother and tell her that he was definitely at the wrong place.

"Please sit down," Michael said, gesturing to one of the black stackable chairs. "Vince is waiting to show you around, but first you should become familiar with some materials."

"Materials?" Charlie croaked. His voice betrayed him again and he realized that he had better grow a set of balls and quick or he was really going to be stuck to the bottom of this guy's shoe. He cleared his throat.

"Would you like a glass of water?" Michael asked.

"Yeah," conceded Charlie glumly as he slumped into the hard plastic seat.

"Alright, look these over and I'll be right back," Michael said, producing two sheets of paper that he had been holding at his side. Charlie took them. Michael left, padding down the hall. The first page read:

DAILY SCHEDULE

```
Monday/Wednesday/Friday
6:30 - Wake up
7:30 - Breakfast
8:30 - First Light Meeting
9:00 - Work Crew
12:00 - Lunch/Dorm Time
1:00 - Academics
3:00 - Raps
6:00 - Dinner
7:00 - Floor
9:30 - Last Light meeting
10:00 - Lights out

Tuesday/Thursday/Saturday
6:30 - Wake up
7:30 - Breakfast
8:30 - First Light Meeting
9:00 - Work Crew
12:00 - Lunch/Dorm Time
1:00 - Academics
3:00 - Experiential
```

```
5:30 - Dorm Time
6:00 - Dinner
7:00 - Floor
9:30 - Last Light meeting
10:00 - Lights out

Sunday
7:30 - Wake up
8:30 - Breakfast
9:30 - Free time/ Afternoon sign ups
1:00 - Lunch/ Dorm Time
2:00 - Free time
5:30 - Dorm Time
6:00 - Dinner
7:00 - Movie
9:30 - Last Light meeting
10:00 - Lights out
```

A water cooler gurgled somewhere in the building. Work Crews? Raps? Floor? What the hell was this? Charlie's hands began to shake. He licked his lips and slid the first page behind the second:

PONDEROSA ACADEMY BASIC AGREEMENTS

1. No violence towards yourself or others.
2. No sex or sexual contact with anyone.
3. No drugs unless prescribed by a doctor.
4. No alcohol.
5. No caffeine or refined sugar unless approved by your family head.
6. No listening to or discussing music that has not been approved.
7. Trendy clothing or hairstyles or use of slang language that would create a street image is not permitted.
8. No discussing the details of your city and neighborhood with other students.
9. No student is to discuss Raps, Disclosure Circles or Propheets with those who were not present. This includes family as well as other students.
10. Shirts must be tucked in at meals and when entering the lodge. Personal hygiene must be kept up and showers taken daily.
11. You must be in your dorm at dorm time. Dorm chores are done each morning and you will not leave the dorm for breakfast until dismissed by

```
    your dorm head.
12. No student may leave the campus or communicate
    with family or past acquaintances without
    approval.
```

Charlie's mouth had gone dry. His peripheral vision became a throbbing and indistinct smudge. He viewed the papers still gripped in his hand through a lengthening red tunnel. He was cold somewhere deep inside and the chill was spreading like an infection down his limbs as if borne by a colony of frosty spiders. A Dixie cup of water appeared on the small table beside him with a click. Charlie stared at it blankly wondering what purpose it could possibly serve. Michael and the boy Vince stood over him. Although they were smiling pleasantly, their eyes were appraising and keen.

"I'm sure you will have some questions for Vince," Michael said, "but before I let you two loose we just need a quick photo for our records."

One of the suitcase women appeared in the doorway with a Polaroid camera.

"Charlie," Michael said, "if you would stand right against this wall that would be perfect."

Mechanically, Charlie rose on rubbery legs and put his back to the white wall. The camera flashed, whirred, regurgitated a white square and then, without a word, the woman disappeared down the hall, casually waving the print at her side. Charlie watched her go, through swimming stars of light from the flash bulb. His vision melted to an azure film, cleared, and revealed again the man beside him, the man with the endless smile.

"Well, that's it," Michael said, "Vince can show you around now. Your clothes will be sent to your dorm room. Welcome to Ponderosa Academy."

Charlie stared at him with eyeballs that felt numb in their sockets. Michael briefly broadened his smile, nodded his head once, turned on his heel and quit the room. Charlie reached for the little cup of water and stared into it for a moment before drinking it in a single gulp.

"He took my clothes," Charlie finally managed looking at Vince. "He took my wallet, too."

"Yeah," Vince said apologetically, "they were probably just looking for drugs."

"DRUGS? I don't have any drugs," Charlie spat. Then, raising his voice--tactically loud enough to save face in front of this boy, but without inviting a real confrontation with anyone within earshot-- shouted towards the hall, "I want my stuff!"

"C'mon," Vince said, "we can go out the back."

Charlie hissed through his teeth, glancing over his shoulder on the way out.

The two boys blinked against the afternoon sun as they emerged from the administration building just feet from the stone wall that spanned the terraced inclination in both directions. To their left about fifty yards away the wall gave way to stone steps sweeping up and right, fronting the wing of a large, half-timbered multi-level building that stuck out past the ramparts of the wall and overlooked the lawn. To the right the wall ended twenty yards away where it was intersected by a steep paved road that began in the parking lot and headed straight uphill and out of sight.

"Maybe we should take the Microwave and go straight to the dorms first. Raps are still going on," Vince said, biting a nail.

"What?" Charlie said wrinkling his brow. "I have no idea what you're talking about."

"Sorry," Vince laughed. "We'll take this road up to our left. We call it the Microwave because there's a microwave tower at the top of the hill, way up top. It's not part of the school; the city or state owns it, I guess."

"What's a rap?" asked Charlie.

"Group therapy, basically. We get together and talk about our feelings. Problems we're having...stuff like that."

Charlie didn't answer. He had heard enough. He had to find a phone and tell his mother what was going on.

"You okay, Charlie?" asked Vince.

"Fine," Charlie said flatly. He was far from okay. He felt hollow. His mind was squirming. He concentrated on calming it down. This problem had to be solved, and solved quickly.

He reviewed his options. It was a long way back to town on foot and they would catch him within minutes anyway. No, that was too rash; a last resort. He needed a phone. There had to be phones around, unattended long enough for a quick call. There had to be.

A deep breath brought a cool wave of calm. His panic would serve no purpose; he knew it. It was best to relax and wait for an opportunity. If he looked as miserable as he felt it would only raise suspicions. In the meantime he would go along with it, gather information, and try to keep cool. It was clear that they had no intention of letting him leave, and if he didn't play this right it would be a hell of a long summer.

A hell of a long one.

"You coming?" Vince asked.

Charlie realized he had stopped walking.

They started climbing the Microwave road. It was steep and before long Charlie was panting. Vince was not.

"What's with those rules?" Charlie asked. He tried to seem casual. He thought he sounded pretty convincing, even managing a flip chuckle for good measure. "Are they serious?"

"Ah," said Vince, "you read the dirty dozen. Yeah, the agreements take some getting used to."

"I didn't agree to anything," Charlie muttered, and regretted it instantly.

"There's the lodge," Vince said, coming to a halt.

The campus was vast. Charlie followed Vince's finger left over a long and broad quadrangle dotted with picnic tables, past the aqua glint of a pool to a grand craftsman-style building whose centerpiece was an enormous stone chimney. The lodge's wings sprawled up the hill into the trees on one side and down the hill and past the stone wall on the other. He looked to his right. A slope tumbled down to a basketball court and a large field beyond. Above them, a path intersected the road and led down left to the lodge and then up to the right where a group of low buildings squatted on a bluff beneath a steep hill of tall pines.

"Those are the girls' dorms on the left," said Vince, following Charlie's eyes. "The boys' are those two on the right."

Charlie looked for signs of life but no one could be seen in any direction. A sheep bleated somewhere in the distance.

"There's animals?" asked Charlie.

"The farm," said Vince. "It's past the fields. If you would've turned right at the parking lot you would've seen a dirt road that goes down there. We got horses, pigs, sheep, goats, chickens, and the whole deal. There's a garden down there too where we grow a lot of our own veggies and stuff."

The two arrived at the path intersecting the road and Charlie looked up the Microwave. It became even steeper ahead and he was glad they had leveled off. They turned right and traversed the bluff over the sports fields and courts and arrived at the furthest of the dorms.

"This is Walden," Vince said. "Home sweet home."

The building was really a series of three rectangular, clapboard buildings, each complex separated by a narrow open courtyard. An arcade of support poles hoisted a shingled overhang that shadowed the porches in front of the numbered brown doors. The place reminded Charlie of the cloisters at Sacred Heart, his last school, where the priests would float around in ecclesiastical silence with clasped hands.

The two paused. Vince consulted a piece of paper from his pocket as a woodpecker hammered a tree somewhere upslope..

"Let's see," Vince said, turning into one of the courtyards, "You're in this one. Number five."

Vince opened the door. Four beds were pushed against their respective chocolate brown faux wood-paneled walls, each with tartan plaid bedspread and matching bolster and pillow shams.

Charlie gasped.

One of the beds had a large cardboard box at its foot with writing on it--his mother's writing. The box had already been opened. The flap holding the packing label stuck straight up, facing him. He stared at his return address.

Charlie felt a wave of homesickness seeing his mother's loopy scrawl and his stomach tightened. It occurred to him briefly that the box had already been violated by a stranger's hands, but whatever indignation he had was eclipsed by its mere, unexpected presence. Vince sat on the bed as Charlie dropped to his knees before the box and unfolded the other flaps.

Clothes. It was clothes. Charlie looked at Vince and then returned his attention to the package. He rifled through its contents: boots, a jacket lined with fleece, sweaters and more jeans.

"I..." Charlie began, "I don't need this many clothes." He laughed nervously, "Jesus, Mom..."

Charlie glanced at Vince who said nothing, but only stared out the window, expressionless.

"Can you believe this?" Charlie said. He laughed again, too loudly, and looked up at Vince.

Vince's face was grave. Something was wrong.

Charlie held up the wool lined jacket. "These things are way too hot for summer." His voice trailed off. "What is she thinking...?"

"They should have told you," Vince said stiffly.

Charlie blanched and dropped the jacket to his lap and looked blankly at Vince. "Told me what?"

"Charlie...this isn't a summer school," said Vince. The boy slowly turned away from the window and looked squarely at Charlie. "It's a two year program."

Chapter 3

"Wait up!" cried Vince. He was alongside Charlie in no time, one foot sliding on a patch of scree that had tumbled onto the path from the hill above. He pinwheeled his arms and grabbed Charlie's elbow for support. Charlie shook him off, stopped walking, and turned to face Vince who regarded him with nervous surprise.

"You knew," Charlie said.

"Of course I knew," said Vince, "I just didn't know that nobody had told you." Vince grabbed his knees and caught his breath. "That sucks."

Charlie figured this was true and felt a hot wave of frustration flood his insides. He scoured the landscape with narrowed eyes for someone to blame.

"Where you headed?" asked Vince.

"In there..." Charlie replied methodically, pointing to the lodge below. "There will be a phone. I will call my mom and tell her I'm not staying here. If my stepfather answers, I will chew him a new asshole."

"Nice," said Vince with contemplative admiration, "but not likely."

Their attention was arrested by the sound of distant voices. They both looked down the trail at the lodge in time to see the building disgorge a wave of teenagers from its double doors. The kids funneled hastily up a set of stone steps to the trailhead fronting the right wing of the lodge and then they jostled up the trail, coming straight for the two boys. In moments the students were breezing past the pair, some with distrustful glances at Charlie, some with polite smiles, and more than a few with swollen eyes and beet-red faces as if they had been crying.

"Dorm time," Vince said. "Raps just got out."

"She doesn't look very good," whispered Charlie, following a straggling girl with his eyes as she trudged towards the cluster of dormitories. She was turned away, wiping snot from her nose.

"Look..." Vince said, his eyes bright and imploring, "let's head back to your room and you can meet your roommates. Dinner is in an hour and we can all go down together. Okay?"

"What happened to that girl?" Charlie insisted.

"Nothing for you to worry about," Vince said. "Sad about something, had a tough Rap; it happens. C'mon Charlie..." Vince swept an arm towards the dorms.

"What do you mean it happens?"

Vince's mouth worked, searching for words.

Charlie's eyes blazed: "You won't tell me? Had a tough rap? That's normal? You're going to ignore her? That's what happens in a rap? Are you KIDDING me? Vince, what's going on here?"

"It's okay, Charlie," Vince said softly, his face falling to anguish.

Judging from the boy's face, Vince was feeling in over his head, nervous about a misstep. His eyes flashed with apprehension. Charlie suddenly felt sympathy for him. He could tell that none of this was Vince's fault. He was being made to walk a tightrope and it was clear he wanted down. Charlie sighed and began to unwind.

Vince brightened a little and tried again: "We'll go down to the House later and you can talk to Toby. He's on the Floor tonight. He's your family head. He wants to talk to you anyway."

"Why is he on the floor?" asked Charlie, squinting with confusion.

Vince coughed out such a genuine laugh that Charlie smiled in spite of himself.

"Lots of lingo, I know," said Vince. "It just means he is the staff on duty. I'm supposed to go to dinner with you and introduce you to him. Look, if you do something crazy it's my ass."

Irresolute, Charlie brought his sneaker down on a large pinecone and rolled it back and forth under the ball of his foot. He felt better as he listened to it splinter. The afternoon was growing old. The sun had fallen behind the tall firs on the ridge above them and now their spiky shadows blanketed the trail. Charlie glanced at the lodge and then towards the dorms.

"All right," said Charlie, "I'll go back, but I'm not staying at this place for long."

❖

Three other boys now occupied North Walden Five. They flung the day's gossip over their shoulders as they weaved quickly around one another, crossing the room and going in and out of the small bathroom. Clothes were removed and tossed towards the hamper with precision, drawers opened and closed, the toilet flushed, and the sink turned on and off in short bursts. Nobody noticed Charlie and Vince, and if they did they were too engaged to inquire as to what they were doing standing in the doorway.

"Shawn," said Vince, "this is your new guy."

A large, oafish boy with a barrel chest and a reddish tint had just implausibly pulled a pair of jeans up his thick legs and was fumbling with the button fly. "Hi," he said distractedly, concerned with getting his pants to accept his burly frame.

"That's Shawn. He's your dorm head," Vince said to Charlie. "The Big Cheese. Look, I got to head back to my room for a bit."

"Wait," Charlie implored confidentially through his teeth, "don't leave. You're leaving?"

"I'll be back in a bit. Just hang out. Now, please don't do anything crazy like split or whatever...we're going to see Toby in, like, a half hour. Okay?"

"Fine," Charlie made his way to his bed where the box of clothes from home still sat, the warm winter jacket heaped on the plaid bedspread. Charlie turned back to look at Vince but he was gone.

Shawn was bent over tying his shoes now, but the two other boys in the room stopped to appraise Charlie.

"I'm Austin," said one of them. He was tall, athletically built and strikingly handsome. He threaded a webbed belt through the loops of his khaki pants and smiled charitably as if he were aware of the dazzling impression he made.

"I'm Jonathan," said the other, struggling with a pullover shirt, eventually managing to coax it down his flabby, doughy white torso. Relieved with the execution of this task, and with flushed cheeks and a triumphant sigh, Jonathan sat down hard on the foot of his bed. The springs groaned in protest. He looked at Charlie and folded his hands in his lap. His face was kind and his eyes seemed to accept the humor of his own existence with a bright twinkle. "So why did you get sent here?"

The question shook Charlie. He realized he was the last one to completely accept this indubitable fact. The rest of the world was sharing a joke and he was the only one who had not understood the punch line. Even as Kurt drove him here--it felt like years ago although only two hours had passed--he had no choice but to concede spending the summer away from home. The Committee had made their decision. Yet he had known there was a nasty detail concealed; a deception of some kind, he had just known it. Now it was clear and it was inconceivable. The joke was on him and "two years" was the punch line. He would be stranded on the top of this mountain until he was 16. Hopelessness clamped his heart and squeezed.

All three boys awaited his reply: the ruddy oaf, the charming prince, and the fat kid. Why was he sent here? He really didn't know. He wasn't sure what this place even was yet. One thing was certain: he had been tricked by his mother and Kurt. He had been lured into a cage.

His anger began to bake his insides into an arid, lonely wasteland. Kurt's treachery, his mother's apathy in the face of it, and the increased vulnerability of his little brother all roiled within him like some foul stew. How did this happen? He had become excised fat, cut from his own family to render it lean, and then thrown away. Tears were inadequate now. He had to make a vow to himself: whatever weakness still threatened him would be shielded from exploitation.

All of these boys who now stared in expectation of an answer shared his fate. Charlie swept his glance over them all and found a cold solace in the kindred sacrifice he saw within them, flickering like a long-tended pyre deep within their eyes. Someone had betrayed them all.

"You don't have to answer that," Shawn said, shooting a punitive glance at Jonathan who deflated sheepishly. Shawn pursed his thick lips as he buttoned up a long-sleeved shirt, watching Charlie carefully.

Charlie had the feeling that the objection to Jonathan's question was a power play. It was certainly not to protect his feelings-which he knew must have been scrawled all over his face-, but rather to preserve Shawn's right as dorm head to grill the fresh meat at his leisure.

Austin dared his own question: "Where are you from?"

"San Jose," Charlie replied.

"Hey, I'm from San Francisco," said Jonathan, excited. "Close by!"

For some reason Jonathan received another withering glance

from the dorm head.

"Huntington Beach," said Austin, with a grunt as he tied his shoe.

Charlie looked at Shawn expectantly.

The dorm head thawed: "Boston."

Charlie went on: "What grade are you guys in?"

They looked momentarily confused.

"I guess..." Jonathan began, "I'm a sophomore, but we don't have grades here really. Everyone is about the same age. Me and Austin are fifteen. Shawn is seventeen. He's in the Upper Family and has been here the longest." Jonathan glanced obsequiously at Shawn.

"There are a few thirteen-year-olds," said Austin, "but mostly no one is younger than that or older than seventeen. Because, of course, if anyone was eighteen..."

Austin caught Shawn's eye. The dorm head was staring a hole through him.

"Never mind," Austin said, swallowing the rest.

There was an awkward silence.

It was Shawn who fired the next question: "Charlie what?"

"Hoff."

"Charlie Hoff," repeated Shawn, chewing the words. He paused, stared blankly and then brightened. "At least you weren't named Jack!" A barking laugh erupted from Shawn. Austin and Jonathan smiled courteously.

Charlie already knew he would not like Shawn. The boy was too much like the loutish construction workers that Kurt would pollute the house with on game day; one would inevitably point out Charlie's weight, or lack thereof, between roaring belches and heinous insults hurled at the opposing team without regard for his mother's ears.

"I don't get it," Charlie teased.

"Jack Hoff," said the dorm head with a suspicious frown.

The other two boys looked mortified. Not that they couldn't appreciate a good masturbation joke--that was verbal ambrosia--it was the obvious toying with Shawn that would have compelled them to drag a cautionary finger across their necks and grit their teeth at Charlie if Shawn had only been facing the other way.

Mercifully there was a knock on the door. Michael DiFranco peered in and then shouldered the door open, wrestling with Charlie's suitcase. Charlie took it from him and hoisted it onto his bed.

"Ah...Charlie," Michael said, "I see you've met your roommates. What do you think of the campus? Had a chance to see the lodge?"

"Not yet," said Charlie.

Way too busy reeling from being kicked in the nuts by the people I'm supposed to trust to care much about sightseeing, thought Charlie, and tried his best not to darken. He sat by his box of clothes, a hand casually resting on the top, and challenged Michael with a steady look to indicate to the man that the punch line had been revealed.

"Well, you boys better be getting to dinner," said Michael pleasantly, evidently unmotivated to explain or offer condolences.

"We were just on our way," Shawn put in as Michael left and pulled the door closed.

Charlie popped the clasps on the suitcase, lifted the lid and discovered what he knew he would find. His things had been removed and carefully refolded by someone.

Looking for drugs, he thought. That's what Vince had said. Was this place really full of drug addicts? These kids were conniving, desperate, dangerous, and rabid drug addicts? Really? It didn't make sense. Then why was he here? He had never done drugs.

He glanced up at the boys. Jonathan was not a druggie, was he? Could that roly-poly, good-natured kid be the kind of boy parents everywhere feared—the irresistible corrupting force that proverbially haunted the shadows of suburbia? And Austin? The guy looked like a model or something. Did guys so perfect do drugs? Austin was a long way from the haggard and shifty-eyed ne'er-do-wells clad in black that frequented the bleachers and the deep left field of the baseball diamond at his old school.

Shawn on the other hand...

Shawn looked like he had a history of some kind; there was something in his watchful eyes. He never let his guard down. Yet, on closer inspection, he seemed more miserably defensive than cruel, like a beaten dog.

Then there was Vince. Wholesome and obedient, he was obviously trusted by the adults in charge. Nice enough guy but, again, a former drug addict? Charlie didn't think so.

Of course, there was still the real question that made Charlie want to scream the birds from their trees: Why had they all been left here? Whatever was in store for them all was not going to be...

"You coming?" It was Jonathan, holding the door open.

Charlie and the other boys of North Walden Five intercepted Vince in the courtyard and started for the lodge. Clusters of girls emptied onto the path ahead of them from their dorms tucked into the trees above. They passed South Walden where another group of students made their way down the short incline to join the trail.

They all walked silently for a while until Austin leaned into Jonathan. "South Six had a dorm Rap. Brutal. Were you in Archie Goetz's Rap?"

"Yep," Jonathan replied, "it was pretty mellow. I didn't get talked to."

"Lucky," said Austin.

Charlie was listening. His stomach clenched.

"Who's on Floor tonight?" asked Jonathan.

"Toby Heiser," Vince offered as they all crossed the Microwave road.

Charlie ventured his own question. "How many students go here?"

"Hmmm..." Jonathan pondered, screwing up his mouth.

"Like a hundred, right?" hazarded Austin.

"About right," said Shawn.

"Hey, Vicky," said Vince. A tall, lanky girl fell into step with them. "How was your Rap?"

"Okay," she said, "what about you?"

"I was touring," Vince said.

"We have a Nate?"

"Charlie here," said Vince, cocking a thumb at Charlie.

"Hi, Charlie," said Vicky leaning forward to see past the group of boys to the thin blond kid on the end.

"Hi," Charlie said with a quick glance before returning his attention to his feet.

Vicky fell behind to regroup with the pack of girls she had come with.

Charlie looked at Vince. "What's a Nate?"

"It just means a new kid," said Vince apologetically. "It comes from 'Nathan the New Kid'. I don't know who came up with it-- someone long before I got here, probably. New kids always...well..."

"Do all the things a new kid usually does," offered Austin.

"Yeah. Like that," said Vince.

"What kind of things?" asked Charlie.

"Breaking agreements. Popping off. Stuff like that," Austin replied.

"Popping off?" Charlie wasn't sure what this meant but it sounded salacious.

"Mentioning bands, unacceptable music, cutting up the streets. That kind of stuff," said Jonathan.

Mentioning bands, thought Charlie. Ridiculous, but evidently, everyone had accepted the rules. The oppressive list of bizarre demands he had held in his hands in the administration building seemed to be not only tolerated but also celebrated with fables of hapless transgressors. Charlie looked at them all in astonishment.

"So I really can't mention Ozzy Osborne?" asked Charlie. "You've got to be kidding."

The boys were silent and had gone pale. Vince put a hand to his own mouth and massaged his cheeks nervously. Shawn released a soft, involuntary groan. Austin and Jonathan's faces lit with awe and then fell into deep concern.

"What?" Charlie asked. He didn't like the affected look of the group but he had to know if the sky would fall. Someone had really been putting the screws to these guys, and the sooner he knew what he was up against, the better.

Ozzy may have been accused of being the Devil a few times, Charlie supposed, but his name alone should not scare a teenage boy. What concerned him the most was Shawn. Here was a guy who could bend him into a pretzel with little effort and the guy had turned white as a ghost. Why?

"That's unacceptable," said Jonathan.

"...and that's a Nate," said Vince glumly.

They were in front of the lodge now and, from this new angle Charlie could appreciate its size. A half-timbered addition sprawled up the mountain to his left and out of sight, to the right the lodge continued downhill past the stone terraces. The pool in front of the lodge, a standard size rectangle, looked murky in the dying light.

The quad, with its weathered picnic tables equidistant on the cement, was deserted save for a hunched-over girl who was sitting on one of the planked tables with her feet on the attached bench, an extended arm between her legs holding a fuming cigarette.

You can smoke? Charlie thought with a mix of alarm and confusion. His eyes swept the quad for authorities, nervous for the girl. Instead, he noticed rusty coffee cans full of sand beneath the picnic tables, studded with bouquets of cigarette butts.

No sugar, but smoking is okay? Why?

Charlie looked back at the girl. She pulled deeply on the smoke and let her arm fall. She looked at Charlie through a tangle of long black curls and deep-set dark eyes and then returned to staring at the ground. She hugged herself with her other arm and comforted herself with an almost imperceptible rocking motion. She looked broken somehow, a picture of unbridled introspection, and she looked utterly abandoned in the gathering twilight. Charlie tore his eyes away from her with difficulty.

"After you," said Vince, holding open one of the heavy double doors to the lodge. Charlie paused, momentarily unsure, and then entered the dark mouth of the building.

Chapter 4

A long narrow room was before him. Five large closet doors lined the left wall, each with its own word burned onto a wood plaque and centered at eye level. "Genesis" read the first door, "Vision" read the second, followed by "Quest", "Evolution" and finally "Source".

The hall ended at a flight of stairs. Underneath were stacks of the black molded plastic chairs with the shiny chrome legs shoved into the dark recess like an army of dormant beetles; he recognized them, he had sat in one in the administration building. To the left was the threshold to the main room of the lodge. Soaring walls of honey-colored, highly-varnished logs rose to a peaked roof in the main room that was dominated by a wrought iron chandelier the size of a wagon wheel. Dark portraits from the Dutch masters hung in gilded frames under brass picture lights. Vermeer's "Woman with Pearl Earring" stared placidly over her shoulder in one corner not far from "The Letter", while Rembrandt's "Man in Helmet", "Night Watch" and "Self Portrait" were mounted above groupings of furniture along the far wall.

In the center of the lodge, in front of the imposing stone fireplace, was a sunken portion of the room, accessed on either side by a set of three steps down, with a built-in semi-circular sectional couch and a heavy coffee table that sat centered on the broad flagstones. Around this Pit--as Charlie would come to know it--the floor was covered in wall-to-wall mousy-brown, short-nape carpet and strewn with many intimate clusters of identically upholstered and finished love seats, end tables, bergére chairs, and low-wattage lamps.

The far side of the room had a long raised landing; at the edge of the landing a suspended staircase snaked its way to the second floor where an open balcony overlooked the ground floor. There were generous doorways along the far wall of the ground level that led to even more unseen rooms.

"Sheesh," said Charlie.

"Wait until you have to clean it," said Jonathan out of the corner of his mouth.

Shawn and Vince had taken the lead and had joined a throng funneling into a doorway across the room and to the far right. Students who had entered the lodge from the other side traversed the expanse of the main room and headed determinedly for the same door.

"Let's try to get a place on the lower level," Jonathan said to Austin who agreed with an emphatic nod.

Through the door, a short hall and an abrupt right turn revealed a long buffet table strewn with the evening's offerings. It was lined on both sides with students holding orange plates.

"Chile rellenos," said a crestfallen Austin. "Crap."

"It's not bad," Jonathan soothed without much conviction. He instructed Charlie to grab a plate and a tray.

As they shuffled down the line, Charlie noticed everyone seemed to help themselves to almost identically modest portions from the chafing dishes. He did the same.

"Milk is on the table," said Jonathan, "follow me."

The dining room had three levels. The middle, where the buffet table was stretched down its length, had a large freestanding wrought-iron potbelly stove--never used by the looks of its insides--on a raised knee-high circular brick hearth that currently supported a metal bowl full of watery salsa to accompany the sodden lumps of stuffed peppers.

The upper level was a few steps up and was comprised of four rows of built in tables under a low ceiling. The lower level, however, was impressive. A few tables on the middle level were built into a low dividing wall that looked down on the sprawl of tables below and the floor to ceiling windows that looked out into space. The view was breathtaking.

Shawn and Vince had intercepted some older students and joined a table on the middle level, filling it to capacity. Charlie, Austin and Jonathan headed down the dozen steps to the lower level, securing a choice table by the window.

The land below the dining hall fell away gradually to a slope of manzanita, chinquapin, and whitethorn, then precipitously disappeared out of sight leaving only deep canyons and valleys that stretched to the horizon. The sun was setting. The pine-filled landscape far below was dark, vast and still.

"You okay Charlie?" asked Austin, "You afraid of heights or something?"

Charlie realized he was standing, holding his tray, with his mouth hanging open. The school was completely isolated. He leaned towards the window and craned his neck left and right. The school was surrounded, at least on this side, by one hell of a drop; the place was built on a cliff. He still had clung to the hope that the school was not so entirely set apart from civilization, that maybe shops and houses full of sympathetic ears were only a stone's throw away. One thing was clear: if you threw a stone from up here, no one would ever find it.

"We're really...up here," said Charlie. His voice shook.

He sat and stared at his plate and, in spite of being ravenously hungry, picked at the soggy egg batter of his supper with his fork. He looked around the lower level and up at the middle level. All of these kids had probably not wanted to come here and all of these kids were still here and jockeying for their piece of waterlogged, incompetently-prepared Mexican food. Had anyone ever just got up and left?

His mind flashed to the long road on which he had come in, with the inviting grand cabins of golden wood. For all he knew, more houses surrounded the other side of campus past the dorms where he had heard the sheep. Maybe he could just talk to those in charge and tell them a mistake had been made, a misunderstanding had occurred. He remembered the look on the girl's face in the quad. He wanted to run back outside and see if she was still there and ask her what happened. Why did she look so sad? Had she tried to leave yet? Did she want to walk back to town with him? Charlie's mind was spinning like a runaway carnival ride. He had to stop it. He set his jaw.

The boys at the table seemed unconcerned with such questions. Jonathan rapaciously shoveled refried beans into his mouth between vacant stares at the land below as he chewed. Austin was similarly unconcerned. He slowly poured a glass of milk from the pitcher, threatening an overflow as he coaxed an alarming amount of liquid into the plastic glass. His brows knit in concentration.

Programmed, Charlie thought with a shudder. They are all programmed. Any talk of leaving the school would have to be done with caution until he knew who to trust.

"You can only have one glass of milk, by the way," said Austin. "If you get it in the glass, it's yours." He looked up at Charlie and set the pitcher down, beaming with accomplishment. Charlie figured the girls must really like him. His dimples were deep and his golden brown hair flopped over his forehead in thick waves. Perfect teeth, high cheekbones, and bright green eyes were not often the tell-tale signs of the fabled loser. Yet, he had been sent here and here he remained, passing on another dismal rule with a guileless smile. In fact, giving the room another once-over, Charlie thought most of the kids looked like good-looking, healthy specimens of American youth.

Charlie's eyes were glazing. Jonathan leaned over the table. "You okay?"

"Yeah..." Charlie replied, "Sure..."

"So..." Jonathan continued, "We're in the same peer group,"

"When did you get here?" Charlie asked, regaining himself.

"About a month ago. Everyone starts off in Genesis and then moves up from there."

"What's Genesis?"

"Just the name of the family. All the families have names. Austin is in Quest now. That's two families above us. He's been here a year."

"I got moved up last week," said Austin.

Charlie remembered the names "Genesis" and "Quest" from the row of closet doors he had seen on the way into the lodge.

"So, I'm in Genesis," Charlie said apathetically. He began slowly eating. His food had gone cold.

A voice from the middle level suddenly shouted above the rest and all attention was focused on a short, dark-haired boy who was just visible over the dividing wall above, his hands cupped around his mouth.

"Excuse me. Can we please keep it down? Thank you." The boy's head sank out of sight.

"Kenny Bootman," said Jonathan with an unaffectionate sigh. "He's in Genesis too."

"The guy's working on his "look-good"," Austin informed Charlie.

The dining room was effectively hushed and the conversations throughout resumed with a self-conscious murmur.

"Oh..." said Austin with revelation, his eyes still trained on the middle level, "no wonder. Jonas Portman is here."

"You're right," said Jonathan, eyes wide.

A tall fat man with a receding hairline and wire-rimmed glasses was descending the short flight of stairs to the lower level. He ignored the handrail bolted to the adjoining wall and surveyed the room with regal confidence.

Jonathan leaned confidentially to Austin: "I can't believe The Boot pulled everyone up in front of Jonas."

"When else would he do it?" said Austin and slugged the last of his milk.

"Jonas and Mary Portman run the school," Jonathan informed Charlie discreetly, keeping one eye on the commanding figure that was now gliding towards them between tables.

"Hi, Jonas," Austin and Jonathan said together.

"Gentlemen," greeted Jonas with just enough of a sardonic lilt as to make perfectly clear that the pleasantry was mere noblesse oblige and that it had not been earned. The big man paused, winded from his journey across the dining room, and breathed audibly through his nose. The boys straightened reflexively in their chairs.

"Charlie Hoff," Jonas said in a silken bass voice, sweeping his eyes towards the blond kid. "Welcome to Ponderosa Academy. I look forward to getting to know you. Toby Heiser, your family head, would like to meet with you in Michelangelo at 7:30, and he will go over your schedule with you and you can ask him whatever questions you may have. I've spoken to Vince Russo, he's been assigned as your Big Brother, correct? He will show you the way. It's a big place, Charlie, but we will make sure you don't get lost. Okay?"

Jonas didn't wait for a reply, and with a nod and a tight smile, took leave of them and glided to an adjacent table where he dispensed some token pleasantries before moving on to the next table to do the same. Before long he had made his way up the stairs and out of sight.

Charlie was chilled. Was that a threat? Jonas would make sure he "didn't get lost." Jonas would make sure he didn't leave and that his whereabouts were known at all times, isn't that what he really meant, or was it just something to say? He didn't know this man but he could see the effect he had on the other boys and he didn't seem like the kind of guy who just blurted things out. He had spoken slowly and carefully as if to make his words indelible. Charlie wondered if paranoia was getting the best of him.

He looked out the window. The sun was now a thin gold band on the horizon; the valleys far below were being swallowed by the coming night.

"Has anyone ever tried to run away from here?" Charlie asked.

The words tumbled heavily from his mouth. Now he had said it. Patience did not seem like a virtue anymore, in spite of what his mother used to tell him. He felt panicked, suddenly starved for information and the boys across from him knew things, had seen things. He had to know sooner than later. He held his breath as the words landed.

Austin and Jonathan flicked their eyes around the room. They were done eating and the milk pitcher was just an empty vessel with a creamy white glaze. They pushed their plates aside and leaned into the table.

"Sure," said Austin.

"Yeah," said Jonathan, "as a matter of fact someone split the day I got here."

Charlie was relieved. He didn't really know what he was expecting. He supposed the two boys could have bolted straight out of their seats, pointing an extended accusatory finger, while making that guttural hissing noise from "Invasion of the Body Snatchers"--it had scared the crap out of him when he first saw that movie--but instead they were so forthcoming that Charlie almost raised a silencing finger to his lips to ensure some discretion. Before long, however, he was listening heedlessly, breathless with curiosity.

"Oh, that's right," said Austin, "Paul Benedict. They found him hiding out in the big woodshed at the lumberyard at the end of School Road. You might have seen it on the way in, you know, the place on the corner? Well, it's usually full of wood, but since the beginning of summer, I guess, there isn't as much wood there now and there are plenty of nooks and crannies to hide in. He would sleep there and wait for food deliveries to the elementary school across the street, which, I guess, happened early in the morning. He would wait for the delivery guy to take a dolly full of food crates or whatever into the cafeteria, and then Paul would rip off some food right out of the back of the open truck. Snack cakes, cookies-- whatever he could get his hands on."

"He was hiding out there for, like, three days," Jonathan added.

"Yeah," said Austin, "and I guess he got tired of it and tried walking to town. Betty Anderton, one of the townies who work in the kitchen, spotted him and she blew the whistle. Some staff picked him up and threw him on Full Time. Can you believe it? Busted by the kitchen lady. Lame."

"Full time?" asked Charlie

"Permanent dishes. If you do something wrong here you get a night of Dishes but if you do something really bad you get a Full Time. You never leave the dining room on Full Time except to go to bed. You got to ask a staff if you want to take a piss. Usually you just sit on the middle level and you're on Bans from the whole school. You can't talk to anyone, you can't even make eye contact with anyone, and you just sit and write in your journal and write down your dirt until they say you're done."

"Paul was on Full Time for at least a week," said Jonathan.

"At least," confirmed Austin. "I think it was more like ten days."

"Why didn't he just knock on the door of one of those big houses on that road...the...School Road?" asked Charlie with instant regret. That question was too specific, way too betraying.

Jonathan let out a convulsive laugh.

"And tell them what?" posed a bemused Austin. "'Hi, strangers. I just ran away from the boarding school for fuckups down the road because I don't want to be there anymore.' If they didn't immediately call the school, which they probably would, they would call the cops. It's not like they would have let him crash on their couch. People who live up here don't want anything to do with this school. That's what I think."

Charlie figured he was right. Why would they want to get involved? It sounded like the town viewed this school as nothing more than a depository for criminal youth.

School for fuck-ups?

His heart was sinking and it took an effort to appear apathetic. He did not want to appear like he was hanging on every valuable word, which of course he was.

"What happened to him, this Paul guy, is he still here?" Charlie asked.

"Oh yeah," Jonathan replied, "he's still here. He shaped up pretty quick."

"At least he didn't get sent to Provo like Kevin Levy," said Austin.

"What's that?" asked Charlie, trying to slow his words down, but his heart was racing.

"Provo Canyon, Utah. It's a lockup. I guess it's in the middle of nowhere. Hardcore juvie. This guy Kevin Levy split and when they found him he had gone nuts."

Jonathan interrupted: "Was that the guy who ate the lizards?"

"Yep," said Austin.

"I remember hearing about that," Jonathan said with wonder. "That guy was in Shawn's peer group."

"So, anyway," continued Austin, "this guy decides to go straight that way." Austin cocked a thumb at the window. "Straight into the canyon. He got pretty lost and ended up grilling lizards for food. The rumor was that he had nabbed a lighter from Anna Bladen's purse. She's a staff here. Old lady. Smokes like a chimney. So a forest ranger finds Kevin walking on an access road, only about a mile from the interstate, and they pick him up. Get this--he's wearing a bloody raccoon pelt on his head as a hat like some bat-shit crazy Daniel Boone. How weird is that? So they get him back to campus, isolate him, and within...like...two or three hours, the men in the white coats show up, throw him into an unmarked white van, and take him to the airport where they load him onto a plane and fly him straight to Provo. Shawn told me all this. He was on a work crew digging an irrigation ditch down on the front lawn and saw the whole thing. Well, I mean, the van part. He heard the rest from Michael DiFranco."

Austin leaned back and contemplatively rotated his empty glass with his thumb and forefinger. The lower level was deserted now. A cricket chirped somewhere in the brush below the window.

Jonathan looked at Charlie, speaking softly, and echoed the unarticulated question pushing on the inside of Charlie's head, "Until you're eighteen, what rights do you really have?"

Silence, sober and thick, fell upon the three.

"Charlie!" It was Vince, calling down from the middle level. "Let's go. Toby wants to see you now."

Chapter 5

Across the lodge and down a short, dimly-lit hall lay Michelangelo, a newer addition in the half-timbered wing that overlooked the front lawn and the parking lot beyond. This room was similar to the other satellite rooms of the lodge in its appointments: a sofa with sage-colored cushions and wooden arms, matching chairs and mahogany end tables holding lamps with amber shades. The walls were warm with dark wood paneling. Charlie could smell the flat scent of years of lemon-scented furniture polish.

It was off of this room, in a cramped office that looked as if it had been adapted from a walk-in closet, that Toby Heiser's back could be seen, hunched and speaking softly into a phone.

"Well, that's it for the main floor," said Vince flopping down on one of the couches. "We can go see the library and gallery upstairs later."

Charlie remained standing and peered out of the window through the dusk. The administration building, along with the other small building beside it, lit the far side of the lawn with porch lights burning inside iron lanterns.

After a few reassuring grunts, followed by the sound of the phone receiver being set back onto the cradle, Toby Heiser emerged wringing his hands.

"Charlie Hoff," said the man, "I'm Toby Heiser. I'm your family head. Please have a seat."

He was short and stout, his limbs compact and his barrel-shaped torso neither thin nor overweight. A close-clipped dark beard encircled his jaw. Deep brown close-set eyes, beneath a heavy brow, surveyed the boys. His hair was receding at the temples leaving a widow's peak that lined up perfectly with his aquiline nose, somehow increasing the impression that he was unusually wise and clever.

Charlie took a chair next to Vince who sprang to his feet and looked at Toby expectantly.

"Thank you, Vince," said Toby, "we shouldn't be long. Can you close the door on the way out? Thanks."

Vince left while Toby and Charlie appraised one another.

Toby spoke: "I just got off the phone with your mother. She has regrets about the way she decided to convince you to come here but she wants you to know that she believes it's the best thing for you right now."

"I want to talk to her," said Charlie leaning forward with his hands on his knees, peering at the office in the wall. Suddenly, Charlie felt close to her. In a way, she had just been here, just feet away.

"We can get to that in a minute. What I want you to know, Charlie. is that we did not approve of the way your parents chose to...misrepresent...the time you would be spending here at Ponderosa. We did advise them to tell you what are program offers and to tell you how long our program lasts. That being said, I also want you to know that your parents felt that you would not willingly consent to the program. They felt the program here would be healthy for you and that it would be a safe environment where you could get the support you need and grow emotionally. It was very important that they got you here without incident and without your brother being subjected to a traumatizing... situation."

Charlie leaned back in his chair and rubbed his face with both hands. It was still hard to believe this was happening. Between his fingers he kept his eye on the pool of dim light coming from the tiny office where the edge of a desk and blotter could just be seen around the slight corner. A phone was in there. It was so close.

There was a pregnant silence. Toby was reading his mind; Charlie could almost feel his brain being suckled by the troll-like man across from him who was now pursing his lips and tenting his fingers under his chin.

"I can't let you call home right now, Charlie," said Toby.

"Why not?" Charlie blurted. Suddenly, it was all too real. Without warning, something inside him began to unravel. "I want to talk to my mom. I don't think she knew it was this kind of school. It was all Kurt's idea. She wouldn't send me here. What did I do that was so bad? It was a mistake. I don't want to stay here for two years. I don't even want to stay here for two days. They tricked me. They totally tricked me! This is BULLSHIT!"

Charlie was leaning forward again, his hands grabbing the side of his head in frustration as he rambled. The man across from him nodded patiently and with each slow and commiserating movement of Toby's head, Charlie was slowly diffused until he eventually slumped back into the cushions with an exhausted stare.

"I know," said Toby soothingly, "I know."

"I don't do drugs."

"We have many students who do not have drug problems."

"Then why am I here?"

"Why do you think you're here, Charlie?"

Charlie expelled his breath slowly and evenly towards his feet, feet that were writhing in his sneakers. He glanced up and began to speak, his mouth working without words.

Toby drew a file to his lap from an end table and opened the goldenrod cover. "I understand you've been expelled from two schools. Is that right?"

Charlie stared out the window.

"I also understand that you have had some problems at home. You live with your mother and your stepfather? Is that correct?"

Charlie looked at the floor and rubbed the back of his neck. His teeth came together and ground. He had been set up. He was sure that Kurt had pulled his mother aside at some point and had suggested this place, probably with an affected concern for his well-being. In the end, The Committee was really just Kurt. It was Kurt's edicts forced on the family, that's all it was. There was no deliberation, and if there was, it would be nothing but a pretense, just in case Kurt needed some gild for the hideous lilies of Charlie's condolence bouquet. In the end, Kurt would have his way. The man had hijacked his mother, his brother and was now free to run his family into the ground without interference.

Toby, still glancing at the file, said: "I understand your real father left when..."

"I have no father," Charlie spat.

Toby closed the file and slid it back onto the table.

There was silence.

"We are here to help, Charlie," Toby said. "Every student here is willing to help you as well. What you need to do is accept that you are here and get the most out of this experience."

Charlie glared at him with crossed arms. Toby rose and

disappeared into the office and emerged with a blue plastic binder. He walked across the room and handed it to Charlie who regarded it scornfully before flipping it open with a flourish.

"I believe you had an opportunity to familiarize yourself with our agreements?" Toby asked, returning to his chair and crossing his legs.

Charlie sighed as his eyes swept down the familiar page. This was intolerable. What twisted mind had conceived of this list of rules? "No sugar or caffeine" was bad enough but "No Music"?

"So I can't listen to AC/DC?" asked Charlie.

"No."

"Ozzy Osbourne?"

"No."

"Iron Maiden? Queen? Kiss?"

"No."

"So I've got to listen to Duran Duran or Men at Work or something?"

"No, Charlie. We've selected music that we feel is appropriate to play in the lodge. No radios or tape decks are permitted on campus. We feel that popular music reminds students of their old lives and we want you to move forward. We have plenty of music to listen to that has a positive message."

The troll man was serious. Charlie was willing to suffer the indignity of listening to pop music just to make this man happy, but the man wanted more. What to wear and how to wear it was your typical private school constraints--he had plenty of experience with those--but these "agreements" were different, very different. And the granddaddy of them all, out of an impressive list of jaw droppers, was number twelve: "No student may leave the campus or communicate with family or past acquaintances without approval".

This was 1983, thought Charlie, could a kid just be stripped of all of his rights? Then he remembered what Jonathan had said at dinner: "Until you are eighteen what rights do you really have?"

Suddenly, he felt like a lab rat that inevitably would be shocked for tripping the wrong lever. He stared at the man across from him. There had to be something he could say, something he could do to convince this man of the mistake that had been made.

"Charlie, you need to accept that you are here," said Toby, "every student feels like you are feeling right now when they first get here, but soon you will find that this environment is a place where you will be listened to, free to explore yourself and make lasting and meaningful friendships."

Charlie knew he was not going to simply talk his way out of this situation. He took a deep breath and was surprised when hope flared faintly within him. There was another way, a smarter way, and it came to him like a prayer whispered on a breeze. It was clear that Toby had no interest in his words, but actions, yes actions, would disarm him. A model student, a model kid, a model human being would disarm them all. From what he had gathered so far, it was the only solution. The plan could take a couple of weeks but he was confident that it would work. It had to work.

"Fine," said Charlie, "okay, I'm here. I don't really understand what's going on yet but I'm here."

Toby seemed amused by the retraction of Charlie's defenses. "You'll get used to things in no time."

"So what are these Raps and...Prah...feets?"

He was genuinely curious, but, more than that, he wanted to keep his eyes averted and change the subject to protect his intentions.

"It's an agreement, not a rule," replied Toby, seemingly delighted by the interest, "We need your help in supporting this environment so that it can be what it is. An agreement is a mutual and accepted arrangement, two parties who are in accord. Therein lies the strength of what we are achieving here. Does that make sense?"

It made no sense to Charlie whatsoever but he offered a thin smile that he hoped was convincing.

"Raps are held three times a week," Toby continued, "they are group sessions where students can take care of their feelings, take care of issues. We just had Raps today so your first Rap will be on Wednesday."

Charlie flashed on the sobbing girl, the one from the dorm trail. His stomach tightened.

Toby continued: "The only thing I can tell you about Propheets is that they are workshops where you are given the emotional tools that you will need. There are a total of six Propheets lasting twenty-four hours apiece. There are two that last several days. Your first Propheet will be the Ascent and you will attend this Propheet while in the Genesis family."

"So why can't you talk about them?" Charlie asked.

"You can," Toby replied, "but only with the people who were in the Propheets with you. Raps and Propheets are a safe zone where nothing leaves the room. It's a trust that must not be violated."

More secrets, Charlie thought. This place was full of them. He remembered walking through the administration building and how he could feel the secrets in the air, stifling, like some strange kind of humidity.

"What does Propheet mean?" Charlie ventured.

"The name was taken from 'The Prophet' by Kahlil Gibran. It is an important book and one that we regard highly. Propheet simply means: giving feet to the words of the prophet." Toby raised his eyebrows with declarative pride.

Charlie stared blankly. This was going to be harder than he thought. He had to pretend this didn't sound crazy.

"Your schedule..." Toby resumed, flipping a page.

"Yeah," said Charlie," what's with the work crews."

"Builds character," Toby quipped dismissively, shelving any protestations. Charlie deflated.

"In Genesis," continued Toby, "you will be on house crew. You and your peer group will be responsible, primarily, for keeping the main lodge clean. After you've been here awhile you will move up to Vision where you will work on the farm and in the garden. After that, you move up to Quest where you will learn about nature and the outdoors. Rock climbing, hiking, and wilderness skills are all part of Quest. After that, you move up to..."

Toby went on. Charlie felt the facade on his face sliding off and reaffixing itself imperfectly. He shifted self-consciously in his seat.

"In a few weeks we can call your folks," said Toby, "okay?"

Charlie's attention snapped back into place. Toby was dangling a carrot, a tasty one. He was good at his job. Charlie wondered if this guy was ever really going to accept his sudden reformation: feigned interest from yet another student who had no real intention of swallowing the bitter pill. He suddenly felt as transparent as a picture window. He swallowed hard.

Toby went on: "In the back of your binder you'll notice there is nothing but blank paper. I want you to use that as your journal and write in it every day. Write down your thoughts, feelings, fears and experiences. If you run out of paper just ask for more. You will be surprised at how clear things can be when they are put to paper. Okay?"

Charlie nodded. Toby stood and Charlie followed suit stiffly.

"I'm supervising the floor tonight so I will be around," said Toby over his shoulder as he ducked back into the tiny office. "Go talk to the other students and get to know them."

Charlie headed for the main room of the lodge, his hands shoved deep into the pockets of his jeans. Alarm flared and he pawed wildly at his pocket for the wallet his grandfather had given him, forgetting briefly that it had been confiscated. Resigned, he returned his hands to the pockets, clenching them in moist fists as he walked numbly down the shadowy hall. He heard faint music coming from somewhere in the building: soft horns, muted strings. It poured down the darkened corridor toward him like warm syrup. It was the kind of music played in elevators.

He passed another small office on his left, the door open wide. He poked his head in: darkness, diamond-paned windows with the night beyond, a desk, a pair of chairs. No phone on the desk. He continued walking.

He saw another room, ahead on the right. This door was ajar; a sliver of pale light spilling into the hall. There were voices coming from the room. He stopped in the shadows to listen: first, he heard a deep voice followed by the murmuring of a young girl, a student.

Charlie crept slowly toward the door. He peered through the crack.

The room was lit only by ambient light through the window. A man was sitting in the room in the dark, his back to the door--a large man with thin hair. The student was on his lap, her face obscured, her head turned away from the man. Just visible past the man's shoulder, pudgy fingers stroked coils of blond hair.

"Yes," the man whispered at the girl's ear. "That's right..."

Shifting, Charlie strained for a better look. The floor beneath him creaked. The man in the room began to turn, little round glasses flashing.

It was Jonas Portman, the big man from the dining room.

Charlie ducked and jerked back, holding his breath, his heart hammering.

No, he thought. It couldn't be what it looked like.

He waited, pressing his back to the wall. Silence thickened. There was nowhere to go. As quickly as he could, he passed the crack of the door, walking stiffly. He headed towards the main room of the lodge, towards the soft music, towards the sound of a hundred murmuring voices.

The dim hall ended and he rounded the corner. What he saw then made him stop in his tracks.

Chapter 6

Astonished, he sucked in a breath, his eyes scanning the great room.

Students were lying on the floor everywhere. They littered the carpeted expanse of the lodge, squirming and writhing in piles.

Charlie stood, gaping.

From the speakers in the eves, the Carpenters were singing about only just beginning to live. Charlie didn't know exactly what an omen was but he was beginning to recognize how one felt.

What is this, his mind groaned. What in hell is this?

The students were on top of one another and murmuring. Groups from three to five students dotted the floor in all manner of repose. The Pit, in the center of the room, had a knee-high wall marking the borders of the sunken sectional couch that commanded it and this honey-colored divide was obscured with pillows that had been yanked from the nearby chairs and loveseats. Students reclined on them with their legs straight to serve as pillows for more students who laid their heads upon the randomly jutting legs and stomachs, perpendicularly, forming a jigsaw of bodies that sprawled from one end of the lodge to the other. It looked like they had all fallen from the sky.

Even the Pit was full of students lying about as was the long raised section of the floor that Charlie was now standing on. Prone kids were everywhere. Some of them were obscuring a staff member at the bottom of the pile, some stroking each other's hair slowly, but all with their arms around each other. Everyone was in physical contact, introspectively glazed, intimate and hushed.

Boys were laying atop boys, girls atop girls. Charlie estimated that every last student in the school must have been sprawled across the considerable length and breadth of the room. He clenched the sweaty fists in his pockets tighter and scanned the room for a pathway.

The pillows propped against the raised landing that was the egress from Michelangelo had a small spot along the step where there was a parting of limbs just wide enough to plant a sure foot. He stepped carefully down the step and towards the center of the lodge along the back wall where the cushion-less furniture groupings seemed to be relatively clear of human obstacles.

He didn't know where he was going, but he kept threading his way through the bodies. Scores of drowsy eyes watched him. Across the room was the threshold that led to the outside, the wide doorway he had entered from earlier with the flight of stairs ascending to somewhere and the stacks of black plastic chairs shoved beneath. With new purpose he high-stepped a group of girls at his feet and focused on the exit. He lost balance slightly and one of his sneakers came down too quick and pinched the side of one of the girls' splayed hands.

"Sorry", Charlie offered quickly.

The girl seemed unaffected and calmly tucked her hand closer to her side and continued stroking the hair of the girl that lay between her legs with the other. The girl on top was softly crying and trying to whisper confidingly to her sympathizer between breathless sobs. The sympathizer looked expressionlessly at Charlie as she cooed comforting words at the crook of her arm where curled, wet strands of hair framed the flushed ear of the crying girl. Charlie tore his gaze away.

Before him, a significant pile of students blocked his way to the exit. He broke left, skirting the back wall, furthest from the Pit and the stone fireplace. He stopped transfixed by a scale replica of the lodge that sat on a wooden table against the varnished logs of the wall. He had not noticed it earlier on his way through the building after dinner.

A perfect miniature of the lodge no more than three feet long and two feet high sat sharing the feeble pool of light from Vermeer's "Girl With Pearl Earring" who seemed to be silently bemused by Charlie's confusion. The great central chimney with its gray stone, the long windows of the Genesis family room overlooking the pool, the half-timbered addition on the left, and the individually crafted logs faux-finished with wood grain had all been rendered with precision. Along the pitch of the shingled roof was a long ballot box slit, sanded and smoothed at its edges. Beneath the slit, in black block letters, were the words: RAP

REQUESTS.

Charlie noticed a neat stack of white notepaper and a mug of pencils on the table beside the model. He peered into the slit.

"Charlie."

He jumped, looking around. It was Jonathan, almost underfoot and leaning against the wall with some guy under his arm and a girl sitting beside him. Jonathan invited Charlie to sit by patting the floor with an open palm. Charlie hesitated.

"C'mon," said Jonathan from behind the other boy's mop of dark brown curls, "smush."

"Smush?"

Yeah, smush," said Jonathan and patted the ground again insistently, "let's get our own smush pile going."

"I was just going to head out," said Charlie.

"Head out where?" asked Jonathan.

"I don't know. Back to my room I guess."

Jonathan seemed amused by this. "You better not do that. Not without an older student or a staff at least. What do you need? Is Shawn in the Pit? He was there last time I saw him. You better ask him."

"I don't need anything. I'm just..." Charlie fumbled for words and colored with frustration.

He remembered the game plan he had just devised while talking with Toby: he was to swallow it whole, no matter how weird it got, until he could confidently stand before those in charge and confront them with their mistaken perceptions of him as a rebel, a loser and a breaker of rules. It was the smart way out. He had to remember that. Yes, no matter how weird it got and it seemed to be getting weirder by the moment. If he had to create a smush pile – whatever the hell that was, and whatever purposes it served – he would do it with a smile. Two weeks, max, and he would be offered an apology. It beat the thought of sneaking down that hill and eating lizards or walking the road back to town and getting turned in instantly, making his life even worse than it was now.

Tipping everyone off by saying "Do you know how crazy this looks?" or "What the hell is everyone doing this for?" would scatter all of his cards on the table, face up, and show them all that he was really holding a whole lot of nothing. Which, he was beginning to believe.

He took a seat next to the girl who hugged her knees and smiled.

She was pretty. She looked like the female analogue of Charlie with her blue eyes and blond hair, but her features were fuller. Her cheeks were red and round like apples and her button nose turned up slightly. Her wavy curls played at the shoulders of her lavender blouse and her thick eyelashes blinked once as the eyes behind them swept down Charlie's body and then back to lock with Charlie's own.

"I'm Carolina," she said.

"Care-rule..." Charlie attempted.

"Carolina," she repeated.

"Oh. Oh. Carolina," Charlie tried again, "I thought you said...well...I wasn't sure what you said. Wow."

Charlie shifted uncomfortably on his knees, not sure what to do with his body. "I've never heard that name before," he continued, "I mean I've heard that name but not...you know..."

Stupid stupid, he thought. Can you sound like more of an idiot?

"It's okay. I get that a lot," Carolina said. "My parents screwed in Beaufort on their honeymoon."

Charlie looked stunned.

"It's a town in South Carolina," she continued. A sweet smile spread across her face like an overturned pot of honey. Her eyes glittered mischievously. "I guess it's pretty. Must have been romantic or I wouldn't be here."

Jonathan and the guy lying on top of him watched the exchange drowsily.

"And you're the Nate," Carolina said conclusively and patted his knee.

"I prefer Charlie."

"I'm just kidding," she said and touched his knee again. He looked at the hand and then at her. A guilty look darkened her face. With a barely audible gasp, Charlie shot her a wide-eyed glance, imploring her not to be dismayed. She received the message and resumed a carefree smile and gave her bent legs an extra hug.

"Relax, Charlie" said Jonathan, "you look uptight. Have you met Aaron? This is Aaron Corrigan. He is in Genesis too."

The thin, dark haired boy extracted a hand from beneath the tangle of limbs and jiggled it in a tight, enthusiastic wave. Charlie leaned on an elbow and tentatively let his legs straighten out.

"Why is everyone on the floor?" whispered Charlie.

"Smushing," said Jonathan simply.

"I know but why."

"That's just what we do at night," Jonathan said, "no television. You just hang out and talk, tell your story. Didn't you talk to Toby? Vince told me you guys were in Michelangelo, like, forever."

"Yeah," Charlie replied, "he told me the whole deal. I don't think I get it but he went over a lot of stuff."

He didn't go over this, Charlie thought, glancing around. In fact, what did he really know? That most things were secrets? That most things he would find out about soon enough? They were stringing him along. He suddenly felt claustrophobic. He had to get out of here, of this room at least. Jonathan said to find Shawn, but that was the last thing he wanted to do.

"Where's Vince?" Charlie asked.

"Vince Russo?" Carolina replied.

"I just talked to him," said Jonathan, "he went that way." Pinned beneath Aaron, he jerked his head left. "I think he was running Dishes."

The soft music had stopped and Charlie looked around the lodge. A girl was leaning over on the open balcony across the room and high above, fiddling with something. She raised a cassette tape to her face, read both sides of it, pulled out the cassette and leaned over again. Music began to play. He saw no Vince, but saw a solitary figure on the landing, in the pool of light from an end table.

"Why isn't he smushing or whatever," Charlie asked, nodding his head towards the boy. He was sitting alone and playing with a stack of checkers, making variegated sandwiches of the chips and placing them on the nearby end table in tall stacks.

"Who is it?" asked Jonathan from his constricted position.

Carolina craned her neck around, "Devon Childs."

"He's on bans from, like, half the school," said Aaron, measuring his relish. "He had a sex contract with a girl and he was caught trying to break into Sonia DiFranco's car in the lower parking lot. He did a Full Time for it. He's still on Bans, though."

"Bands?" asked Charlie.

"Bans," Carolina whispered, "you get put on a ban from people if you get contracted up with them. Like plotting to do something wrong"

This Charlie pondered, looking back at the boy with the checkers. The guy was pale and had thick dark hair. His eyebrows arched and met in the middle. His eyes were close together and focused intently on stacking the checkers. His skin was the color of his plain white t-shirt.

The song that was now playing from the balcony was something about riding through the desert on a horse with no name.

"America," said Carolina, "actually, this group isn't bad." She quietly hummed the words she didn't know and sang the parts she did know in a breathy falsetto that made Charlie's body tingle oddly. "In the desert you can't remember your name, 'cause there ain't no one for to give you no pain."

"So, Charlie," said Jonathan struggling to sit up until Aaron obliged him by reluctantly rolling his head off Jonathan's chest, "did Toby tell you what goes on tomorrow?"

"Shit," said Charlie suddenly, "My binder. I left it. It has the schedule and my journal." He sprung to his feet. "I'll be right back."

Charlie high stepped through the crowd towards the landing and found a gap in the bodies wide enough to pass. He stepped up and to the left, through the threshold to the back hallway. He paused before passing the room where he had seen Jonas Portman and the girl, but the door was open wide. They were gone. Quickly, he continued down the hall and into Michelangelo. His binder was still on the couch. Relieved, he yanked it up, turned to go and then stopped.

He was alone.

The phone, he thought.

He stared at the closed pocket door. The room was dark, but the little brass plate where the door locked shone.

Maybe Toby had forgotten to lock it, he thought. Or maybe the lock wasn't very strong.

His heart began to hammer in his chest.

Or maybe Toby is still behind the door, waiting.

Charlie strained to hear anything, the scratch of a pencil, the creak of a chair.

He held his breath. The room was dim and quiet. He heard only soft music coming from the Floor along with the a distant and ghostly muddle of purring voices.

Slowly, as if the muscles in his neck would creak like the moorings of a ship, reverberate through the logs of the lodge and betray him, he looked back at the open door he had come through. Feeble light glinted on the wood paneling in the dim hall. He pricked his ears for the slightest sound of approaching shoes whispering on the carpet. He looked back at the pocket door.

Don't get caught, his mind warned. Don't you get caught.

He took one crab-step towards the office, eyes flicking back at the open door of the family room. He took another step.

Now, he was standing within reach of the small brass handle of the office door. Slowly he reached for it. The brass was cold beneath the fever of his fingers.

Quick, he thought. Do it quick.

With one deliberate movement, he tugged the handle. The door did not budge. He exhaled, muttered a curse and walked stiffly out of the room.

Toby Heiser was standing at the end of the hall.

"Hello, Charlie." said Toby.

Charlie's blood ran with ice and his mouth dried.

"I left this," Charlie said, a little too quickly, extending the binder. "I left this in the room."

"Ah," said Toby, "you don't want to forget that."

Charlie was shaking. A breath shuddered through his lips. A cold lump was pounding in his chest. He stared at Toby.

"You scared me," said Charlie.

"I'm sorry," Toby said, and took a step forward. "I was talking to Shawn Flaherty, your dorm head. He informs me you haven't had a chance to put away your clothes so I'm sending you up to the dorms with him so you can tighten up your area."

Relief came like a warm wind and it made Charlie's knees weak.

Toby continued: "You have to keep your personal effects in good order. It's one of the agreements here. Shawn will take you up."

Charlie wasn't listening. Still not completely convinced he was in the clear, he scanned the man's face for signs of suspicion, evaluating his tone of voice for notes of accusation.

"Okay?" Toby asked with raised eyebrows.

Charlie determined that he was in no trouble, but it had been close. Too close. He shifted the now sweaty binder to his other hand.

"Okay," said Charlie faintly.

Shawn appeared at the end of the hall alongside Toby. Charlie watched them exchange some kind of look, little nods of their heads, before Toby left.

Charlie gripped his binder tighter.

Shawn was staring at him now, holding open one of the heavy

doors of the lodge. Beyond, night had fallen.

"Let's go," said Shawn.

Chapter 7

The alarm by the dorm head's bed shrieked a warbling, lunatic cry with its failing batteries. Shawn slammed a hand down on the black plastic clock on his night stand, upsetting a bottle of lotion which tumbled to the floor. Groans of protest filled the room from all quarters.

"Feet on the floor," Shawn said thickly.

"Yeah, yeah," muttered Jonathan in an irritated lilt, sitting up and absently rubbing the back of his neck. He saw Charlie, free of sleep's hold, scribbling in his journal and cocked an eyebrow.

"How long have you been up?" Jonathan mumbled.

"Huh? Oh...not long," Charlie replied, pushing the pen's button to retract the stylus before tossing it back in the cubbyhole under the bed, "Had a bad dream. Just writing it down."

"'Bout what?" asked Austin rolling over to face Charlie, his head propped up with an elbow.

"Just a nightmare," Charlie replied.

He wasn't going to tell them, couldn't tell them. He couldn't think about it anymore: Brandon, his little brother, beaten beyond all recognition, slowly crawling towards him across the bedroom floor leaving a trail of bloody handprints on the carpet as he inched towards Charlie's bed. Brandon, staring up at him, gurgling, his lips purple and puffy, his mouth full of splintered teeth. "Why did you leave me, Charlie," he had said. "WHY DID YOU LEAVE MEEEEE..."

"Oh come on," said Austin, "You won't tell us?"

Charlie looked at him, and Austin's smile slid from his face.

"That's okay," Austin said, "You don't have to."

"Feet on the floor, Austin," Shawn barked, making his way to the bathroom.

"I got a boner, Shawn," said Austin irritably.

"Don't care," muttered Shawn over his shoulder as he disappeared into the bathroom and slammed the door.

Austin stood up and smiled mischievously. He pressed a finger to his lips. Jonathan rolled his eyes at Charlie and grinned. Austin crept to the bathroom door, flung it wide and stood in the pale pool of light arching his body with his hands on the small of his back. From the direction of Austin's focus, Charlie could tell Shawn must have been sitting on the toilet.

"Morning, Shawn," said Austin, feigning an exaggerated yawn. "What a glorious day! Oops. Didn't know you were in here."

"God damn it Austin!" snapped Shawn. A hand came into view groping for control of the door.

Austin left the doorway, laughing with theatrical malevolence. He scampered past Charlie.

"Maybe next time he'll believe me," said Austin before flopping back onto his bed.

Charlie smiled and then broke into a laugh. Jonathan joined him.

"Just for that," yelled Shawn from behind the bathroom door. "You're on porcelain today, Austin."

"What's that?" Charlie whispered

"I got to clean the crapper," Austin replied, "and the sink. Eh...it was worth it."

Charlie was third to shower. He was startled when the timer that controlled the bathroom lights expired and left him in the pitch dark, soaking wet. During their awkward time together last night, Shawn had informed him of yet another Agreement. Showers were not to exceed ten minutes as the school was on well water. The timer made sure you didn't forget. Fumbling for his allotted towel and a firm grip on the timer so he could twist it afresh and comb his hair, Charlie stepped onto the cold tiles.

The image of his brother's face from his nightmare, that bloody face looking up at him, still haunted him as he stared into the mirror. He hoped it would go away soon. He needed his wits about him.

His chore for the morning was "Bisseling" the Berber carpet with the plastic, powerless vacuum that stood in the corner of the coat closet. An industrious silence fell over them all as they worked to get their tasks over with, and the work helped Charlie forget. Before long the boys, save the dorm head, were standing on the promontory, at the end of North Walden, overlooking the sports fields and waiting for Shawn's permission to go to breakfast.

The morning was still and the sky an unblemished pale blue, the color of a baby's blanket. A red-tailed hawk soared high above. A bleat of a sheep from the farm beyond broke the silence. Charlie could just make out the sweep of a corral fence through the distant pines.

"What's taking him?" Jonathan grumbled.

"Okay guys," came Shawn's voice, "let's head out."

Shawn lumbered down the open corridor from the dorms to his waiting charges with a humorless grin.

"What's up?" asked Austin as the boys began the trail to the lodge.

"Just talked to Craig Shepherd, "said Shawn, "some chairs are missing from the lodge. The good ones."

"You think?" Austin asked breathlessly.

"Yep," said Shawn, "we knew it was coming soon. Looks like it's here."

"A Propheet?" asked Jonathan, his eyes wide.

"The Evolve," said Shawn. "I'm sure of it. It's the next one due and there has been a buzz about it coming for a while."

"That's Shawn's next Propheet," Jonathan informed Charlie. "It's a big'un. It's three days long."

"I'm shitting a brick," Shawn conceded, his face sour.

"So you know this because some chairs are gone?" Charlie asked.

"Yep," confirmed Austin, "every time there's a Propheet, the staff that are running it gather comfortable chairs to sit in and drag them up to the New Wing. That's how you can tell. Other than that, it's a surprise. "

"Of course," said Jonathan. "Students all have to sit in black Rap chairs."

"So I may be leaving you guys for a while," said Shawn, his eyes fixed on the trail, "I guess we'll see."

They passed the girl's dorms, and intercepted groups of girls who joined the trail. Pleasantries were exchanged, but the hour subdued further conversation.

After a long silence Charlie said, "You realize that I don't understand half of what anyone says here."

"Like what?" offered Austin.

"Like, what exactly are these Propheets?," asked Charlie, "How often are they? All I know is that you can't talk about it. It's like a secret club or something."

"Kind of," said Austin contemplatively, "guess it kind of is. Well, there are...how many?" he asked, turning to Shawn for help.

It was apparent that Shawn was lost in his anxiety. He didn't answer.

"Well," continued Austin, counting them off on his fingers, "there is the Ascent, the Survivor's, the Children's, the Values, the Dreams, the Imagine, the Evolve, and the Summit."

"The last two are the ones that last for days," Jonathan said.

"They're very long," confirmed Austin, "and you don't get to those until you are an Older Student. That's all I'm going to say 'bout that because I definitely don't want to get contracted up with a Nate."

"See," said Charlie, "what does THAT mean? Contracted up?"

Jonathan leaned towards Charlie as if the subject required at least token discretion. "Getting contracted up with someone is making an agreement with someone that you will permit them to break agreements around you if they will do the same for you. Or if I knew you had dirt and didn't bust you on it then I could be accused of being Contracted Up with you."

"You had me until the end there," said Charlie. "What dirt?"

"That's just what we call..." Jonathan faltered.

"Guilt," Shawn put in suddenly. "Shame. If you're dirty it means you are hiding something. If you don't take care of it in a Rap, and you're still holding on to it, then you're dirty."

Take care of it in a Rap, Charlie thought. Like that girl had been taken care of, the one who had been sobbing on the dorm trail, and no one seemed to be fazed by it, like it happened all the time?

Charlie knew his first Rap was coming, and soon. He shuddered.

The dining room was still cool from the night. Breakfast was granola, fruit and yogurt. The boys chose the middle level – the thought of stairs daunting before breakfast – and ate quietly and efficiently before Charlie spoke: "Toby never told me last night when he plans on letting me call home. You know, just to check in."

Charlie looked at the other boys nervously and then to his cereal, where he began slapping the gravel-like clusters into the milk.

"Two weeks," said Shawn, his jaw disinterestedly sawing the grains like cud, "Maybe more, maybe less. He'll give you fifteen minutes. Timed and monitored."

Charlie stopped in mid chew and looked at the other two boys, waiting for them to refute or confirm this new intelligence. They met his eyes briefly and returned to their breakfasts.

"Really?" said Charlie. "Monitored?"

Shawn grunted that it was so. "Got to make sure you don't tell a bunch of lies about how you're being mistreated or start begging to come home 'cause it was all a big mistake."

Jonathan and Austin laughed dully and continued eating. A wad of oats stuck in Charlie's throat. He swallowed hard.

Chapter 8

Toby Heiser held the First Light meeting in the Genesis family room. Charlie was introduced, roll call was taken and then the day's chores were handed out.

A girl named Karen, a member of the Evolution family who was close to graduation, was in charge of Charlie, instructing him how to use newspaper and vinegar from a squeeze bottle to clean glass. He polished countless diamond-paned windows, cleaned Michael DiFranco's office overlooking the front lawn, and removed all of the books from the library's shelves, dusting the cavities.

Charlie watched other students from the library balcony as they traversed the main floor of the lodge, busily beating cushions, dusting picture frames and mopping the stone floor of the Pit, rolling industrial buckets of sudsy water behind them on rickety casters.

In the corner of the library the daily newspaper hung in segments from mahogany rods on a little rack. He picked up the front section of the newspaper and read the headline. He replaced the rod on its hanger and looked through the other sections. He couldn't find television listings, news of upcoming concerts or local events. It seemed that several sections of the paper had gone missing. Or, they had never been placed there to begin with.

"There you are!"

Charlie jumped and spun around.

It was Karen.

"Didn't mean to startle you," she said. "are you about finished with the library?"

"Done," he replied. "Just one more set of windows. I also did Michael's office. Just looking for more to do."

Karen put her hands on her hips and smiled approvingly, "Looks pretty tight. Well, keep up the good work. I'm impressed."

Charlie watched her leave and then approached the windows.

The sky beyond the glass graded from pale blue to the hazy indigo of the valley floor far below.

Karen was impressed. She had said so. His plan could work. He would be off of this mountain soon enough.

He crumpled another newspaper, squirted vinegar on the panes, wiped the squeaking glass and smiled at his reflection.

Vince Russo turned the backgammon chip around in his hand indecisively before committing to his next move. Keeping one eye on Vince, Charlie scanned the room.

During Floor Time, it appeared that board games were the only acceptable alternative to being involved in a smush pile. The dim corners of the lodge were hosting chess, checkers and a few card games on their slickly waxed coffee tables while the floor, once again, was littered with students, hushed and entwined.

Charlie answered Vince's move with a 3-1 and made his 5-point.

"So how was your first day at Ponderosa," Vince asked as he led a checker with his index finger and clicked it into place atop another at his own 4. Charlie rolled a Lover's Leap but was thwarted by Vince's bar point and was forced to leave a man open on his own 7.

"Better than this game is going," Charlie replied.

Jonathan wandered by, spotted the two, stopped in his tracks, raised his eyebrows in greeting and pulled up the only nearby chair that had not been harvested for its cushions by the floor dwellers. "Who's winning?" he asked.

Charlie rolled a 4-3 and rescued his open man at his 7 with a point at his 5.

"No way!" cried Vince at the board, "Boy, did you just luck out."

"I may have a chance now," Charlie told Jonathan and leaned back in relief.

"I was just asking Charlie how his first full day went." said Vince.

"Not bad," ventured Jonathan, "We were in Archie Goetz's Algebra class together. He's better at math than I am"

"I liked Archie," admitted Charlie, "he kind of reminded me of my grandfather."

"Yeah, he's pretty cool," said Jonathan, "He's on Floor tonight with DiFranco. I saw him earlier. I think he's supervising Dishes."

"Your turn," said Vince.

Charlie rolled double fours and the two discs at Vince's ace point were promptly gathered up and airlifted to Vince's 9.

"Looks like the race is on," Vince said, rubbing his hands.

"What's with Dishes?" Charlie asked, staring at the board. "It seems like a big deal or something."

Vince bit his thumbnail and pondered his next move as he replied, "Well, you are assigned a bunch of work in the dining room and kitchen. You don't leave until you are checked out by whoever is running Dishes, and there's no talking. You got to hustle too or you'll never get off. It's a ball-breaker for sure."

"And let's not forget," added Jonathan, "you miss the weekly movie on Sunday and have to sit in a Cerebration."

"What's that?" asked Charlie.

"You are shut into a room with everyone else who had Dishes that week and..." Jonathan faltered, his expression falling. "I don't know. It depends on who is running it."

The table had grown quiet.

"Well," said Charlie shaking his dice cup, "guess I'm not going to get Dishes then."

Jonathan offered Charlie a smile, but a grave and humorless one: "Everyone gets Dishes...eventually. Walking into the lodge with your shirt not tucked in, wearing a hat in the House, leaving your coat somewhere, being late for a class or work crew or just because a staff is in a bad mood. It all gets you Dishes"

Vince shot Jonathan a look that suggested caution, but confirmed to Charlie with a nod of the head.

Charlie frowned, turning his attention back to bearing his checkers off his home board, trying to clear his mind, but the game was all but over. He was piled up on his 6 and Vince was in better shape. Vince rolled double fives and that was it.

"Two out of three?" asked Charlie.

"It's your funeral," Vince said and raked the checkers into place.

Charlie stretched his neck and glanced around. He saw that boy again, Devon Childs, sitting alone. Tonight, the boy was not stacking checkers. Instead, Devon sat on the landing under the stairs, a pair of dark, watery eyes peeking at the gathered over the top of a book from the upstairs collection of classics, a shock of raven black hair pasted across his pale forehead. He could have been holding the book upside down for all Charlie could tell. Passing students ignored him.

Charlie watched the boy, the House's stereo system cooing Bread's "It Don't Matter to Me". Vince was watching him too.

"Don't worry," said Vince, grabbing the arm of his chair, preparing to spring. "I can talk to him. I'm allowed to. I'm his dorm head. It looks like he needs some company." He thrust the dice cup at Jonathan. "Want to finish him off?"

"Sure," said Jonathan. Charlie peeled his gaze away and smiled at Jonathan. Vince leapt up and made his way to Devon.

Taking his seat slowly, Jonathan stared past Charlie's shoulder and whispered: "Yikes. Speaking of dorm heads, there is ours. He's at the Rap Request Box. Yep...he's filling one out alright."

Charlie turned towards the far wall, towards the mini replica of the lodge he had seen last night. Shawn was hunched over it. He saw Shawn straightened, briefly looked around the room and then dropped   the slip of paper into the slot in the model's roof. Then, he glided away casually, crouching and disappearing into a group of reclining students.

Charlie spoke flatly as he watched Shawn: "What's the point of that? I haven't been in a Rap yet so I don't know what the big deal is. I have no idea why you would want to request someone to be in your Rap."

"It's not to give them a hug," Jonathan replied, under his breath. "It's bad news if you get requested by someone. You'll find out soon enough. I just hope it's not me. Nah...it can't be me. Shawn and I are okay."

Charlie decided to leave it alone. He was content with playing backgammon for a while. There was one thing he couldn't shake though. A storm had passed through Jonathan's eyes. Charlie had seen it in other students as well. It seemed anything might bring it on. There seemed to be such gravity attached to the simplest acts or the most unobjectionable words. Trying to keep up was grueling.

Aside from trying to decipher ahead of time what was inevitably going to unfold at a masterfully predetermined time and place-- whether he wanted it to or not--Charlie was physically exhausted as well. His plan to free himself from all of these concerns was not proving to be easy. He had single-handedly cleaned the entire second level of the lodge without being asked during the morning work crew. The model student approach was not without its drawbacks. His feet, along with his mind, were throbbing from his efforts.

Jonathan said: "So why are you here, Charlie? You never did answer the question."

Charlie didn't want to talk about that especially, but Jonathan seemed earnest. He was trying to reach out. Maybe he was trying to find an ally. There was something about this guy that Charlie trusted.

Charlie put down his dice cup, let his reluctance melt and then leaned back in his chair. "They want me out of the way I guess. I had no idea this would happen. I got booted from a couple of boarding schools, but they sucked. My parents...I mean, my mom couldn't have known that this place..."

He faltered. He didn't like how he was darkening, how confusion was beginning to gnaw at him.

He fortified himself with a deep breath and continued: "My mom and stepdad tell me I'm going off to summer school, I get dropped off, and then I'm told I'm not going anywhere for two years."

"Well, look at it this way," Jonathan said, fiddling with the chips on the board, "at least you weren't kidnapped."

It became clear to Charlie that game time was over. Jonathan absently held the remaining game pieces and clenched them as if he would turn them to powder. Charlie slumped in his chair, all ears and wide-eyed. Jonathan looked at him gravely. He had just popped open a big can of worms. Something unpleasant and starved for oxygen was about to crawl out.

Charlie hesitated to follow up with the obvious question. Hadn't he just decided to leave the devil-in-the-details alone for the night and just relax? Only moments ago he vowed to not worry about secrets, plans of escape and the answers to an almost inexhaustible supply of questions that he still had about this place.

He swore within his head as he listened to the words slide from his mouth: "What do you mean kidnapped?"

Upstairs on the balcony, Michael DiFranco was bent over and flipping the cassette in the House stereo. A mellow tremolo filled the lodge. It was another soft rock lullaby and it made Charlie's head swim.

Jonathan spoke: "They thought I was crazy...my parents, I mean. I was sleeping--dead asleep. I woke up and two men were standing over me. The overhead light was on and I was looking right up into it. It was bright. I couldn't really see at first and then all I could see was their shapes. They were tall and big guys. I had never seen them before. They said 'Jonathan, get up and get dressed'. I was really freaked out. I called for my mom and then I heard her somewhere behind them, it sounded like she was watching from the hall. She said 'It's okay Jonathan, they won't hurt you, just do what they say'.

"It sounded like she had been crying and I didn't believe her. I called her name again. I could see better now and I saw that one of the men was holding something in his hands. I asked the men who they were and then yelled at my mom, 'What's going on?' I think I said it over and over."

Jonathan stared up at one of the oil paintings on the varnished log wall, a little bridge over a pond done in blotchy dots of color. It was Monet's "Le Pont Japanais a Giverny" and it seemed to be soothing Jonathan, beckoning him to its peaceful   and indistinct world.

Jonathan continued, his voice distant: "They were handcuffs. The man was holding handcuffs. They told me to get dressed again and said they didn't want any problems from me. Of course I asked where we were going and they said they were going to take me to a very nice place where I could get some help and..."

He trailed off and tore his glance from the painting and looked at Charlie, "They didn't use the handcuffs. I begged them not to. I told them I would go. It was the longest ride of my life but I went, me in the backseat, between these two gorillas, another guy driving.

"Turns out they were hired by my mom, like a service or something, to get me to Ponderosa. I guess my mom thought I was going to freak out and not want to go, hurt somebody or go running through the streets and cause a scene. I didn't care really. That's the funny part. I didn't want to be home anyway at the time. I do now. But then, I couldn't have cared less. So...your parents lied to you. My own mother hired a goon squad to take me here against my will. You're not alone"

Charlie was suddenly thirsty. His mouth clicked as he worked his tongue in a vain attempt to moisten his lips. "Shit..."

The humor returned to Jonathan's face, the twinkle--like a rainbow celebrating the end of a storm. It was back in its familiar place, in the corners of his eyes. Yet there was more than just good humor or relief that suffused his features, there was bravery. That was it; he wore a brave face, one that he had earned. Charlie now saw that this boy was prepared to take the blows and remain unsurprised by their arrival.

Jonathan was underestimated. That's what Charlie wanted. That trait would be an invaluable commodity at this place. The stealth that comes from being discounted, the luxurious advantage afforded those dismissed as sufficiently subdued.

Yes, Charlie thought, sticking with Jonathan would not be a bad move, not bad at all. Maybe he had made his first friend at Ponderosa.

"At least it's a nice place," Jonathan said, his grin devilish, glancing around at the art-lined walls. "These paintings aren't cheap, even if they are re-pros. Do you know how much it costs to go here?"

Charlie pursed his lips and shook his head.

"Four grand a month," Jonathan said, leaning back in his chair.

Charlie whistled, "No kidding?"

"Four grand a month," Jonathan repeated.

"Well, that explains it," said Charlie, "my mom just got a whole bunch of money since my grandfather died. I guess this is how she wants to spend it...getting rid of me for awhile."

"Was he rich or something?" asked Jonathan. "Your grandfather?"

"He owned Morgenson Electronics. His name was Peter Morgenson."

"I think I've heard of that."

Charlie continued: "We called him Papa Pete. Well, my brother Brandon and I did. He was like our father. I don't know my real dad..."

Before his heart could sink, Charlie continued: "Anyway, he had a huge house in Chicago, lots of science stuff everywhere. He was really into the power of the sun, the power of light, you know? He made the solar panels that power most of the satellites orbiting the earth. He was really smart. He was very...nice to me. I miss him..."

"Sounds like he was a cool guy," said Jonathan.

Uncomfortable with the blooming silence, Charlie reached for the scattered chips and slid them around the felt and into position for a new game.

Suddenly, a girl was yelling from across the room: "House around the Pit!"

Soon the directive spread like a wildfire and students throughout the lodge began cupping their hands to their mouths and yelling into the adjacent family rooms. A boy next to Charlie sprung to his feet, training the phrase up the library steps and then sat, expectantly watching the stone fireplace.

"House around the Pit?" Charlie asked Jonathan, crinkling his nose.

"We're fine," said Jonathan, "I bet I know what this is about."

Archie Goetz was descending the three steps to the stone floor of the Pit.

Charlie's first class of the day had been Archie's algebra class. The class-just like all of the others-had been peculiar, informal, no textbooks, no blackboards, and no desks. Instead, students sat on couches in the satellite rooms of the lodge with notebooks.

Archie's class had been Charlie's favorite, and he was glad to have at least one mandatory requirement on his schedule that he might even begin to anticipate with relief. Moreover, the man's similarity to Papa Pete was uncanny.

Archie patiently waited in the Pit, hands clasped, sartorially ostentatious amidst the tousled hair casualness of the evening's smush piles. He sported a crisp white button-down shirt the color of his close-cropped hair under a hound's-tooth jacket. His thick-rimmed glasses reflected orange in the dim aurora of the wrought iron chandelier hanging above as his head followed a few stragglers who had come in from the dining room. The tardy group of students walked hunched for the remainder of the distance before crouching self-consciously near the rim of the Pit.

"Okay," Archie began in his quavering high tenor. "I think we are all here now. That's good. Well, I have a special announcement to make."

A murmur swept through the House. It sounded like wind blowing through tall grass. This led to sporadic shushes proffered behind index fingers pressed to puckered lips. Finally, silence took hold.

Archie continued, "Thank you. Okay. We have an Evolve going in tonight. Those attending have already been informed and would like to say farewell before they head up to the New Wing. As you know, the Propheet lasts three days so they will be doing some significant work and, well, I'm sure they would appreciate your good wishes and support. A good portion of the Upper School will be gone until Friday so if your dorm head is missing then we will make arrangements to appoint their replacements until their return. So...let's give some hugs and wish them well."

Respectful applause pattered across the Floor as students rose to their feet and began milling and looking for the attendees who were making their way through the room. Clusters of bodies formed in valediction. Charlie and Jonathan watched stonily, standing by their chairs.

Charlie remembered walking down to breakfast. The guys had seen this Propheet coming. They had noticed chairs missing from the lodge. It seemed that some things could be anticipated. That was good to know.

"Goodbye gents." It was Vince. He had come up behind the two and put his arm around them both.

Jonathan turned around and hugged Vince. Charlie smiled uncomfortably. A tall brown haired girl tapped Vince from behind, and before he spun to greet her, Vince volleyed a goodbye to Charlie over his shoulder before being absorbed by the throng. Charlie said goodbye, but too softly, and was sure he hadn't been heard.

Students jostled all around him as Charlie peered through the crowd. Shawn appeared suddenly to his left, hugging Jonathan. Shawn turned and grabbed Charlie's shoulder, vowing to return soon. His face, ruddy by nature, was flushed crimson and his eyes were wide, lit with the oddest mix of pride and panic.

Charlie had no idea what was in store for the guy, and could offer no words. Charlie was consumed with his own thoughts as he watched Shawn go, knowing that if his plans failed he would be next one of these days.

Eventually, the group assembled at the threshold across the room that led to the stairs-the stairs to somewhere. Charlie could see a portion of the ascending flight behind them from where he stood, drenched in shadow. Charlie and Jonathan watched in silence. Music began to play again over the House's stereo, some song about "a long, long road".

The participants waved at the spectators a final time, and like astronauts boarding a rocket they filed ceremoniously up the staircase and out of sight. They were not seen again for three days.

Chapter 9

Charlie was thankful his nightmares did not return that night and he slept dreamlessly.

The dorm was unusually subdued. Austin had been appointed the surrogate dorm head during Shawn's absence and was changed by the burden of his office. His playful insubordinations had no target and North Walden Five was calmed, reverent with the mystery unfolding in a room, deep inside the lodge below.

On the way down to breakfast, a summer wind gusted up and down the steep slopes that surrounded the dormitory, a warm, pine-scented whisper like some secret surrendered by the deep forest above. They walked in silence, lost in their own thoughts, pine needles crunching beneath their feet, until they heard the scream.

It came on the wind. It came from the lodge. Charlie's blood froze at the sound of it. It was guttural, wrenching and unmistakably human. The boys stopped walking.

The scream had come from the New Wing, somewhere within the blond, half-timbered addition that herniated from the weathered main lodge and clung to the slope, partly shrouded by the bushy arms of the pines.

It had come from the Propheet.

Charlie snapped his gaze to the dark squares of diamond-pane glass in the upstairs windows beneath the peaked roof, but they only stared back like dead eyes, revealing nothing but a reflection of grey sky.

The scream faded into the surrounding hills and it did not come again. The stillness that replaced it was somehow worse and a shiver worked its way down Charlie's spine. The boys made no comment, but settled instead for an exchange of nervous, sidelong glances at each other. It was somehow understood that mentioning it aloud would make it worse; give it legs to trample their spirits.

Instead, the boys continued stiffly into the lodge.

They shuffled down the long breakfast table and inspected the offerings: granola, honey, and dark muffins that smelled of nutty soil. They ate mechanically and talked little. Conversation was attempted but every topic seemed irrelevant when compared to whatever was going on upstairs, a mystery they were not allowed to talk about.

Among them, only Austin had been in a Propheet--two of them so far, he had confided—but he, of course, was prohibited from discussing the details. Even Austin was in awe of the extended upper-school Propheets and it was plain in his face that his mind was having difficulty extrapolating his past Propheet experiences to three whole days. As a result, ticks of incomprehension marred his otherwise perfect face as he gazed out the window at the milky blue swirls that filled the canyons. Charlie was looking out the window too, looking for signs of life below. He could see none.

At First Light, the Genesis family gathered again in their designated room and Toby asked everyone to state a goal they would like to achieve for the day. The question made its way, clockwise, around the room. Some answers were indecipherable to Charlie and comprised, undoubtedly, of jargon that he had yet to learn. He answered, "to do a good job" and was promptly pressed by Toby to be more specific. He amended his goal to "work hard and do a good job" and the question, to Charlie's obvious relief, was allowed to progress to the girl on his left.

Giving voice to his goal made him feel vulnerable suddenly. He fidgeted at his place on the couch, aware of how visible he was and how astute Toby had proven to be. He hoped his sincerity would remain unquestioned, his ulterior motive safe. Still, stating his goal aloud had sounded like a confession.

The work crews were assigned, and again, Karen dispensed chores to the waiting circle of students. Charlie was given the Quest family room and finished the two other adjoining rooms before Karen had returned to check on his progress.

"Way to bust ass," said Karen, clearly impressed. She nodded with appreciation.

The Da Vinci, Source and Michelangelo family rooms soon all

fell victim to Charlie's kinetic dust rag and were ticked off Karen's " to do" list in short order. The work was hard, but he welcomed it today. It helped Charlie forget the thing that was gnawing at the back of his mind: his first Rap was in less than two hours.

Lunch was a debacle of ingredients intended, once positioned correctly, to form a sandwich, but the homemade, health-conscious bread was cut too thick and was of such a coarse grain that Charlie abandoned it altogether and was forced to wad the cold cuts into his mouth.

He couldn't find Jonathan after work crew so he sat with Carolina Eversol--the girl he met his first night on the Floor—as well as Aaron Goldenberg and an oversized boy with heavy eyelids and a low forehead that everyone called "Smitty". They sat at a large round table on the Lower Level.

Carolina attempted to eat demurely, nibbling on the sides of a farcically bready sandwich. She aborted a proper bite when she realized halfway through that she would have to unhinge her jaw like a snake to do it.

"What?" she asked, as all eyes trained on the indelicate results of her ambitions, mustard ringing her mouth.

"That's not bread," Charlie said, wracked with giggles. "It's like eating a wicker couch."

The table erupted in laughter and Carolina put her sandwich down, comically deflating with a pouting glare at her companions. Then, defiantly, she raised her sandwich to her mouth again. An anemic tomato squirted violently out of the back of it, plopping on her fruit salad. The despair on her face produced another raucous laugh and Carolina dropped her sandwich to her plate with a thud.

"Oh, forget it," she sighed, "Charlie has the right idea."

She began hastily dismantling the sandwich and wadding cold cuts into her mouth with a victorious smile. Charlie was surprised to feel a flush of heat rise to his face when Carolina mentioned his name. He had been publicly complimented by Carolina. Not only that, but the act of her simply uttering his name made him curiously happy. He beamed and tried to force his goofy smile to stop spreading.

Michael DiFranco was suddenly standing over them at the edge of the table. Carolina gasped.

"You guys," he began, with a casual tap of his fingernails on the worn tabletop, "you're out of agreement. Let's break it up. Okay?" A tight smile was locked beneath his feathered hair. He gave the table a final decisive rap with his knuckles and moved on, fielding a barrage of salutations from the other students at the adjoining tables before coolly drifting away.

Carolina gathered her plate and glass, stood up and mumbled a parting before ascending the stairs to the Middle Level. Charlie watched her head bob around upstairs and then sink out of sight as she found another table. Charlie looked back at his company, gaping.

"I didn't notice," said Aaron sheepishly.

Scott "Smitty" Smith--the slow boy who looked too big for his age--began to speak, staring at the end of his raised sandwich: "A girl cannot sit with three guys if all present are in Genesis. The girl to boy ratio is one to one for Genesis family members unless there is a Quest student or older present, in which case, the ratio can be three to one or possibly more. Although still not preferred, the configuration would, technically, no longer be in violation of agreements."

Grimacing and trying hard not to roll his eyes at Smitty, Aaron had to confirm the statement with an apologetic shrug. "We are all in Genesis. It was three to one. I didn't even think."

Charlie fumed, picking at his fruit salad. He was sick of this. As soon as he seemed to get a handle on things another absurd nuance blindsided him. He suddenly disliked DiFranco in a far more significant way than he had before. The man never stopped smiling as he took from you. Worse, he had made Carolina feel bad, dirty somehow. DiFranco's easy manner as he warned you--the guys had called it being "pulled up"--was worse than the old-world barking admonitions Charlie had received from the septuagenarian priests at his old Catholic school. At least, one could brace for those.

DiFranco, on the other hand, used breezy cordiality to tell you that he was the keeper of your freedom and could deplete your reserve with no more effort than a lazy wave of his hand.

Charlie scanned the room, but Michael was gone. He slugged the last of his milk, got up from the table and marched to the Middle Level where he was to scrape his plate into three different garbage cans for composting and recycling.

The "Veggie Prep" area it was called. Everything had a name and every move you made was choreographed. He scraped the fat bread and chunks of fruit into the compost can with shrieks of his fork and dropped his dirty plate into the designated gray plastic bin. The piles of muck would be dealt with later by whoever had been punished with Dishes. The whole thing was as irritating and pervasive as a throbbing toothache...this place...this weird little city.

He had been at Ponderosa Academy for just short of forty-eight hours. Already he understood how precious free time was at this place and how the prospect of losing even a minute of it would eventually compel you to comply with just about anything.

Time was the thing, the only thing, you could call your own and there wasn't much of it allotted for idle purpose. It was a ration and needed to be coddled and kept safe at all costs. That is how those in charge were motivating the students; at least that was part of the picture.

Charlie turned and headed back through the Middle Level to offer Carolina a consoling smile, but she was turned away from him talking to another girl. He reconnoitered, saw Michael DiFranco coming down from the Upper Level, and decided to leave before a confrontation was forced.

Then there was the scream he had heard this morning coming from the New Wing. That was obviously part of all of this too, a part he didn't want to think about. He gathered from what Toby had told him that first night that The Academy was an emotionally therapeutic environment, but what did that mean? Whose idea of therapy? What kind of therapy? A therapy that made you scream like you were being ripped apart? Being erased from the inside? That is what it sure sounded like this morning: a death throe.

He knew they weren't actually murdering kids here, it didn't make sense. Who would stick around for torture just to avoid doing some dishes? But there was Provo, he remembered: A place where no one could find you, where men in white coats came to disappear you. Was that threat enough to make you tolerate pain? What would be the difference at trying your luck at Provo if something horrible was happening here? Maybe Provo didn't even exist. Maybe it was just a scare tactic to make you digest the absurdities that were thrown at you for fear of far greater ones.

Clearly, however, the students here were afraid of more than just

Dishes. What it was they were afraid of was sure to be revealed eventually, unless he could get out soon.

That, of course, was the best option, the only option.

But now, he had something more pressing to deal with: he was headed to his first Rap.

Light-headed, he shouldered open the heavy door from the dining room and entered what he was learning to call The Floor, the main room of the lodge. He was headed toward the broad door that led to the Quad and what he hoped would be a rejuvenating breath of air. But, it was not to be.

A girl who had just come from outside, was walking briskly down the hall towards him and shouting: "House around the Pit!"

Charlie turned and reentered the big room to see students beginning to line the semi-circular low wall surrounding the Pit, staring expectantly towards the stone fireplace.

Charlie flinched. Jonas Portman entered The Pit and stood staring out at the gathering crowd. His face, plump and topped with wisps of brown hair, was expressionless. He began to speak in a resonant bass voice that tranquilized the gathered with impressive efficiency.

"Welcome to Wednesday Raps," he said. He allowed a small ironical smile to play at the edges of his mouth, clarifying that he was aware that no student wanted to be there and that he was indifferent to the fact. "We have a Propheet going on right now so we're going to consolidate everyone a little differently today. Shake things up a bit. How about that?"

Anxious giggles rolled through the room and died quickly.

Charlie seized on the distraction, crouched and sat by Jonathan, suddenly relieved to see a friendly face.

"Hey," Charlie whispered.

"What's up," whispered Jonathan.

Jonas began reading a list. "In Da Vinci with Sonia..." He then read a dozen names. "In Genesis with Toby..." Another dozen or so names were read. In total, five rooms and five counselors were paired, followed by a handful of names apiece. Jonathan's name was called. He was in Michelangelo with Pat. Charlie hadn't met Pat. Jonathan sighed in relief.

"Is that good?" whispered Charlie," Being with Pat?"

"Yes," whispered Jonathan.

They continued listening.

"And with me," Jonas continued, "in the Source family room..." He read off more names. "Charlie Hoff" was the seventh on the list.

"Oh, boy," Jonathan chuckled, "your first Rap with Jonas..."

Charlie's head numbed. He cursed silently.

"Don't sweat it," said Jonathan. "You're a Nate. I doubt you're going to have any problems. Good luck. I'll see you later."

Jonas raised his voice against the ensuing bustle, "Have a good Rap," he said and waddled out of the Pit and towards the Source family room.

The students all rose at once and began weaving around each other towards their assigned rooms, steps brisk with nervous energy.

In the Source family room a dozen of the black molded plastic chairs with the chrome legs were arranged in a circle. A gap between two of them at the doorway allowed for access into the ring where a few students were already deciding where to sit. One of the room's resident, tobacco-brown wingbacks capped the circle of chairs, turned inward to face the center of the room. Charlie entered the small ring and sat in the first available black chair, instinctively avoiding the anomalous luxury of what was obviously to be Jonas' seat.

The chairs filled quickly and Jonas entered, the gap in the circle woefully inadequate to accommodate his frame and the two students in the way had to get up briefly and scoot them out of his way. The circle reassembled, chrome legs clicking together before Jonas could impose his body into the wingback.

Charlie's nerves flared. He looked around. He recognized only five people in the room: Kenny "The Boot" Bootman – the guy who acted like Jonas' pilot fish in the dining room his first night, Dana – the sad girl that had been smoking alone in the Quad, Devon Childs--the guy stacking the checkers and later "reading" the book on the landing, Karen--the Older Student who ran work crew for Genesis, and good ol' Austin Spencer. Charlie smiled at Austin who suggested with his own brief smile and quick nod that this was not the time to pal around.

Jonas repositioned his girth. "We have a new student, Charlie Hoff, who you may have seen around. I would urge you all to help him along and tell your stories to him. I know you remember what it is like being new and I'm sure Charlie would appreciate you reaching out to him. Now...would someone explain the rules to

Charlie?"

Several students opened their mouths but Kenny Bootman sounded first: "The Rap lasts for three hours. You cannot indict someone next to you. You have to switch places with someone across the room if you want to indict someone next to you..." Kenny faltered and shot a servile glance at Jonas.

Jonas continued for him, "If someone goes like this..." Jonas held up a beckoning finger, "you trade seats with them. Otherwise, you cannot leave your seat. A part of your body must always be touching your seat. Once the Rap begins, no one can leave the room for any reason until it is over. Also, nothing anyone says is to leave this room. What happens in this room stays in this room. Do you understand?"

Charlie nodded dumbly.

A strange, prickly anticipation filled the room as if it had suddenly been drained of all oxygen, like in a storm's eye. Several students, with their hands flat on their knees, rocked in place as if they were braced in a starting block. All faces were masks of anticipation, jaws set and eyes wide and steady. There was a moment of thick silence, unnatural and complete.

"Okay," said Jonas, "let's begin.

Chapter 10

Shouting, sudden and fierce, detonated from the twisted faces surrounding him and filled the small room with a deafening roar. The burst of sound was so intense and so unexpected that Charlie reflexively slammed his back against the molded plastic of his chair. He rode the euphoric wave of adrenalin that poured into his body as his skin danced and   prickled with the shock, his mouth fell open and his vision sharpened in defense.

At first, no words were discernible through the noise. Half of the dozen students in the room were yelling simultaneously with passion and fury. Confusion and fear tugged at Charlie's brain as he tried to gather himself, his eyes darting.

Oh God, his mind cried, they were yelling at him, right at him. A vitriolic wall of sound pressed him further into his seat. They were attacking animals, their brows furrowed, their eyes narrow and their mouths foaming with spittle. Charlie's own mouth had gone dry. He worked his tongue in a vain attempt to find moisture but his insides were swathed in the peculiar laminate that only pure dread could produce.

Devon?

Wait a minute, his mind urged, listen.

The inarticulate boil was cooling to a simmer, save for the bellowing of one. A straining voice belonging to a boy he did not know out-screamed the rest and some words began to make sense as they rose above the vanquished sentiments of the others.

The realization that he had overwhelmed the competition gave this boy a burst of energy and he leaned forward in his chair shouting, beet-red, with an accusatory finger trembling at the end of his outstretched arm and pointing just to the left of Charlie.

Not me, Charlie thought. It's not me. He snapped his head left to where Devon sat recalcitrant, arms folded across his chest, staring the finger down.

"YOU KNOW WHAT, DEVON?" the boy across the room

screamed, "FUCK YOU! I'M SO FUCKING TIRED OF YOUR SHIT! I REACH OUT TO YOU AND YOU SHIT ALL OVER ME, YOU SHIT ALL OVER THIS HOUSE! THIS IS MY HOME!"

Charlie was stunned by the intensity of the words, but a relief so profound that he felt like sobbing eclipsed it. He realized he had been holding his breath. He exhaled steadily. His stomach felt hollow and poisonous, like a drum of acid. The cold cuts from lunch were swimming in that corrosive bath and threatening to mount an escape. He swallowed hard. His bladder ached and he pressed his knees together.

The boy across the room continued, his eyes locked with Devon's, "ALL YOU DO IS HIDE BEHIND YOUR FUCKING WEIRDNESS! You walk around here like some psycho and make things totally unsafe for all of us. This is my home and you should have some FUCKING RESPECT FOR THAT!"

A girl across the room cut in, "What was that shit in art class Devon? I don't think it's funny at all to be huffing markers or paint or whatever, or even pretending to! THAT SHIT IS NOT OKAY, DEVON, AND YOU KNOW IT!"

Another boy across the room spoke, "And what's with your personal area in the dorm Devon? Why is there nothing but a calendar with exes marked off it? You're just doing time! You have no intention of letting anybody into your life! You just push people away! If you hate it so much here THEN JUST FUCKING SPLIT!"

The first boy spoke again with an exhausted intensity, "You may be on bans from the lower school, and you should be, but you're even pushing older students away. AND THAT MEANS no one, BUT NO ONE, is going to trust you, Devon. No one is going to trust what you're about. "

Jonas interrupted, "Jeff, tell him that it's you who doesn't trust him. Speak for yourself."

"I don't trust you," said the boy tightly.

Charlie kept track of Devon with uneasy glances at the boy between staring at the floor. Devon was pale, but somehow still managed a slight, haughty pursing of the lips. His dark eyes quietly returned the hostility as they glittered, motionless, beneath the arch of his eyebrows.

Jonas spoke, "What do you think of what they are saying to you, Devon? I think it's right on. How about you?"

Devon didn't speak. One of his cheeks twitched.

Jonas continued, "So you've been trying to get your hands on anything you can to get high? So you're a fiend? Are you a bad kid Devon? Are you proud of that?"

Devon croaked a reply, "I was just playing around."

A burst of disbelief from the accusers across the room rose to a din but was quickly quashed by Jonas' raised palm.

"Playing around?" said Jonas thoughtfully.

Devon shrugged.

An explosion of sound came from Jonas. Charlie recoiled so that the cramped, chrome legs of his seat clicked against the neighboring chairs. The fine hairs on his neck straightened.

Jonas roared, seemingly without effort, "YOU CAN'T BULLSHIT A BULLSHITTER, DEVON! I KNOW WHAT YOUR KIND OF THINKING DOES, PAL! I HAVE BEEN THERE! I'VE SHOT UP MORE DOPE IN MY TIME THAN YOU'VE HAD HOT DINNERS! Now, you have a choice. You can follow the path you are on or take the fork in the road that you're being offered here because where you're going is DOWN, SON!"

Devon mumbled.

"What's that?" asked Jonas

Devon mumbled again, his voice trembling, "I'm not your son."

"Are you going to do any work in here today?" asked Jonas.

Devon glanced away, his arms still folded across his chest.

"Okay," said Jonas, "then sit in your shit. Let's move on."

Another blast of voices shook the room. The volume was not quite as intense as before but no less jarring. Charlie jumped again, looking from one side of the circle to the other. The shouts were coming from his section of the ring this time, directed across. A girl opposite him beckoned with her finger, her face urgent. Charlie tentatively rose on his rubbery legs. The girl was upon him instantly, brushing by and sliding her butt into Charlie's chair. Charlie tottered to the girl's vacated chair across the room and sat down stiffly. They were yelling towards him again, but this time, further to the right, two chairs to his right. They were yelling at Austin.

Austin was being accused of "cutting corners" and "slacking off" on work crews. He was also being charged with flirting, a charge that seemed to spark his indignity as he leaned forward, a quizzical look on his face, and shook his head in disbelief.

Charlie felt a need to come to his dorm mate's aid, to champion him in some way, but was burdened by inexperience. Was that the worst thing he could do? Was it what he was expected to do? He didn't know. The last thing he wanted was their guns trained on him, ripping him apart. Would Austin resent him for not deflecting the attack? It was all happening so fast.

Charlie noticed that Austin was paying him no attention; no pleading look came to Charlie. In fact, Austin was beginning to turn the table on the girl who accused him of flirting.

"BULLSHIT, BECKY," Austin yelled back, "all I said to you was that you were a beautiful girl and you should take care of yourself more. I have NO intention of getting contracted up with you, Becky!"

This seemed to be an effective response and several students nodded knowingly, believing Austin's intentions to be benign and not as lascivious as Becky--looking pale now – had probably fantasized them to be.

It wasn't over yet for Austin however. He was still battling two boys regarding his allegedly shoddy work ethic.

Austin turned his attention to one of them, "You're projecting, Collin! I chopped twice as much wood as you did today while you and Steve bullshitted in the woodshed! Now you're in here piggybacking on an indictment? Make sure your shit doesn't stink before you come at me with a fucking look-good indictment, Collin!"

Collin clammed up, his eyes darting nervously around to see if Austin was getting any traction. He was. Evidently, there was truth in Austin's defense and Collin was inviting his own slaughter if he were to continue. That left one accuser. It was someone Charlie didn't know but the boy seemed to be adamant and not willing to back down. Charlie was impressed by the deft way Austin had deflected the majority of the onslaught but his roommate couldn't seem to shake the final charge.

Jonas aided the accuser, "I believe what he's saying Austin. You have been slacking off lately."

Austin's fight left him and he slumped back in his chair, not willing to take on Jonas as the boy's wingman.

Jonas continued, "I understand you're having some problems getting up in the morning."

The Rap Request box, Charlie thought instantly, flashing on the little model of the lodge. It had ben during the backgammon game last night. It was Shawn who had slipped the folded piece of paper into the roof of the model. That piece of paper must have had Austin's name on it as well as Shawn's own. The piece of paper was a warrant, a joust to be resolved in this stuffy little room in front of everyone. Shawn had called Austin out, and if Shawn hadn't been yanked into the Propheet he would have been sitting across from Austin now, screaming at him on all cylinders. Instead, the complaint had been logged and forwarded to Jonas.

But, Shawn had known he was going into a Proheet. He mentioned the other morning that some chairs were missing from The Floor and that the Evolve must be coming. It seemed like cowardice to Charlie. Shawn had effectively hunted Austin down for not putting his feet on the floor the other morning and for the harmless tease that had followed, but Shawn was able to leave the unpleasant business of decimating his dorm mate to others.

Maybe Austin's laziness was a constant problem and for all Charlie knew it had been going on for a while before Charlie arrived, but it was still disturbing to think that Shawn would offer up Austin to be publicly chastised for something so petty: a rule that clearly, no one cherished anyway. Charlie felt a sense of betrayal on Austin's behalf.

He also realized that confrontation was to be part of his performance at The Academy. Petty or otherwise, every move he made was grounds for reprisal in one of these rooms. Everything was to be exposed, and the unsettling reality was that it was to be his peers that exposed him.

The motivation for such betrayal was self-serving. The "us against them" creed of Catholic school--hell, of all schools--was coldly absent. It was brother against brother. The students were policing each other and, somehow, benefiting.

Perhaps the benefit was some measure of immunity from the character assassinations he was witnessing. It seemed that a well-placed show of orthodoxy, a preemptive attack on your fellow student, could deflect unwanted scrutiny and provide a temporary measure of relief.

It was conniving and primal; the flexing of a collective survival instinct, a sort of emotional cannibalism. The oddest part was the ferocity of the verbal assaults. They were suspiciously disproportionate and furtive glances at Jonas while they were exacted told Charlie something interesting: the students were not as concerned with the solutions to their grievances as they were with the sheer theatricality of expressing them.

There was a lot to learn. Charlie watched Austin in awe. Austin had parried with assertions of his own and effectively disabled one of his attackers by exposing the attacker's self-interest as inexpertly blatant. A "piggyback indictment" he had called it.

Of course, Austin had been here a year, was in Quest, and had plenty of experience but even those advantages did not exempt him from everything. Shawn, in absentia, had nailed him with a reputable complaint that he wasn't going to shake so easily.

Austin regrouped, trying a different approach: "That's right on. I can hear that. I am bad at getting up in the morning. No doubt about it. What can I say?"

Jonas said, "You need to pull your head out of your ass and quick. Why do you think it's okay to be out of agreement Austin? What kind of example is that setting? How is that living with the tools you have learned?"

The dark-haired girl from the Quad interrupted awkwardly as if she had been working up courage, "I think you coast on your looks Austin. I think you're used to getting your way because you're good-looking. You walk around like Prince Charming, like you don't have to try."

Jonas spoke, "How does that make you feel Dana?"

"I resent it."

"Say it again."

"I RESENT IT!"

Jonas rubbed his jowls, "This brings up some issues for you, doesn't it, Dana? You're not very happy with yourself are you? Tell Austin why it pisses you off, Dana. Tell Austin why you resent him."

Dana looked at Austin, and for the first time, Charlie was able to get a good look at her face. She was kind of funny looking, not ugly but her face had an inharmonious air as if none of her features could agree on a common aesthetic. He hadn't noticed when her hair was in her face, looking at her from afar, but her face was oddly angular. Her nose was large, her lips were thin and her teeth were like weathered, listing fence posts. Her eyes were astonishingly pretty though and they welled with tears as she flipped her hair back, sniffed and steeled herself.

"I RESENT YOU!" she yelled, "It's all so easy for you!"

Jonas incited her, "That's right, Dana! Run it!"

Dana balled her fists, "FUCK YOU, AUSTIN! YOU THINK YOU CAN DO A HALF-ASSED JOB, FLASH A SMILE AND EVERYONE WILL FORGIVE YOU! WELL, THAT FUCKING SUCKS!"

"That's right, Dana," Jonas cooed. " Why don't you just feel that."

Dana leaned over in her chair, yelling at the ground, "I'M SO FUCKING TIRED OF HATING MYSELF!"

Jonas urged her on, "How do you feel inside Dana? Forget what the mirror tells you, what do you feel inside..."

Dana sobbed, "I FEEL SHITTY INSIDE!"

Beneath every third chair in the ring was a box of tissues. One of these whispered across the carpet and came to a stop at Dana's feet. Kenny Bootman had expertly pitched the floral printed box, like some shuffleboard pro, and now straightened himself back into his chair. Dana ignored the tissues and continued crying with deep, wracking sobs. She rambled on: hating herself, missing home. She was hunched over, screaming at the ground, her hands clasped to the sides of her head as if to prevent her skull from exploding.

Charlie finally saw what had prompted Kenny to act. He was horrified. A thick rope of mucus was hanging from the girl's nose. Charlie tried to catch someone's eye so that he could widen his own and gesture urgently with his head at the girl, but the surrounding faces, were solemn and unconcerned with the growing dilemma.

The late afternoon sun was slanting into the window, illuminating the tube of snot as it descended towards the floor. Now, more than a foot of translucent goop was feeling its way towards the carpet like a blind cave snake.

Charlie shifted in his chair with embarrassment and wrinkled his mouth in frustration and revulsion. He didn't want to look at it, he wanted to spare her the indignity but his eyes kept traveling to the viscous rope as if it were a hypnotist's chain.

Jonas spoke in a syrupy baritone, "Isn't that what your mother told you, Dana? That you would never be good enough?"

A plaintive moan escaped Dana. The snot rope was now less than two feet from the ground.

Why doesn't she do something about it? Charlie thought. She has to know. Still, Dana's hands clutched the side of her head, her elbows propped on her knees.

Jonas prodded: "What do you want to tell your mother, Dana?"

Dana screamed: "I FUCKING HATE YOU!"

Jonas leaned forward: "Say it again, Dana!"

Dana did, and to Charlie's horror, the fresh burst of emotion had set the opalescent lanyard swinging. The arc was sending the rope of snot out into the middle of the circle, and then on its return, between Dana's legs and under her black chair where it threatened to adhere to the lip of the seat.

Karen, who was sitting next to Dana, quickly tore four sheets from the slit of the box at Dana's feet and hastily assembled a bed of tissue at the projected point of impact. The snake attached itself to the first sheet, and as Dana kept talking about her oppressive mother, the mucus slowly began to coil onto the padding.

Suddenly, without seeming to notice how precarious the situation had been, Dana took an absent swipe at her nose. The snake broke in the middle, one half collapsing to the floor and the rest affixing to the leg of her jeans. Between her concluding sobs, Dana irritably plucked a wad of the Kleenex and removed the pearly stalactite that still hung from her nose.

Charlie was relieved. He averted his eyes and relaxed his muscles, tensed for longer than he had realized.

Jonas exhaled thoughtfully through his pudgy nose and leaned back in his armchair: "Just take a moment to feel those feelings, Dana. I want you to think about the power that you have and the power that you give away. Who decides what kind of person you will be? Who is in charge?"

Dana sniffed and nodded at each of the rhetorical questions. Strands of hair were stuck to her face. She produced a final affirmation in a thick voice before settling back in her chair with a bracing flip of her hair, the long black waves calming into tufted piles.

"Okay," said Jonas. "Who needs to clear some space?"

Karen quickly spoke: "I have something to say to Charlie."

Charlie went cold. Karen sat across from him, stone-faced, and they locked eyes. She was backlit by postmeridian light.

She spoke flatly: "I'm a little concerned with your performance on house crew."

Charlie tried to contain his astonishment but it spread across his face like a rash.

Impossible, he thought. No. It couldn't be. What could I have done?

But, all eyes were now on him. They all stared at him gravely. This was it. He forced his mouth closed.

Karen continued: "I'm concerned because I have a feeling that you are trying to impress me. You do a very good job but it seems that you are doing a good job because you believe it will allow you to go home sooner."

Charlie's stomach tightened like it was being wrung out. His vision swam for a moment before he locked eyes with Karen again. Disbelief, a miserable disbelief gusted beneath his skin like icy wind.

Karen continued: "I've seen this before. I appreciate your hard work but I don't want you to be working hard because you're trying to pull one over on us, Charlie. I want you to work hard so that you feel a sense of pride."

Jonas turned his head slowly to Charlie: "What do you think of what she is saying to you, Charlie?"

Betrayed.

How could Karen expose him like this? He was a fool. He should have known. But, he did know didn't he? He had always known. If he had stopped deluding himself he would have seen that his ploy was obvious, rudimentary. How many kids had been here before? How many had tried everything a thousand times before? Stupid. He was stupid to think he could have fooled them. It was stupid to think he ever could have won. His fight was leaving him as if through a puncture in his heart.

Jonas stared: "Charlie?"

Charlie looked at Jonas. The big man leaned forward and his little round glasses caught the sun and flashed, just like they had the night Charlie spied him in that darkened room with the girl. Charlie was shaking and the trembling of his lip threatened tears.

"Charlie?" Jonas asked again.

"Yes..."

"You want to go home don't you?" Jonas soothed.

That voice. It was tugging at him. It was tugging the water out of his eyes. He swallowed hard. Weakness was not an option. He had been beaten but he didn't have to surrender everything. He was not going to bawl and empty his head of snot in front of these people. Not today.

"I was just trying to do a good job," he said bleakly. His voice trembled and he hated himself for it. His soft underbelly was now exposed to their gnashing teeth. He had nothing. All he could hope for now was mercy, to be spared emotional defilement, the kind that had ripped Devon apart.

As he listened though, he realized they were donning their kid gloves for him. Perhaps they knew that, as he sat there peeled like an onion, that the airing of his last, private hope was sufficient compensation for his folly.

Karen spoke to him. Jonas spoke to him. A girl he didn't know agreed with Karen and confirmed that she had tried something similar when she was a new student. The two girls shared a brief laugh about it. They asked Charlie what he thought of the Rap and of The Academy. His answers were short and he couldn't remember them later.

Jonas moved the Rap on and Charlie was left hugging his own body. He flashed on the folded up schedule in his back pocket, slating Raps three times a week, three hours apiece. His mind began desperately tripping over itself to multiply the number of Raps by the number of days he was to be at The Academy. The number startled him. He reworked the figure, hoping he had made a mistake, but still the number remained. The number was inconceivable. His mind squirmed with despair and dread, refusing to accept it.

Three hundred and ten, Charlie thought numbly, three hundred and ten more Raps to go.

PART TWO

POTTERS AND CLAY

Chapter 11

Charlie was finally going to call home. But, Toby was late. Charlie looked over his shoulder, saw no Toby, and continued gazing over the back of the couch and through the window of the Genesis family room at the pool.

No one seemed to use the pool much; there was no time. Its deep waters were still and relegated to reflecting the cloudless sky above. The quad beyond it bustled with students choking down their last cigarettes before work crew. The smoking didn't seem so strange anymore. Charlie supposed there were those who felt they had nothing more to lose.

A plump bee floated lazily on a current of air, perilously close to the glassy surface of the water. Then, it plunged, dipping its fuzzy abdomen into the pool. It hydroplaned for a moment before it tumbled into the water. Its body drifted slowly towards the filter.

A month had passed at The Academy. Charlie had attended a dozen Raps, three hours apiece: a total of 36 hours of witnessing his peers reach into each other to churn their souls. His dust cloth had scrutinized every surface of the lodge. He had inadvertently broken a good share of the rules-or had come dangerously close from simple lack of reflex-and all of his prayers had gone unanswered.

Reprimands came from staff and student alike and were proffered with the leniency afforded to newer students who were still protected by inexperience. However, he knew that his grace period was coming to an end. From now on, his wits would have to be sharper.

There was so much to learn and being a step behind his peers was always a disadvantage. A quick study would be armed with a bit of cautious nerve. A slow learner however, well, they would be fodder for the rhetorical cannons of the Rap. Charlie knew that he was teetering somewhere in between.

For a school that concerned itself primarily with the destruction of image and the dismantling of cliques, the institution required nothing short of uncompromised assimilation. Any rebels would be instantly singled out as paradigms of noncompliance and dashed against the tongues of the devout, or at least of the illusory devotees who had somehow managed to maintain their "look good".

Culture shock came from all aspects of life at Ponderosa, but none more so than the complexity of the jargon. Sure, the words were simple and familiar. But, their definitions took some getting used to.

"Dirt" was simply that which remained hidden from the scrutiny of others. By strict definition, the word referred to an act or thought that one felt bad about. In practice, it became a word that defined what one *should* feel bad about. An important distinction since "dirt" was only as debilitating as the owner's perception deemed it to be. A "dirty" student was withholding a lie, impurity or misbehavior that the staff deemed significant. Often it was synonymous with being "out of agreement". Learning the difference between what you actually felt bad about and what you *should* feel bad about was an important step in appeasement: establishing a supposed pattern of emotional growth, thereby validating the methods of those in charge.

It was common knowledge that dirt was to be produced when requested. If one were asked to "cop out" (divulge) one's dirt it was best to have some at the ready. Having no dirt whatsoever just raised suspicions.

"Going fast" meant running away from your feelings whereas "going slow" meant that you were "in touch" with them. A "crack" was an emotional hiding place, a position of denial. A "flag" was a harbinger of negative behavior patterns. "Going for broke" was the opposite of "doing time" and "busting ass" was the opposite of "slacking off". A "bagger" was full of dirt and a "look-good" was probably full of dirt too, they just deflected scrutiny by deftly "pulling up" (admonishing) other students preemptively.

"Needsy" was a good one. The term was applied to a student who would "run an indictment" at another student with motives that were impure: perhaps a selfish need to see that person humiliated. More often, it was usually to debilitate someone preemptively for a more strategic reason. Yet, any confrontation sensed to be motivated by anything less than compassionate motives faced challenges to its validity. The danger was that during these "needsy indictments" an astute Rap group could come to the victim's aid and expose the attacker's motives as self-serving, provided the majority of the attendees were politically sympathetic to the victim over the attacker.

In this instance, a charge of projecting might be leveled at the attacker. "Projecting" was the unconscious attributing of one's own unresolved emotional issues and imperfections upon another. This charge could turn a Rap back on the attacker. Not only did projecting open one up for scrutiny, but it also branded the aggressor as "out of touch" with their own motivations, belying their understanding of self and diluting the validity of their attack with their own clinical ignorance.

It was confusing-no doubt about that-, yet Charlie was beginning to limp along with a modicum of skill. Using the mental gymnastics and developing the cunning required to endure the incessant confrontations was playing emotional chess. However, the rules of this chess game were not easy. A super-intuition had to be honed. Only the skilled knew how to move confidently, and only the skilled would resist the temptation to move too quickly, or to keep an indecisive hand atop their piece and fail to move at all.

Meanwhile, the intervening hours served to fuel the next Rap with an endless combination of behavioral dynamics. What was solid, ideal behavior to one might spark the ire of another. Charlie remembered Austin being "blown away" for being good-looking. So, it seemed, you could be blown away for the unrelated crimes of being a 'look-good' or good-looking, it hardly mattered. Really, there was no anticipating the countless possibilities, so the only solution was to get better at the game, because no one was ever immune and participation was always mandatory.

It was clear that some students had already swallowed the bitter pill, and it had gone down their pipes as smooth as a lick of ice cream. Others were kicking and screaming. A good portion of the students seemed to be stuck between orthodoxy and defiance, but in the end the tightrope wobbled beneath all.

Charlie had found out the hard way (the only way to find out at The Academy) that his nameless predecessors had explored every possible angle. Every Rap became an opportunity to destroy the contrivances of others while new ones were devised. Each subtlety of behavior had been donned like a disguise, deemed ineffective, and then discarded, every generation clinging to a renewed hope in their worth. The game was to sift through this wealth of tactics abandoned by those before him, and seize on one that might preserve him, at least for a while.

Charlie felt foolish looking back at his first days at the school. He had really thought he was onto something: Work hard and they will think that a terrible mistake had been made. Show them you're a good boy and they'll leave you alone. He chuckled derisively to himself. To be fair, he had suspected his plan would fail, but he had no idea just how elementary it had been until he had witnessed the impressive scope of the emotional surveillance at Ponderosa Academy.

He remembered thinking that Toby, Michael and Jonas had been looking through him. Of course, they had been. With luck, Charlie thought he might someday gain the power to scrutinize others in such a way, peering into their eyes-the windows to the soul, or so he had heard them called- to look upon them uninvited, to gain unfair advantage.

Until then, he was still learning and still grappling with the same question: Why was it all tolerated? It was amazing really-this school, this camp, this repository of abandoned youth. It had no fences, no guard towers or machine gun nests in which to pick off straggling prisoners who didn't fall in line. Yet, it was rare for a student to leave. Something was keeping them here and it had to be more than the logistics of leaving. The thought of leaving, making your own way and risking the consequences was daunting but the act was certainly possible.

Of course, there was the threat of something worse: Provo. But, the details were fuzzy. Supposedly it was a lock-up at the bottom of a canyon, in the middle of nowhere. Yet, no one had ever come back from Provo so there was no way to know if its existence was only a legend, a ghost story for a crackling campfire. For all Charlie knew, tales about the place had trickled down from the top.

Still he wondered why there was no revolt. Could it be that easy to strip a population of their freedoms with a menace that could not be seen or proven? He thought back to the scream that came from the New Wing. He couldn't stop thinking about it. He had wanted to ask Vince or Shawn about it the day they were released from the Propheet, but he knew they wouldn't talk. Though, he had seen the look on their faces. Yes. *That* they were not able to hide.

Each day made it clearer to Charlie that he didn't know the half of what was going on here. All his gains, as hard won as they were, still amounted to nothing more than introductory knowledge. Charlie wasn't sure how long mere curiosity would sustain him, and although he wanted to know all, he knew that discovery would be painful.

Nobody was allowed to exchange puzzle pieces. One conversation with an older student who was close to graduating could reveal everything. Of course, there was no way they would break agreements to appease him or aid in his prying. Everyone had to wait; everyone had to pay their dues. The older students owed him nothing.

So far, he could vouch for one significant upside: it was safe. Aside from being verbally mauled three times a week the place was free of physical violence. Charlie could not conceive of another place on earth where physical violence seemed so unlikely. He had not witnessed a single scuffle, a single bodily threat or even a surreptitious shove the entire month. He had no fear of bullies or of defending his honor and manhood, which for a 14-year-old boy, was luxurious indeed. Perhaps the price of safety was loss of freedom. Maybe new fears were better than old fears.

Utopia also had a demand: the individual must be sacrificed. The staff maintained that the individual was exalted, but it was a thin deception. Conformity was fostered and rewarded while all deviations were quickly destroyed before they ever had a chance to become influential.

But, the real taxes for this society were paid in tears. All were to be stripped of their defenses and explored for any in reserve. A peeling of the psyche was in store for all as the infection in one's soul was indentified and excised without anesthesia. In exchange, nobody would hit you anymore. Nobody would drag you up the stairs by your hair. Nobody would get drunk and tell you that you were never going to amount to anything. Nobody...

❖

Charlie, still on the couch in Genesis, stared out the window, his daydream glazing his eyes. He blinked hard and absently shifted his cramped leg from beneath him. The quad was empty now. He had no idea how late Toby was for this home call for he was not allowed to carry a watch. Only public clocks were used and there was not one close by. It certainly felt like an eternity though.

He sighed and looked down at the water. The maw of the filter framed the bee in the pool. Half submerged below the waterline, the filter's dark hole waited patiently for the water which ebbed before it to bear the morsel into its black mouth. Helplessly, the bee floated on the glassy surface in the shadow of the lodge.

Charlie was pretty sure the bee was not dead. He could save it if he wanted. He remembered the pool back home, after his mother had married Kurt and moved into his apartment building. Charlie spent a lot of time at the apartment's communal pool-mostly because Kurt never went there. It was a place he could always find peace. He and his brother had spent hours laughing and playing in its turquoise waters.

Brandon had spotted a bee on the side of the pool once and they had saved it from drowning. Charlie had been surprised to find that if a bee was lifted gently out of the water in cupped hands and placed on dry ground, the sun would revive it and it would eventually fly away to continue its quest for sweetness.

Someone had to care enough though.

Charlie mumbled a felicitation at the window, wishing his words were backed with conviction.

"Good luck," he said. "I hope you make it."

Charlie was startled by Toby Heiser's voice from behind: "Ready to call home?"

Chapter 12

Toby hurried into Genesis. Charlie twisted his neck to see Toby sweep his arm towards the room's small office.

"Thanks for waiting," said Toby.

Charlie stood on cramped legs and hobbled to the office.

Finally, he was going to call home. He had waited longer than he had thought possible. It turned out that Toby was only ten minutes late but it had felt much longer. What if his mother had given up? Maybe something came up and she couldn't wait anymore or someone else called and tied up the phone. He was sure Toby would not wait around for another try. Charlie tasted anxiety on his tongue.

Toby, in a green velour tracksuit that seemed way too substantial for the summer heat, had already unlocked the sliding glass door to the office and was seated at the desk before Charlie peered in cautiously.

"Have a seat," said Toby without looking up. He picked up the canary yellow base of the phone, wiped some papers aside with his other hand, and dropped the phone onto the clearing. The phone's bell clanged.

"Okay," Toby continued, "how this works is..." He drew out the final consonant in a long sibilant leak that pulsed with antsy deliberation as he pawed around the desk, searching for something. He produced a plastic dial timer from behind a stack of phone books.

"How this works," repeated Toby, "is that once we get a hold of your parents, I will set the timer for fifteen minutes. When the timer clicks off, I expect you to say your goodbyes and return the phone to me before you hang up. Do you understand?"

The bits of information Charlie had gleaned about Home Calls were apparently true: monitored and timed.

Boy, they weren't kidding, Charlie thought. Toby was going to sit here and listen to every word, just sit and watch him in this tiny office as he talked to his family for the first time in a month.

The desire to not screw up the opportunity to make this call far outweighed the indignity of self-censorship. Clearly, if one were to pour their heart out to their family with the honesty and emotional insight that was so valued at The Academy, then one would not be likely to call home again for a very long time.

No kid in their right mind would wax gratefully about the peace of isolation, the effectiveness of the therapy, the vigor coursing through them from the health food and work crews, or the charming lack of freedom on their first call. Yet, all must have done just that. All must have lied to the one person who might have saved them.

Charlie wondered if his mother would save him if she knew what he had endured, what he still might endure. He shuddered, because the truth was, he wasn't sure of the answer anymore.

This call was to be a performance. To make matters worse, it was presented as a privilege. There was an unspoken understanding that the call had better be a ringing endorsement of the program, or at the very least, convincingly indifferent. If one had the nerve to be critical then the piper would surely have to be paid.

Currently, the piper in question was flipping open his notebook, his lips protruding through his beard in concentration, his thick index finger gliding down a page and landing beneath the number to Charlie's home.

Fine, thought Charlie, I guess it's better to lie to the ones you love than to not talk to them at all.

He wasn't sure what he would say. When he heard his mother's voice, Brandon's voice, would he just crumble and beg for another chance? He had worked for a moment like this: searching for unattended phones, exploring the perimeters of the property for escape routes, and spitting vows to reclaim his former life. And now that the moment had arrived, he felt further than ever from resolve.

Why beg his mother? She had betrayed him, tricked him, and chosen Kurt over him. His cries had fallen on deaf ears. She might not even miss him, she might even be relieved. But, she was still his mom. Wouldn't she always care?

Toby finished dialing the phone: "Sara? Toby Heiser, Ponderosa Academy...very good...thank you. Well, I have Charlie here and he's looking forward to talking to you. Sorry to have kept you waiting."

There was another pause. Charlie took a deep breath. Toby continued, "I'm sure he feels the same. Here, let me give you to him."

Toby held out the receiver, the coiled tangle of cord dragging a pencil to the floor. Toby twisted the dial on the timer to 15 minutes.

"Mom?" said Charlie.

"Hi, honey," she said. "How are you? We miss you."

Charlie's eyes throbbed and then detonated. A hot, salty stream of tears bathed his cheeks.

"Mom," said Charlie. "I miss you guys. I miss you so much."

His eyes gushed. His nostrils burned within as if they had been packed with bleach. His chest heaved to bridle the sobs but a force within him chafed for release. He was going to break down. He was going to cry forever until the men in the white coats came.

His mother sounded worried now. She said his name again.

Good, Charlie thought. She's getting the picture. Maybe she will demand to know why her baby is an inconsolable basket case.

Toby put a calming hand on Charlie's shoulder and with the other, removed his reading glasses and met Charlie's eyes, a sympathetic offering on his face.

The timer ticked frantically on the desk. Charlie steeled himself with a sucking breath.

"I'm here, Mom," he said.

"I hate to hear you so sad," she muttered. She sounded so far away.

Charlie couldn't respond. He was torn between a need to alleviate his mother's pain and indulge his own. He could actually feel the tug within him. Finally the roiling anger overtook him.

"Why didn't you tell me!" he cried.

"Charlie..." his mother attempted.

"Why did you send me here?"

Charlie wiped his nose with the tissue that had lit upon his hand. Toby's eyebrows were raised, suggesting caution.

"Charlie," pleaded his mother, "I couldn't handle you running away from me again. A woman at the office has a daughter that went to Ponderosa. She said it really helped her and I wanted the same for you. Honey, I don't know how to help you any other way. I want you to be safe; I want you to be happy."

"It was Kurt's idea," spat Charlie, "wasn't it."

"It was my idea and, yes, Kurt thought it would be good for you too. Don't you like it there? Isn't it better than public school? You and Kurt weren't exactly getting along anyway. I was tired of the fighting. I was tired of always being forced to choose sides. You are my son. I will always do what's best for you. It may not always be easy, it may not always be what you want but I will always make sure you are safe and cared for."

"I just want you, Mom," said Charlie. A sob wracked him, choking his words. "I just want you."

"Honey, don't..."

Charlie wiped his nose, covering his face. Still, the tears kept coming. Now, it didn't matter how or why he was here. It only mattered whether he would continue to be here. Desperately he tried to get a hold of himself. He had to find out what he needed to know. Time was short.

With a deep breath, he lowered the tissue and flicked his eyes to Toby and posed the question to his mother: "Am I going to stay here? The whole two years?"

Charlie kept an eye on Toby who was listening, affecting preoccupation with a stack of papers. The question was clever. He wasn't begging to return home. No, he simply asked if he would be staying. Toby could not fault him for that. He hoped.

After a moment, his mother spoke: "They would not accept a part time student. The program is designed for that amount of time. Look, honey, I miss you lots but I can't take the thought of you getting in trouble, falling in with the wrong crowd, and I can't deal with you and Kurt constantly at each other's throats. Brandon's grades were starting to slip too. You affect him Charlie. He looks up to you. Whatever is going on inside needs to be...I don't know...healed somehow."

Charlie was disarmed by the mention of his brother. Homesickness weighted his heart so that he bent forward in the office chair. He put his free hand to his forehead and rubbed his temple.

"Can I talk to Brandon," said Charlie.

His mother muffled the phone with a hand and yelled for Brandon. A rustle on the mouthpiece was followed by an admonition from the background to "not talk too long".

"Charlie?"

"Brando!" A smile lit Charlie's glistening face.

"When are you coming home?" asked Brandon.

"I don't know. I get a home visit in the fall for, like a weekend or something. Probably around Thanksgiving."

"Is it like your old school with priests and stuff?"

"No. No priests," confirmed Charlie.

"That's good," said Brandon with relief.

Charlie laughed. "So you're going to be a bad-ass sixth grader this year. Did you go shopping for school stuff?"

"Yep, Kurt got me a Star Wars binder. You can clip your folders to the inside and it even has a zipper bag for pencils hanging from the inside cover so you don't lose them. It's pretty cool. I found out I got Mrs. Schwartz this year. Not so cool."

"Lame," said Charlie. "No Mr. Freeman? Schwartz is a witch."

"Tell me about it."

"How's Bowser?" asked Charlie.

"He's okay," Brandon replied. "A big pain in the butt actually. We just gave him a bath. Mom thought he was dying because his poop was red, but it turns out he had just eaten one of my Starbursts."

"Gross."

"Totally."

A pause, swollen with unspoken words, worked Charlie's tongue as if taffy was stuck in his molars. Too much gushing would be unnatural and awkward. It would only serve to worry his brother. Saying, "I love you" to him out of context would surely sound alarm bells in the little guy's head.

"Hey!" said Brandon with inspiration. "Remember that Mom said that Papa Pete left us some of his money? It was a lot! We're rich!"

"How much?" Charlie asked.

"We get a hundred thousand a piece! Mom gets more of course. I think a lot more. We won't get it until we're eighteen though. Wait...Mom is freaking out. She wants the phone back."

"Okay," said Charlie, "I...I'll see you soon."

"I love you," said Brandon.

Charlie's heart swelled. "I love you too Brando," he said, a wide smile stretching his wet face.

Silence, a consuming emptiness, seeped into his ear and infected him with loss. For a moment he heard only the timer ticking on the desk. Finally, there was a crackle on the other end of the phone, and then...

Kurt's voice: "How are things, sport?"

Charlie's insides constricted. Going from Brandon to Kurt was emotional whiplash. He stomped his vulnerability back into the hole in his heart. He gripped the receiver tighter, as if to crush it to powder. He straightened in his chair.

"Fine," said Charlie.

"We all miss you," said Kurt without a trace of sarcasm and without swagger. It was convincing. Kurt sounded almost...what? Sorry?

"I'll be home in the fall," said Charlie. "They said I can go home for a Home Visit in the fall."

"Good," said Kurt. "That's good. Well, we'll be happy to see you. You know...Tony has been asking about you. Says for me to tell you that while you're at that fancy boarding school he will be a freshman at the mercy of San Jose High, without his wingman."

"Tell Tony he'll do fine. Tell him I said hi."

His mother's voice broke in on another extension.

She must have gone upstairs for privacy, thought Charlie. Maybe she has something to say that Kurt isn't supposed to hear.

"I got it, honey," she yelled half into the receiver.

Charlie heard the other extension click off. He knew very well that a diligent finger could produce the same click as a handset and there was no way to know if Kurt was really off the phone. Brandon would just have to get his back on that one.

"So I guess Brandon couldn't keep his trap shut about Papa Pete's gift," his mother said.

"It's true?" asked Charlie

"Yes it is and once escrow is closed on the Evanston house we will get our own house, with our own pool. How does that sound?"

"Awesome. Are you going to quit your job?"

"No, They need me right now. Plus, I don't think it would be wise to retire in my forties. I could eat that money up pretty quick sitting on my ass for another forty years."

They shared a laugh. Charlie then heard about the project her employer, Knight Ridder, was launching. She spoke of Kurt becoming the foreman on a massive high-rise project that was to help revitalize the downtown area. She regaled him with a tale about their crazy neighbor backing into a retaining wall and destroying the rear end of his Mustang.

The timer's incessant tick slowed as the spring slackened towards zero.

Charlie, glazed with the enriching words, listened with vague interest to the details, but mostly just to the sound of his mother's voice. Suddenly, he felt as if the distance between them had been obliterated. That beloved voice, reciting tales of a simple, prosaic suburbia, soothed him as if she were blowing gently on his wounds.

"Charlie," said his mother after a pause, "are you going to be okay?"

If he was ever going to beg, if he was ever going to attempt to articulate the things he had witnessed: the work crews, the Raps-emotional scabs scrubbed raw by the lashing of tongues, the mute zombies on Dishes, the Propheets-screams flushing the birds from the trees-it had to be now. If she thought this was an extension of a summer camp, as it had been presented to him, then she needed to open wide for a foul dose of reality.

"Mom," he began urgently, his pulse thumping through his neck, "I don't think you understand what kind of school this is. I think you've been..."

The timer's hammer struck the bell. A jarring peal shimmered through the room and through Charlie's brain like a silver nail. Charlie started. He bent over and pressed the receiver to his ear, his grip tightening.

"Time's up," said Toby. The metallic warble of the bell still vibrated through the wood panels of the office. Toby's stating of the obvious made anger flare in Charlie's gut.

"What was that bell?" asked Sara.

"I'm being timed," said Charlie. "My time is up."

His mother sounded vexed: "I knew they wanted to keep the conversation to around fifteen minutes but I didn't know they were going to be so strict about it."

Charlie barked a bitter laugh. "Wow, you don't know the half of it."

"Say goodbye Charlie," said Toby firmly. He half-extended a hand to suggest that the receiver be placed in it soon.

"Well," said Charlie's mother, slowed by her son's sudden sarcasm, "behave yourself. That school is highly recommended and you will only get out of it what you put into it. Try hard for me. Okay, honey?"

"Sure," Charlie said tightly.

"I love you," said his mother

"I...I love you too, Mom"

The line went dead. The receiver, slick with sweat, moved

through the air to meet Toby's outstretched palm. As if in a dream, Charlie watched Toby's lips mutter some assurances into the mouthpiece, followed by a chugging, insincere laugh. There was a polite "goodbye", and then the receiver hovered over the base of the phone for a moment before clicking into the cradle with the finality of a lock's tumbler.

Chapter 13

Charlie made his way towards the outskirts of the property, along the Farm Road that would lead him to his assigned work crew. It was hot, and although he was glad to be off of House Crew and outside, he wished the opportunity hadn't come at the end of August. No breeze stirred the thick heat. The smell of acres worth of downy beds of brown, baking pine needles filled his nostrils with the fuming acridity of decay. A red-tailed hawk shrieked somewhere along the vault of heaven, its cry relayed by the granite sentinels that peered over the canopy of the forest above.

He walked past the Muir Hut where his art classes were held–a building adjacent to the almost identical Administration building. Past the oval lawn, the broad parking lot, and the incline to School Road, the Farm Road began in earnest. The asphalt gave way to hard-packed dirt, louvered with furrows that grabbed at Charlie's work boot and threatened to twist his ankle. Tufts of weeds poked through the arid shoulder of the road. The ground sloped gently downhill as the way narrowed. To the right, the Portman's and DiFranco's houses crouched behind a copse of ponderosa pine and black cottonwood. To the left, bracken fern beneath the shade of white fir, bordered the sports field. The eroded face of the dorm's promontory loomed beyond.

Charlie pulled up the bottom of his t-shirt and wiped the sweat from his brow. Something big buzzed into his ear and he flapped a convulsive hand at the side of his head. He loped past the deserted riding ring, then past the corral where a chestnut mare swished its tail and stared at him with a dark, wet eye.

Now, Charlie could hear the students in the distance, somewhere in the Leech Fields. A new enclosure was being built for the new flock of sheep, and for the second day--in a rare consolidation of lower family resources--Genesis was to join forces with Vision and Quest to get the job done.

He hoped that he wouldn't be expected to talk about the call home or the details of life beyond the crispy pine needles of Bear Creek. But, word had a way of getting around and he was sure that everyone would know why he was late.

"Charlie!" said Pat Conner, the Vision family head. He was pulling work gloves off of his hands as Charlie approached. "You're just in time; we're going to start mixing the cement. We got to get those poles in the ground pretty quick once we start mixing." Pat cupped his hands around his mouth and shouted towards the field, "Robert! Let's do it to it!"

Pat had presided over a couple of Charlie's Raps and he thought the guy was cut from a different cloth than the rest of the staff. Charlie liked him. With his mousy brown curls wobbling atop his head, his goofy large glasses and his push-broom moustache perched above his generous grin – nothing about Pat Conner demanded caution. Moreover, Pat liked Charlie and Charlie could tell.

Pat lowered the cupped hands from his mouth and turned to Charlie, asking confidentially: "How did it go?"

"It was okay," Charlie replied. "Hard."

"I know," said Pat, "I know."

A moment of reflective silence passed, mercifully cut short by a brisk clap of Pat's hands.

"Alrighty," said Pat, "grab a round-nose shovel, Chuck. Your see-ment awaits."

His attempt at a Texas drawl cracked a smile on Charlie's face. Tucking his gloves into the back pocket of his jeans, Pat headed for the Leech Fields, the gloves bouncing as he walked away, like the ears of a poorly concealed rabbit.

Heading for the tool shed behind the barn, Charlie met a boy named Kevin DeWilt who was returning from the work site to exchange tools.

"You call home?" asked Kevin.

"Yeah."

"First time, right?"

"Yeah,"

"How did it go?"

Charlie figured that his eyes were still swollen and his face still red from the emotionally draining call. He clung to the hope that maybe no one would notice. After all, it was hot and the fields were disgorging freshly disturbed allergens into the stagnant air and everyone probably looked the same. Kevin's crooked nose appeared to be bursting with histamines and even Pat had looked a little rosy and scorched. So, who could really tell if he had been bawling on the phone?

Not that it was a big deal, someone was always bawling-or "dumping" as it was known- somewhere on the property: alone in a family room with a staff member for a special dumping session, sitting in the corner of the lodge with a friend at Floor Time, blubbering in front of a group of twelve, or rocking themselves to sleep on their wet pillow. Crying was considered progress; the more tears, the better. Preferably, dumping should be done with a flourish and in front of as many witnesses as possible.

Nonetheless, this wasn't the time or place to get into his feelings again. Besides, he wasn't close to Kevin. In fact, Charlie thought him to be untrustworthy. Charlie was sure that if the shielding Agreements were not in place, Kevin would have been the first to laugh and point his finger. Second only to Devon Childs, Kevin was always getting blown away in Raps for making things unsafe. Unlike Devon-who was not allowed to be acknowledged by the Genesis family as he was still on Bans, rendering him invisible to all but older students-Kevin had to be treated with good, old-fashioned mistrust.

"You gotta see this," said Kevin as the two left the tool shed, Charlie with his shovel resting on his shoulder, Kevin jabbing his post-hole digger into the earth like a walking stick with each alternate step.

Kevin pulled ahead and spoke over his shoulder, "Check it out." He flapped a hand, beckoning Charlie into the barn.

The barn was stuffy and stank of sweet urine. A rhombus of hot light fell on the dirt floor from the hayloft window. In the shadows, hay rustled as sheep struggled to their feet to press their black faces against the slats of their pen. Charlie followed Kevin's finger. To the right of the barn door, in the corner, leaning against the wall beneath a wispy spider web was a tall white wand with a red grip at one end and a glint of metal at the other.

"Cattle prod," said Kevin, beaming. "See what cool stuff Vision gets to play with?" Kevin grabbed the device and thumbed the power switch. "It's electric. It's for zapping animals. You know...to get them to move. You wanna try?"

"No...no," said Charlie holding up a flattened palm.

Undaunted, Kevin crossed to one of the pens where a ram stood broadside to the boys, chewing its cud. The horizontal slit of the animal's pupil regarding them coolly. Kevin crept closer to its backside where an obscenely large, wooly scrotum dangled between its haunches like a half-inflated balloon. Kevin touched the prod to the ram's testicles. A brief sizzle of electricity sent the animal leaping forward and scampering to the far side of the pen. Kevin bent over and slapped his knee, but his braying laugh was cut short by the sound of clanking tools approaching. Kevin quickly ditched the prod and headed for the door. Charlie, stunned and sickened, followed numbly.

"What were you guys doing in there?"

It was Steve Valentine. He emerged from the tool shed with a jug of creosote and a grimace that expected answers.

Steve was a Quester and Charlie didn't know him well. Charlie was relieved it hadn't been Pat. The thought of disappointing someone he respected and liked, someone like Pat, by being even passively involved with such a stupid and cruel act made Charlie's own testicles constrict.

Steve hadn't seen anything. Steve was just being a hard-ass. Questers could get that way, even more so than Evolution or Source kids who generally wanted nothing to do with the lower school and couldn't care less if they were a bunch of baggers; their lives just didn't intersect often enough to care. Quest students, on the other hand, loved to bust the chops of Genesis. Whenever the younger students ran afoul of the most orthodox of Questers, there was sure to be a bloodbath in the next Rap.

"Well, come on!" said Steve. "Stop slacking off. Pat is mixing up the cement."

Kevin flashed an insolently raised eyebrow at Charlie and then left, trudging towards the fields behind Steve. Charlie paused, shook his head, filled his lungs with a restorative breath and then followed the two boys; the dry brush in the field whispering past the legs of their jeans as they went.

On Tuesday and Thursday afternoons, Raps were not held and Experientials took their place. After four hours of sinking creosote-coated posts into the ground of the Leech Fields, Charlie was ready for anything else.

Experientials could, indeed, be anything. Sometimes they required some type of exertion; sometimes they required problem solving skills or the fashioning of some useless craft. Charlie hoped for the latter. So did the rest of Genesis who were gathered along the shoulder of the Microwave Road at the edge of the sports field waiting for Michael DiFranco, who'd been rumored to be leading the afternoon's activity, whatever it turned out to be.

It was even hotter now and the blacktop of the Microwave seemed gooey under Charlie's tennis shoe. Some students had straggled onto the field to take advantage of the wispy shade cast by the sapling pines that fronted the green.

"Why do they call it the Leech Fields anyway?" asked Charlie to no one in particular.

Jonathan's eyes rolled up in thought, Kenny Bootman had no intention of answering and Aaron Golldenberg , squatting on his haunches with his limp arms before him, looked like he was in the beginning stages of heat stroke.

Carolina Eversol sidled up to Charlie and mischievously purred in his ear, "I think it's to keep you from running away into the woods."

"There's nothing past there, anyway," Aaron mumbled to the ground, fiddling with a pebble, "just more trees for miles. If you were going to split why wouldn't you head for town down School Road?"

"Leech Road," put in Vicki Brennan. "They should call it Leech Road. Or Man-Eating Tiger Road."

"If I was going to split..." began Kevin DeWilt.

"Hey! Hey!" cried Kenny Bootman, grabbing the sides of his head. "This is not okay. We can't just sit here and talk about splitting. It's unacceptable, totally out of agreement. It's a split contract? Ever heard of it?"

"We were just saying..." Aaron trailed off bleakly.

Jonathan casually walked past Charlie, and without moving his lips, whispered: "Feel The Boot up your ass."

Kenny Bootman was "The Boot" for his tendency to constantly "pull you up", ostensibly out of your "personal bullshit" and up to a higher level. Thus, the pull-up was a favor to you and to all. Kenny was the highly effective mole that The Academy's system of rewards and punishments seemed to foster. Kenny also excelled at the art of avoiding being pulled-up himself while he hunted diligently for transgressors. The Boot's "look-good" was clever and hermetic.

Smitty, on the other hand, had a different kind of "look-good". His was a sincere willingness to swallow anything, to trust everything and to not question the wisdom of the Ponderosa staff. Unlike The Boot's insidious brand of unctuous hypocrisy--for all knew that Kenny was really just as cynical as they were--Smitty was just a half-wit pawn, and therefore, far more dangerous.

Also, something was very wrong with Smitty, but nobody knew exactly what. He always looked at you vaguely and just below the line of your eyes, as if he was watching a bug on your cheek. Smitty also had too much spit in his mouth at all times, and when excited, the spit problem increased. No one really knew what was wrong with the guy, but Charlie thought he might be slightly mentally retarded, or from Europe or something.

It was Smitty who happily answered the question about the naming of the Leech Fields: "It's spelled totally differently. The Leach Fields have a well under them. Those black pipes coming out of the ground, the ones we had to go around when we sank the back fence, are wellheads. So, Leach Fields means...leaching water from the ground. There aren't any blood-sucking creatures out there except maybe mosquitoes."

Charlie looked past the boy and up the hill to where the dorm trail crossed the Microwave. He saw Devon Childs in the distance, walking to the dorm with Vince Russo.

"It isn't spelled at all," Charlie said absently, his eyes fixed on the two boys above. "It isn't written down anywhere."

Smitty's gloat slid from his face as he realized his moment of deference had passed. Everyone was now watching the bluff.

"When is Devon going to be off Bans?" asked Charlie. "He never gets to do anything with us."

Images of the boy stacking checkers and reading upside-down books alone in the shadows flashed through Charlie's head.

"Just ignore him, Charlie," said Jonathan. "I don't think he'll be around for long. I think he's Provo material."

"He can't even take a dump without an escort," said Charlie.

"I think he needs meds," said Jonathan.

"Then why doesn't he take some?" Charlie asked.

Smitty answered: "It's out of agreement. No psych drugs."

"I thought if it was prescribed..." Charlie began.

Smitty cut him off: "No psych drugs. The Academy doesn't allow them."

"It's a crutch," confirmed Kenny Bootman.

"They allow smoking," Charlie challenged.

"That's because smoking is harder to quit than psych drugs," said Kenny. "They tried banning cigs years ago and I heard it was a disaster."

The conversation died. Michael DiFranco had appeared at the end of the Quad wearing a nylon warm-up suit. It wasn't a good sign. Jogging was likely, probably to the end of School Road and back

"I still think the Leech Fields are just a way to freak us out," said Aaron, raising from his haunches and kicking the blood back into his legs.

"Afternoon," said Michael DiFranco in the distance. "You guys ready for a jog?"

No one had been ready for a jog. Two miles to the elementary school at the end of School Road and back had thoroughly exhausted Genesis. Bone tired, their t-shirts mottled with dark sweat, the kids' final climb up the Microwave to the dorms evoked the zombie movies of George Romero. Limp armed and staggering bodies groaned as they gained the dorm trail and infiltrated the living quarters in search of cool showers.

Charlie emerged from dorm time with a fresh set of clothes for an evening on the Floor: a pair of indigo jeans that he hadn't worn yet and a dark green button-down shirt. Crumpled in his hand was a dollar bill.

Walking Around Money, or WAM, was handed out to Genesis students once a week. A dollar was the standard pay once a student had received the privilege, and raises in increments of twenty-five cents were awarded periodically. Eventually, as a member of the upper families, a student would receive a stipend of a more substantial amount. WAM, however, never exceeded more than a couple bucks and change.

There were only two possible ways to spend WAM. One was to sign up for a supervised shuttle to the Bear Creek Market on

Sundays for a Store Run and the other was to visit Mary Portman's makeshift shop in the STC. Whatever a student's choice, the imposed sugar limit was still in effect: only one dollar's worth of products containing refined sugar could be purchased in a week, regardless of how much change a student had the discipline to amass. Mary's store with its tailored stock and cheap prices usually won more Ponderosa customers than Bear Creek.

The door of the annex building, on a hill above the dining room, was standing open. Mary was doing business. As Charlie mounted the last of the recumbent logs and began crossing the gravel drive to the looming shade of the building, he mentally double-checked his shopping list for possible blunders in judgment: one grape soda at twenty cents, one cream soda at twenty cents, two bags of spice drops at fifteen cents a pop...

Not bad, he thought as he entered the makeshift store in the basement, thirty cents left. He decided to buy one more soda, a root beer, and roll over the dime.

Charlie ditched his spoils back in the dorm and then headed down the dorm trail, to the lodge for dinner. He scanned the Quad. A couple of smokers sat at one of the picnic tables blowing their plumes of smoke into the tepid evening. He entered the lodge through the heavy doors, past the coat closets, and onto the Floor.

He reconnoitered. Shawn was across the room at the other side of the Pit talking to DiFranco–not his favorite pair of people. Charlie turned away from the two before he could be spotted and almost ran squarely into Toby Heiser.

"Whoa," said Charlie, "sorry."

"Tuck in your shirt, Charlie," said Toby. "That's a night."

Charlie glanced down at the green tail of shirt that had worked its way out of the waistband of his jeans. He looked up to shoot Toby an incredulous look but Toby had already breezed past. Charlie's mouth gaped like a hooked fish. He whipped his head around to see Toby enter the Genesis family room and disappear from sight.

Everyone knew what "that's a night" meant. Charlie stood rooted to his spot in the lodge, fuming, his insides flooding with cold despair. It had finally happened. Just like that, his night was gone.

He was on Dishes.

Chapter 14

"It's about time," said Austin, shoveling a forkful of shepherd's pie into his mouth.

"A full month is a long time to avoid the axe, Charlie," said Jonathan.

The boys sat in the Upper Level of the dining room on Charlie's behest, its low ceilings and moody lighting never failing to attract the despondent.

"I knew I was going to get Dishes," said Charlie. "It was because of the call home, I know it."

"I didn't want to ask," Jonathan said. "What happened on the call?"

"Nothing," Charlie replied unconvincingly, picking a sinewy bit of flank steak from between his front teeth. "I thought I held back a lot. I mean a LOT."

Austin pondered this. "Hmmm...well, your shirt was untucked so, technically, you were out of agreement." He trained a wide grin at Charlie. "You bagger."

"Yeah," said Charlie, "but he wouldn't have popped me if I hadn't..." He faltered, searching for words.

"Hadn't what?" asked Austin.

"I don't even remember what I said," admitted Charlie, glumly. He reached back in his mind, but the phone call was an anxious blur. He only remembered that he had been on thin ice for a moment, but he thought he had pulled it out. Evidently, he had not. His mind flashed to the paneled walls, the tears, and Toby's admonishing stare. Maybe he had gone too far at the end.

He glanced at the wall clock on the Middle Level. His nervous stomach announced the approach of Dishes with a sour back flip.

"Oh, well," said Jonathan, swigging the last of his milk. "I guess we will see you on Floor."

"See ya', Charlie," said Austin. "Work hard. Oh, and I expect to see myself in the back of every spoon." He clapped Charlie on the shoulder.

"You would," mumbled Charlie.

Austin and Jonathan gathered their trays and left. Charlie stayed put. It wasn't long before the day's malefactors were made to gather on the Middle Level for punishment. The thought of more work after a day of backbreaking labor and physical exercise made Charlie want to whip his fluted plastic cup at the wall. He raised it, paused, sighed and then set it back on his tray.

Steve Valentine walked briskly into the dining room holding a clipboard. A few students trailed disconsolately behind him. Aside from James – an introvert burdened with a wicked humor and a sharp tongue that occasionally served to carve his name onto the Dishes clipboard--the ever-detained Devon Childs was the only other Genesis kid in tow, the rest were from Vision.

Charlie knew exactly why there was a disproportionate amount of Vision kids on Dishes tonight. He recalled his last Rap, where he had been privy to the recent Vision work crew debacle.

Pat Conner had made a run to town for some sheep dip and had left the most faithful student in charge. According to said student, a few kids had been caught sitting down in a clearing between two boulders some distance from the barn, doing nothing. Their chatter had betrayed their position. The rest of the Vision family, who had been working the farm in the heat, absolutely annihilated the trio in Wednesday's Rap and Dishes had been handed out on the spot. Dispensing of discipline during a Rap was rare, but not unheard of-especially for a Sonia DiFranco Rap. Sonia's hand of justice was reputedly a heavy one.

Steve Valentine leaned on the brick hearth of the potbelly stove. He swept a shock of dark hair back into its lofty cowlick and reviewed the names on the clipboard with icy blue eyes. An imperious sneer twisted his thick red slug of an upper lip.

Charlie rose and quietly joined the group. Why Steve Valentine? Out of all older students, Steve was the most power-drunk boob to ever be allowed to wield a clipboard.

Steve completed roll call and then raised his head to meet the eyes of his charges. "There's no talking, smiling, laughing or slacking off on my crew," He set the clipboard on the hearth, laced his hands before him and tented his index fingers, stabbing the air before each student to punctuate his edicts: "Devon, you're on the

Sterilizer. Susan, you're on Lower Level. James, Middle Level. Chris, Upper Level. Robert: pots and pans. Charlie, you're on Veggie Prep."

Charlie's eyes wanted to roll, but the last thing he wanted to do was give Steve a reason to ride him all night. He knew Steve was good for it.

"When you have your area tight," Steve continued, "check back with me and I'll give you something else to do. Alright?"

Barely perceptible nods from the students appeased him.

"Then let's show some hustle!" concluded Steve with a clap of his hands.

Charlie had stumbled upon Dishes in progress enough times to know what pace was expected: breakneck. His legs were rubbery from the day's exertions, but he made them move towards the Veggie Prep. Why they called it that he would never know. It was a pile of shit, pure and simple. A mountain of plates, trays and flatware waited in the gray tubs, stacked into wobbly towers. He skidded to a halt before the mess and realized he had no idea what to do. He turned on his heel and ran back to the Middle Level and to Steve.

"I..." he began.

"What?" Steve replied, glaring.

Charlie tried again: "I'm not sure...I mean I'm new...not new but I've never been on Dishes before. How do I do the Veggie Prep?"

Steve sighed, "Come on." They approached the mountain of plates. "This is Veggie Prep from here..." Steve swept his right arm to the wall. They turned the corner into the industrial hallway. Steve extended his left arm, "...to there." He indicated the end of the hall, 25 feet away.

Charlie listened to Steve's directive with growing despair. "You use this sink to spray off the plates and then you bring them to the back and give them to Devon who is running the Sterilizer--same with the silverware. The cups you stack onto these plastic pallets, upside down on the pegs, and give them to Devon. Stack the pitchers on a separate pallet.

They rounded the corner: "Once that's done, you sweep and mop the floor and take out these three trashcans--this one goes in the compost pile near the parking lot and these two go in the dumpster. After that, clean the sinks with the soap in that jug and then wipe down the faucets and the back splashes. Sponge, mop, broom, soap and trash bags are in these closets.

Steve faced Charlie: "When you're finished, and you think it's tight, come see me and I'll find something else for you to do."

James and Robert darted by, in the throes of their chores. Steve smiled thinly at Charlie, suggesting that it would be wise to adopt a similar pace.

It was a show, thought Charlie. Just like everything else here. It wasn't necessary to run from place to place to insure an ideal result. It was another ridiculous contrivance to add to the repertoire of behaviors that might, just might, aid a student in avoiding their fellow cannibals who would gladly rat them out if it meant a pat on the back. One misstep, or in this case one slow step, was sure to train the dancing red dots of countless laser-sighted tongues right on your forehead in the next Rap.

Charlie's thoughts shattered like a dropped glass. Someone was behind him. Charlie turned.

It was Devon Childs.

The boy's dark, beady eyes were narrowed and his black, sweaty hair lay flat against his scalp. The boy, grunting like a cave man, was gesturing frantically with his hands at the plastic tubs. He was attempting to reprimand Charlie for something, or to urge him into some action, but he was not allowed to talk. Eager to help, Charlie struggled to understand and began guessing.

"What?" asked Charlie.

Devon looked stung by the word. It took a moment for Charlie to realize he had broken the no talking rule himself by speaking aloud; he whispered a reflexive apology, compounding his folly. Exasperated, Devon grunted afresh, turned with a squeak of his sneaker and disappeared into the back kitchen.

This sucks, Charlie thought, spraying the meaty gore off of the plates with the high-pressure nozzle. Slicks of gravy soaked mashed potatoes clung stubbornly to the plates as the blasting water sent tiny peas flying into the stainless steel sink. Hundreds of dishes and cups still waited in the filth of the tubs for Charlie's attention.

"Another thing..."

Charlie jumped.

Steve had come up behind him. "Something has been brought to my attention. I forgot to mention it. If there is any milk left in the pitchers, then we consolidate. Wash one pitcher and dump all the leftover milk into one pitcher, or two if there is enough, and then cover the pitchers with plastic wrap and put them..." Steve walked down the hall, Charlie followed. Steve yanked the handle of the walk-in refrigerator, swung the large steel door open and gestured, through the swirls of fog, at an empty space on a wire shelf just inside the cold vault, "...and you put them on that shelf." Charlie nodded and the two retraced their steps.

The milk pitchers arrived sporadically from the students who were working all three levels of the dining room. Some of the pitchers were full, probably from tables where no one sat. There were only three of these, and out of three, two had dead flies floating in them. Most of the pitchers were completely empty, but several had puddles at the bottom. Charlie poured the tepid milk together into one pitcher and filled it almost to the top. With a nervous glance over his shoulder, he poured the full pitchers that had been polluted with dead flies into the drain. This left two full pitchers of milk. He found the spool of plastic wrap down the hall and attached to the wall, wrapped the pitchers and carried them to the walk-in refrigerator with shuffling steps to prevent sloshing.

After the pitchers were placed on the walk-in's wire shelf, he paused and looked around. He stayed inside the refrigerator and pulled the door closed, but not so it latched, because he wasn't sure if it would lock. Nobody would be able to hear him banging on the thick metal door if he was stupid enough to become trapped.

Instead, he gingerly pulled the groaning slab door closed only until the latch glanced against the jam with a soft, metallic click. The garish light of the hall was replaced with the dim glow of a bare bulb screwed into the steel ceiling and encircled by a wire cage. He took a moment to appreciate the silence, the chill, the isolation and the whisper of the refrigerator's fan. Tendrils of cool fog weaved in between the shelves and curled up from the floor in icy fronds of white vapor. He peered through the mist at the items on the shelves: crates of milk, large wheels of orange cheese, tubes of hamburger fastened at the ends with metal clips, palettes of yogurt, big yellow mustard jars, big red ketchup jars, boxes of all kinds and...

"Carob?" Charlie said aloud, wiping the mist off of a box's label.

He remembered his mother buying him a carob bar at a health food store in San Jose. It tasted like chocolate, but according to his mother, it was better for you. It wasn't exactly chocolate, and really, Charlie had no idea what carob was at all, but he liked the taste of it.

He crouched over the white box with the black lettering:

Carob Chips 5 lbs

The box had been opened. He pulled back one of the loose cardboard flaps, keeping an eye on the door. Thousands of tiny brown chips were packed into the plastic bag inside. The top of the bag was wadded closed. His hand began to fish through the folds of plastic until it seized a handful of the cool morsels. With his eyes on the door, he threw the chips into the back of his throat. They crunched like cold gravel.

Quickly, his hand dove into the box and grabbed at the cold pebbles of carob and seized on a handful, shoving them into the pocket of his jeans. He cursed. A few of the dark brown chips fell from his tented fingertips and skittered across the smooth floor.

He kept his eyes on the dark line where the massive door met the jamb. He expected at any moment to see a crack of light appear and widen, the door groaning open like a breached mausoleum to reveal a backlit Steve Valentine. Or maybe it would be Toby, or DiFranco or maybe even Jonas Portman himself.

An old idiom blew tauntingly through Charlie's mind like an ice-throated wind: '...hand in the cookie jar...caught with your hand in the cookie jar.'

He gulped. There would be no way to explain a handful of carob chips to whomever threw open the door. He didn't know exactly why it was illegal to help himself to a bit, but he was certain that it was. He doubted it would count towards his sugar limit, that wouldn't be the major violation. Acting autonomously was the real violation. The candy was sweet and enjoyable, and therefore must certainly be earned no matter how allegedly "healthy" it was. Of course, there was this little fact: he was standing alone in a refrigerator with the door closed, blatantly stealing something that he knew he could never gain the permission to take – not exactly a situation with a whole lot of wiggle room.

The plastic bag was wide open; he could simply toss the morsels back into the bag in seconds.

No, he thought. It felt good. It felt good to get away with something at this place. A current of exhilaration flooded through him and rippled his skin. He relaxed his tensed fingers, slowly fed the chips into the lining of his jeans pocket, wadded the plastic bag, and smoothed down the cardboard flaps of the box. He breathed again as he stooped to sweep away the errant chips on the floor, under the shelves and out of sight, with a flattened palm.

Charlie emerged into the thick warmth of the hallway, looked both ways, closed the walk-in's door with a clank, and returned to his station. He worked alone and in silence for another hour-and-a-half before he was finally released from duty.

Bodies littered the Floor. From one end of the lodge to the other, students were smushing atop each other in sprawling piles as John Denver serenaded the tangle from the speakers above.

Out of all requirements at The Academy, the onus placed on hugging, smushing and constant bodily contact with staff and other students was the hardest thing for Charlie to get used to. According to staff that had waxed philosophically on the topic, touch was healing. To Charlie, touch was confusing. Either it produced a sexual response in the case of girls or tension in the case of other boys.

As with all things Ponderosa, abstaining from any method of therapy was not an option. The only alternative was board games, and too much of that would lead to indictments in a Rap. It had already happened to him once. His directive was to share more of himself with the Floor, to open up and to tell his story to as many people as possible or else it was likely that he would spend every Rap, bathed in the flying spittle of his accusers. Worse, more Dishes could be handed out for failure to fully engage in the program. He was in danger of being labeled a loner, and loners--by the Ponderosa definition--were always hiding something, always dirty.

Charlie weakly traversed the lodge on numb legs. He flexed his fingers, which were wrinkled and bleached; his joints throbbed. Dishes had been more grueling than he had realized when he had the luxury of pondering the prospect with fresh muscles. Perhaps it would be best to be seen smushing tonight, perhaps even in tears, or at the very least, to engage in a humorless conversation that to onlookers would appear to be of some consequence.

Aimlessly, he walked across the Floor, expertly avoiding the bodies.

"Hi, Charlie."

He looked down. Carolina Eversol was leaning against the wall of the Pit on a forest-green cushion. Her blue eyes sparkled; her blonde waves of hair framed her face and splayed across the dark fabric of the cushion like a halo. She smiled sweetly. She was alone.

"Come sit with me," she said.

"Okay," said Charlie, "are you sure? You're not sitting with someone?"

"No one anymore," she replied. "I'm all alone now."

Out of all possible scenarios that the thin remainder of his evening might have produced, this one pleased Charlie the most. He smiled and sat beside her.

"I want to get to know you better," she said. "I still don't know much about you. You're kind of a mystery."

Charlie exhaled and laid his head upon the pillow beside Carolina. His shirt was rolled up to his elbows. She wore a short-sleeved blouse in pale yellow. Their bare arms touched, her warm skin soothing Charlie's like an emollient. Lying on the floor, inconspicuous in the sprawl of limbs that stretched across the lodge, Charlie closed his eyes gratefully.

"You look shot," she whispered.

"Dishes," he said, the word barely making it past his lips. "Toby gave me Dishes."

"Aw," she said with genuine sympathy, "after that hellish work crew? I don't blame you for looking half-dead. What did you get nailed for?"

"Untucked shirt."

She giggled softly. "Looks like your Dishes cherry has been popped. Plan on more where that came from, slugger. Did you know that I got Dishes last week?"

Charlie shook his head.

"I forgot my pencil during Archie Goetz's math class and he gave me a night. Archie! Can you believe it? Okay, so I did forget my pencil three times that week, but he never gives out Dishes. Boy was I wrong. Someone must have pissed in his Wheaties."

Charlie laughed. He thought Carolina a cool girl, and he liked being near her; it was restorative. Her voice was sweet, like a birdsong, and her hair smelled like apples..

He liked her in a different way, a new way. He had to conceal his unwieldy affections though and that was turning out to be as nerve-wracking as smuggling a loaded gun onto an airplane. He knew that if anyone picked up on what he hadn't the skill to conceal yet, he could be suspected of having a sex contract – or at least attempting to have one.

He couldn't imagine initiating a sex contract. Not here, not at The Academy; eyes were everywhere. Besides, he didn't have the first idea how to broach the subject of a secret romance anyway. In fact, he had never had even an above-board relationship with a girl, much less one that was likely to bring severe punishment. Girls made him goofy and nervous. Being in Carolina's presence was good enough for Charlie and it was all he needed to recharge his spent cells.

He propped his head up on an elbow and turned to look at her.

"You want to know more about me," he said, "and I want to know about you. Plus, you remember what I got talked to about in Wednesday's Rap? I have to tell my story. People think I'm too closed off."

"Well," she replied, "then let's tell our stories. You relax. You just got off Dishes. I'll start. But, brace yourself. It's not going to be pretty."

Chapter 15

"My mom married her high school sweetheart in her senior year of high school. I guess they got married young in those days. Anyway, they were only married for about a year when she found out she was pregnant after a vacation in South Carolina. Remember, when I first met you, I told you that was where my name came from? I guess it must have been a good vacation.

"According to my mother, my father didn't want children. The thought of having kids freaked him out, I guess. He was a musician. From what I heard, he was getting pretty popular. He played the organ in a psychedelic rock band that got signed to a small label. I guess he figured having a kid would cramp his style, ruin his chances of making it, and pin him down or something.

"When my mother was seven months pregnant my father screwed one of the back-up singers, some blonde, and they became an item. He took off on a U.S. and Canadian tour and never came back. He packed his stuff when my mom was at work one day. My mother was devastated and moved to Shreveport, Louisiana with her grandmother. She knew that she couldn't have an abortion and still face our super-religious family, and it was already too late for that anyway.

"When I was one my mother remarried and the guy adopted me. They divorced when I was six. My mother didn't marry for love, but for the money and power his family held in the small town where he came from. I guess they were old money – that's what we call it in the South. You know, antebellum mansions, uncomfortable furniture--the works. Nobody knows where his money came from originally, but it was probably from back in the slave days.

"So, she took me and fled to Atlanta, where my grandfather lives, and wouldn't let my adopted father see me for quite a while. She was really greedy about the child support. I remember that. I remember her yelling at him on the phone. Threats like: 'I'll take everything you've got. You won't have a pot to piss in.' Stuff like that."

Carolina rubbed her forehead and spoke from behind her palm, "My mother has made no secret that she has blamed me my entire life for my father leaving her. She has made statements to that fact many times. One of the stories she has told that hurt the worst was in front of my grandfather and great-grandmother when I was seven or eight.

'We were visiting with my grandfather and some of their friends. They were talking about things they regretted doing as teenagers. Right before we left, she made the remark: 'Well, I've only been drunk once in my life, on my eighteenth birthday. Nine months later, this thing comes along.' She points at me. Of course, I was born almost nine months to the day after her eighteenth birthday. She laughed like it was a joke. It wasn't a joke, though. Not to me. I knew she was serious, I felt it. She turned her back to the company and she looked at me...like she was accusing me of...I don't know, it was just the look in her eye."

Carolina stopped talking, a distant look trained at the high ceiling. For a moment, Charlie thought she might not continue, but with a slight shake of her head, she went on: "My mom remarried when I was nine to a man fifteen years her senior. He had two daughters from a previous marriage who were already out of the house and married before he married my mother. The oldest daughter was only four years younger than my mother and has always been against the marriage, still is. The younger daughter was usually very sweet. He, on the other hand, didn't want another child to put up with, and he only accepted me because he didn't really have a choice; it was a package deal.

"The funny thing was, I always thought of myself as a good kid. I was always pretty good in school. I was in the advanced placement program in public school, but school still wasn't really challenging me. I was getting bored and I stopped trying. I don't know what my problem was. My mother and stepfather were getting upset that my grades were less than perfect and grounded me for about a month because I got a C in my Advanced English class in the seventh grade.

"I was allowed to go only to school and church. I was not allowed to have friends over at all. I was allowed two calls per day-- incoming only--and only from females, and each call was limited to five minutes. When summertime came and I was at home all day, the doors were to remain locked at all times, with me inside, and my mother would take all phones to work. I was not allowed to go outside with my friends in the neighborhood or even to speak to them. Most of my seventh grade was spent locked in my bedroom trying to pretend I had a different family.

"Sometimes my mother would make me sit in the spare bedroom. There was no furniture in there, just a hardwood floor, some boxes and some old moth-eaten clothes that she couldn't bear to throw away. There was no light in that room. I had to just sit there and 'think'. I had to sit there for hours."

Carolina's face darkened. "He began...abusing me that year. My stepfather realized that no matter what he did, my mother would idolize him and shut me out. So, he started screwing with my head when she wasn't around. First it was just words, cruel words. He would call me a dirty slut, a loser, and a mistake. He began beating me with different objects--whatever he could get his hands on. Then came...the sexual stuff.

"This man, in his late forties, would walk around the house completely naked in front of me and thought it was perfectly normal. His pastime, when he wasn't out working, was to sit at home completely nude in his recliner in the living room and watch TV while he played with himself. I couldn't believe it. He had two adult daughters and he still had no shame. I even confronted Susan--one of his daughters--about it and she said he never did that in front of her. It probably got back to him that I brought it up. Maybe that was stupid of me to have trusted her; she owed me nothing.

"Eventually, he began to use whatever opportunities he thought he could get away with to try to touch me in various ways. I remember one time in particular I had come home from school and he was there, alone. He told me I had done something wrong that day and I needed to prepare for a spanking. I don't even remember what it was I was accused of, probably not washing out my cereal bowl before school or something stupid like that.

"Anyway, he always had me remove my pants and underwear for spankings, even at thirteen. He told me to bend over the couch. He went to get his belt. He returned, with the belt doubled-over and he was cracking it by letting the two strips of leather get slack and then tugging on the ends of then quickly so they would slap against each other. I hated that noise; it scared the crap out of me.

"I was bent over, shaking. Then, instead of swatting me, he bent down and looked at me, right in the eyes. I was crying, I was asking why he was doing this. Before I knew what was happening, he suddenly leaned down and kissed my butt cheek. He laughed and whispered: 'If you want me to kiss your ass around here, well, I just did.'

"I felt sick. He left me there with my pants down. I heard him crack a beer in the kitchen, flop down on the couch. He ignored me, watched TV, laughing at the set like nothing had happened.

"When I finally began telling my mother about this, she didn't believe a word of it. She said: 'You just have to fuck things up for me, don't you? Why can't you just be happy I'm finally in a relationship with someone I want?' He was a totally different person when she was around, all sweetness and light--like my grandmother used to say. You know, I honestly don't think she would have cared if she knew for sure."

Charlie groaned sympathetically and slid his hand across the short nape of carpet to Carolina's, and placed it atop hers. Whatever sexual tension Charlie thought existed was being replaced with something new, something more profound. Charlie had never loved anyone but his family, but now he was feeling the fetal kick of a new emotion within him.

Carolina glanced at Charlie's hand, wiggled her fingers in appreciation, smiled, and continued: "I finally got fed up with it all and realized I wouldn't get any help from anyone. One night, after a particularly nasty argument with them over why they would not let me take band anymore-my one extra-curricular activity-I ended up getting a beating for not agreeing with them and talking back. My mother claimed that the only reason I wanted to take band was to get noticed by boys. That doesn't even make sense, does it? Like, band is a dude magnet? Well, I finally got sick of it all. I went in my bedroom and pushed my dresser against the door. I packed a small bag and jumped out of my window.

"My parents found me wandering around the park-I had no place to go-and they beat me again. I heard the car start later that night, and my stepfather – Bob is his name, by the way – came into my room and dragged me to the waiting car. They drove me to the local youth shelter and told them I was an uncontrollable runaway.

"I tried to tell my pastor what was going on, when he came to visit me at the shelter. He didn't believe me. My parents decided they needed to take care of the problem once and for all, so they left me there for two weeks while they made arrangements to take me to a Christian school for girls--in Louisiana. They didn't tell me where we were going, and just dropped me off there.

"I was allowed to visit home during the Christmas season. I figured they would have missed me, even a little bit, but they didn't. The abuse continued.

"I wanted a bike for Christmas. I didn't get one, but I got enough money from my grandparents to pay for half. I asked my mother if she would pay for the other half, and she said I would have to ask her husband. Bob said he would think about letting me earn it. I said okay.

"On the day before I was to return, he was doing his usual naked TV routine, so I went into their bedroom to watch the other TV by myself. My mother was still at work.

"I was watching Brady Bunch, I remember, when I noticed him standing in the doorway, posing with his hand on his hip. The hall light lit up his thing. I don't think I'll forget that for a long time. Anyway, he was being cool, like nothing was out of the ordinary. He said, 'What are you doing?' I told him I was watching TV. I was sitting on the edge of the bed, trying not to look at him. He just stood there for a few minutes, and then he stood between the television and me. There was not much room between the bed and the TV cabinet. I tried to ignore him, but it was impossible. Still, I pretended like I was watching through him, like it didn't matter that he was there.

"Eventually, he lay down on the bed beside where I was sitting. He was staring at me. I kept my eyes glued on the TV. I remember how fast my heart was beating. I remember, on the television, Jan Brady was dancing with pom-poms, trying out for the cheerleading squad. I remember he smelled like beer and potato chips. He finally looked at me and said: 'So you wanted that bike, right?' I said I did. I looked over at him quickly; he was smiling. He said: 'Well, what were you planning on doing to earn that money?' I freaked out. I got up and I ran. I ran as fast as I could. I locked myself in my bedroom until my mother came home.

"I tried to tell her what happened. Of course, she thought I was lying--that I was just out to get him. I begged her to let me live with grandma and not to send me back to that crappy school in

Louisiana. I didn't realize that Bob was standing behind me. He heard the whole thing. He pushed me forward. I lost my footing and fell hard. He said: 'We don't want you here anyway, you lying little bitch! Tough shit if you don't like it! You're going back to that school! Those nuns will teach you some manners!'

"I continued to try to talk to my mother as Bob went into the garage and slammed the door. He came back with ropes – the kind you use for water skiing, you know the blue and white, scratchy, nylon kind? They took off my skirt and top and tied me to the bed in my underwear so I wouldn't 'run away again'. I was in my room, and they stood between me and the door.

"They called our pastor; they told him I was possessed by demons. Good ol' Southern Baptist stuff, huh? They still believe that crap. So, while they waited for the pastor, my mother sat on my chest while I screamed for help, and Bob sat on my legs. My mother shoved a stuffed-animal in my mouth to stop the screams. She said: 'It's not my fault you're possessed. Why do you hate me? What have you done? Where do you get this evil?' Then, my pastor arrived, so my parents released me and told me to get dressed.

"Pastor Martin sat on the edge of my bed and talked to me. I tried to tell him what happened that day. Then, he went to talk to my parents. He came back in and sat down. He looked at me for a long while and then sighed. In a sweet voice he said: 'Now, that didn't really happen, Carolina, did it?' My heart sank."

Carolina propped herself on an elbow and looked at Charlie, "I really know how that feels – your heart sinking, I mean – it feels like someone is trying to drown it, weigh it down so it can't breathe. It feels like it's dying; it hurts in such a...different way. You know? Anyway, I knew then, there was no use. I was truly alone in the world. Still, I pleaded with him, but he just shook his head like he was ashamed of me.

"I returned to the school in the swamps, but it closed down six months later-something about not making enough money from new enrollments, at least that was what I was told. My mother found a placement councilor in Atlanta who recommended Ponderosa Academy. My mother and Bob couldn't afford the tuition, but I qualified for a government grant. The last thing my mother said to me was: 'I hope for everyone's sake this place can straighten you out.'

"So, that's how I ended up here. That's my story."

Chapter 16

Charlie was stunned. At some point during Carolina's story he had stopped holding her hand. Now, his hands were in his lap, trying to wring the words from them.

"I'm sorry," he said in a small voice. "That's terrible."

"Thanks," she replied, "I'm okay. At least I'm okay now."

Kenny Bootman glided past them, stepping over their feet, and spoke to Kevin DeWilt who was playing rummy with two other students at a table nearby. "Can you take your feet off the coffee table?" he asked   the boy. "Thanks." Kenny continued breezily through the lodge and disappeared around the far side of the Pit. Kevin complied resentfully.

Carolina and Charlie followed Kenny with their eyes and then exchanged a bilious look.

Carolina said: "You know, even with The Boot on the rampage, the Agreements, and everything else that is annoying around here, I would still rather be here than at home. Not at first, at first I was freaking out. But now, I'll take this over being at home anytime. I'll stay here until they drag me off campus"

Charlie considered this. He had only thought about what he was missing, not what he had gained. It was strict here, but it was safe- at least safer then home could be sometimes.

He looked at Carolina, "I don't...I mean my story is, well, not as bad."

"Everyone has problems," said Carolina. "Yours are just as bad if they control you, if they prevent you from feeling at peace with yourself. Have you met Jonas' wife, Mary Portman? She runs Raps sometimes. She told me that once.".

Clearing his throat, Charlie began, "Well...I was born in San Francisco. I never really knew my Dad. He left when I was three..."

Charlie didn't know why, but he knew he was going to edit the part about his father out, the details at least. His father did leave when he was three; it wasn't a lie, it just wasn't the full truth because there was a lot more to it than that.

He felt conniving as he passed over the subject as if it were an insignificant detail, but the reflex to do so was as powerful as a rubber mallet to the knee.

Carolina had told him things that were hard to hear, and undoubtedly, hard to say. She had not only endured her past, but, she had trusted him and told him all. He knew he owed her some honesty.

He tried again to say the words, to squeeze them through his throat and past his lips. He couldn't, and every time he attempted to exhume the tale of his father from the tomb somewhere within him, his mind would recoil as if it had touched a hot wire.

He wanted very much to present Carolina with a comparable scar that would make her feel less vulnerable for all of her candor. Surely, his anger, shame and guilt could not be as bad as hers; yet, it tied his tongue in hopeless knots.

With effort, he managed one additional detail: "He left my mother when she was pregnant with my brother, Brandon. Just disappeared..."

Saying the words aloud stung. Volcanic anger rumbled somewhere in his darkest corners before his mind slammed its heavy door on the simmering black heat. His cheeks puffed and he blew out his breath.

I'll tell another day, he vowed. I promise I will.

Charlie licked his lips and continued with measure, "My mother had to raise us both, alone. My grandfather was the only father I knew. He died. I guess it's been almost a year since we lost him.

"Huh," Charlie considered. "It sure seems longer. Anyway, my brother and I called him Papa Pete. He was a cool guy. He invented the solar panels that they put on satellites. He was always talking about the sun, about light and how it could power everything. He was rich and he had an awesome house in Chicago – that's where my mom grew up.

"As I said, he was the only father we had. My mom dated a bunch of guys when I was little, but none were that great. She finally met a guy named Kurt Burns when I was, like five, I guess. He is a construction worker, a foreman. He was building something in the City and they met at some community center, at some party for single people.

"When I was 8 we moved to San Jose because that was where Kurt lived. Mom wanted to be closer to him so we moved into his apartment. He was cool at first. He didn't act like a father, more of just a guy, you know? Then, he married my mom about a year later. Soon after, he started having a lot of free time. Work wasn't that great back then, not for construction. He always drank, but then he started drinking a lot more.

"I remember the first time he actually hit me. My mom bought me a bike for Christmas, and a month later it was stolen. I laid it down on its side in front of 7-11 while I ran into the store to buy something-a Spiderman comic. I was only in the store for, like, ten minutes. When I came out, my bike was gone.

"When I got home, Kurt freaked out. My little brother actually tried to save me, but he was thrown against the wall and sent to his room. Kurt continued swearing at me. I reminded him he wasn't really our father. He didn't like that. This happened a lot. Usually, he would throw a beer at me and screw up the wall and the carpet. I guess he figured out that doing that left too much evidence when my mom came home. So, this time, he slapped me hard across the face.

"My mother had just gotten a job at Knight-Ridder – they're a news company. She was new and worked long hours. She came later that night and saw that I had a big ol' welt on my face. They fought that night; it was a big fight, lots of things breaking downstairs. She came into my room later and told me not to worry about the bike and that she had reported it to the police, but we never did find it.

"As time went on though, my mom defended me less and less. I don't really know why. My grades weren't good. I would hide my report cards because I knew that Kurt would kick my ass if he saw my grades. During my first quarter of 6th grade I cut school three times because my friend Tony wanted to go to the arcade and see the new games. Centipede and Super Asteroids were out, so I went with him. The absences showed up on the report card. The school mailed a copy to the house. I didn't know they were going to do that.

"Kurt walked into my room, holding my report card. He asked about the absences. His face was already red. I was afraid so I lied. I told him I didn't know what they were talking about. My A.J. Foyt racetrack was all put together on the carpet of my room. Kurt leaned down, grabbed a section of the hard-plastic track and started beating me across the face and shoulders. I screamed for him to stop.

"Finally, he left, slamming the door so hard that it never closed right again. Brandon tried to come in and see if I was okay. I remember him getting the door open a crack and then Kurt's hand landing on his shoulder. He was yanked away from the crack in the door before the door slammed shut again and then all I could hear was Kurt screaming at my brother to leave me alone and that I was in big trouble. I heard a slap and then I heard Brandon crying and running downstairs."

Charlie paused, "I think that is when he became my enemy. But, he was far from done with me. The worst thing he did happened later that year. I had taken quarters from the coffee can in their bedroom closet to play video games a few times. They caught me in the act once. Kurt always called me a thief after that. One time, though, he claimed I ripped off a bunch of money from his wallet, which I didn't. He questioned me, and when I wouldn't admit it, he dragged me upstairs by the collar of my Raiders jersey. It was a well-made jersey, an official, one and the collar was tough. In fact, I wore it here. It's somewhere in the Admin building now.

"Anyway, I prayed it would rip but it didn't. He screamed as he dragged me: 'You're going to rot in your room until you grow the balls to admit that you're nothing but a petty thief.'

"I tried to get my feet underneath me, but I couldn't. I was flat on my back, being dragged by my throat. Each stair pounded me in the back as he headed for my room. I gagged, I couldn't breathe. I clawed at my throat but it didn't help. I thought for sure that I was going to die, that he was going to finally kill me.

"I remember the next day at school. The teacher asked me to stay after. The last thing I needed was to be in trouble, but the teacher said she just wanted to talk. Anyway, I remember she looked at me frowning and she said: 'Charlie, what happened to your neck?' She pulled down the collar of my shirt. I'll never forget the look on her face.

"I was freaked out by her expression, so she pulled out her make-up mirror and showed me. I had a purple band of bruising around my neck. It looked like I had been hung from a noose and had come back from the dead or something. She wanted to know what happened, and for some reason, I made up something. I didn't want to make things even worse at home. I have a feeling she called my mother anyway because things calmed down for a bit. Kurt laid low for a while.

"My mom believed Kurt's accusation though. That was the saddest part. She admitted what he did was wrong, but she believed him. I had stolen quarters before, she said, so why should she believe that I didn't steal from his wallet? I said: 'Kurt is always drunk! That's why he can't find his money.' She told me to watch my mouth. I felt like I had lost her, like he had stolen her from me forever."

Charlie broke off. Now it was Carolina's turn to offer a comforting hand. Her warm palm lit upon Charlie's and squeezed.

Charlie continued: "I was sent to Sacred Heart School for seventh grade. Just before he died, Papa...I mean my grandfather suggested that my mom put me in a boarding school to get me out of the house. He said he would pay for a private school so that I could get a better education and more attention. He didn't approve of the Catholic school-I mean he wasn't religious at all – but my mom said it was close by and had a good reputation for college prep.

"The school was hell and I was miserable there. Benedictine monks ran the place. They were straight from Hungary, and not one of them was under 60 years old. They were hard-core corporal punishment junkies. It sucked. But, the worst part was that I had to learn Latin. I wouldn't wish that on anyone."

Carolina laughed. "Sorry," she said.

"It's okay," said Charlie and continued: "This one priest, Father Bernard, taught my Latin class. He was a pissed-off little man. You know? Some people are just always pissed off. Anyway, one day I was cutting up in the back of the classroom with this friend of mine. Father Bernard called me to the front of the class. Everyone teased me and whispered 'busted' as I slowly past the desks on my way to the front of the class to face the priest.

"I stood in front of everyone and Father Bernard squared off with me and yelled, in his thick Hungarian accent: 'You will behave!' I must have smiled, I mean, that accent was hilarious. I couldn't help it. And then, do you know what he did? He slapped me. It was one of those old man slaps, a sucker-punch. He kept his arm at his side and just bent his arm at the elbow with lightning speed. It connected hard with my cheek and it stung like hell. I was humiliated. Before I realized what I was doing, I had slapped him back."

Carolina clapped a hand over her mouth.

"Oh yeah," Charlie assured, "the whole class felt the same way. The oxygen was sucked out of that room pretty quick. I knew my ass was grass.

"I was expelled the same day. Kurt beat the tar out of me. I mean he really went ape-shit. I remember we had a big yelling match. Finally, I said: 'I'm getting out of here.'

"I opened the sliding glass door off the living room and headed through the little, enclosed backyard we have at our apartment, going for the gate. Kurt caught up with me. He said: 'You're not going anywhere.' and he grabbed at the barbecue tools that hung next to the grill. I kept walking. The next thing I knew, I was being smacked on the back with something. Soon, I was lying on the cement, tucked into a ball, with my arms around my head. Kurt whipped my spine with a metal spatula until he ran out of breath.

"I was grounded to my room. I couldn't leave my bedroom for a week; they even brought my meals to the room because they 'couldn't stand the sight of me.' They told me I wasn't to leave my room for any reason; I had to ask permission to use the bathroom.

"I finished up the second quarter at a public school where I knew nobody and the teachers couldn't care less if I was there or not. There was only three weeks left until the holiday break so I just wandered around the city.

"It was kind of a downhill slide from there. There were more beatings and I was sent to another hard-ass school–Collins Preparatory–where I didn't even try. My grandfather died in the middle of the second semester and, I guess I just gave up. It hit me really hard; I didn't even know he was sick. A brain tumor got him. I didn't really care about anything after that.

"Collins Prep was a hell hole. There was this eighth grader who made fun of me all the time. He would ask me: 'Are you a boy or a girl?' and he called me a "fag", stuff like that. One day, I was sitting on a bench while he was running by; he was late for class. I stuck out my foot and tripped him. He fell hard and cracked his forearm. I didn't know that then, but he was definitely slow getting up. I beat him over the head with my backpack. A teacher, way down the hall, saw me and came running over. I was suspended.

"I spent the early part of this summer in my room. They never let me leave. No swimming, no friends, no calls, no nothing. I couldn't even talk to my own brother. I could hear mom and Kurt from my bedroom window if they had the downstairs slider open. All they talked about was Papa Pete's money. My mom knew she was going to have a bunch of cash soon so they began looking around for a place to put me, somewhere permanent. Money was no object now.

"Anyway, I just talked to her about it on my Home Call and she said someone at work recommended Ponderosa Academy. She said it wasn't Kurt's idea, but I'm not sure if I believe her; Kurt controls pretty much everything she does. So, after lying to me and telling me that I was only going to a summer camp to 'build character'...here I am. Mom couldn't miss work to take me, and I guess this place only takes new students on weekdays, so she had Kurt do it. It was the longest ride of my life, that's for sure. The longest..."

Carolina stared solemnly at the ceiling. Charlie exhaled and rubbed the back of his neck, staring at his shoes.

"I don't know what you're talking about," said Carolina, "'that story is pretty awful too. I know what it's like to have no one to turn to. It's lonely. At least you have a brother. Is he okay?"

"I don't know," Charlie replied. "I'm not there anymore. I really don't know."

A silence, fueled by Charlie's dawning anxiety, sedated them both. There was nothing more to say so they just lay beside each other, staring at the ceiling. Carolina patted his hand absently, lost in her own thoughts. Charlie glanced down at their clasped hands.

A trail of carob chips had worked their way out of his pocket and were scattered on the carpet, inches from their hands. Charlie's heart iced over.

"Well," said Carolina contentedly, "We are okay now."

Horror and shame filled Charlie. His heart hammered. His brow tingled with cold sweat. Carolina began to lift her hand from his. If she slid it off across the carpet she would feel the chips. His only hope was that she lift her hand quickly.

Oh God, he thought. Please...

A voice from behind them yelled. Charlie jumped. "HOUSE AROUND THE PIT!"

Carolina lifted her hand quickly, skirting the chips. She rose on one elbow, and craned her head the other way. Charlie got to his knees in a flash and scrambled for the chips, plucking them wildly off of the carpet. He cradled them in his palm, flicked his eyes to survey the room and then jammed the chips into his pocket.

Soon, everyone was jockeying for a place at the low wall in the center of the room. Pat Conner was standing before the stone fireplace, waiting for the unwavering attention of all.

"Last Light already," said Carolina, swiveling to face Charlie again. She got to her knees. "Hey, are you okay?"

Charlie tried to steady his voice. He smiled weakly. "Long day."

"True," said Carolina. "By the way, thanks for sharing your story with me."

"Thank you too," said Charlie. He noticed one more chip on the carpet. He quickly slapped his hand over it, shifting his weight to lean on the palm.

"I think Pat will dismiss us pretty quick," she whispered, staring expectantly at the counselor. "He never drags this out."

A flurry of shushes rushed through the lodge.

"God, I hope so," said Charlie under his breath.

Horrified, he spotted a streak of melted carob on the knuckles of the hand that concealed the final chip. Scooping it up, he jerked the hand under his knee.

Carolina glanced back at him. Charlie smiled at her.

Chapter 17

Charlie woke from another nightmare. In this one, he was being chased by something, something with no face and very long arms. He gasped for air, his eyes popping open. Moonlight, pale and indigo, was splashed across the walls of the dorm room. A high-pitched ticking, like a bomb-or maybe it was crickets-greeted his thawing ears. He listened, his eyes twitching. Shawn turned over in his bed and grumbled irritably. Austin and Jonathan made no sound.

Charlie threw back the moist bedclothes and went into the bathroom. He twisted the light timer on the wall and peered at his reflection in the medicine cabinet mirror. His red-rimmed eyes stared back at him, squinting against the harsh light of the fluorescent bulbs.

"Bullshit," he mumbled. "A bunch of bullshit."

He returned to the room, grabbed his latest journal from the drawers beneath his bed, and returned to the bathroom. He gave the timer an extra twist, lowered the lid on the toilet, sat on the cool porcelain and began writing, purging his trembling mind onto the pure, white spiral-bound pages.

He slept deeply and dreamlessly for a while before he heard the footsteps.

His eyes popped open and he turned his heavy head, but the high windows of the dormitory revealed nothing but dark sketches of pine boughs on the hill above, against the ripening sky. Again, he listened: nothing but the three other boys in the room purring with sleep. He craned his neck to see the alarm clock behind him on Shawn's nightstand. ·

5:40 a.m.

Then he heard it: gravel crunching outside the door. He held his breath. The doorknob turned and the door creaked open, sighing a draft of cold air into the room.

He gripped his bedclothes as the intruder entered. The beam of a flashlight danced in a tight circle on the carpet as the intruder paused before soundlessly closing the door. Then the flashlight beam raised, swept the room once, and with a decisive trajectory headed straight for Charlie's bed. The flashlight clicked off; there was a long pause. Charlie didn't move, didn't breathe. A hand touched his shoulder and shook it gently.

"Charlie," a man's voice whispered.

He knew that voice. It was Toby Heiser.

"Wake up," Toby insisted.

"I'm awake," Charlie responded thickly.

"You're going into your Ascent Propheet today," said Toby. "Get cleaned up and dress in comfortable clothes. Bring nothing in your pockets. Be down at the lodge in 20 minutes. We will meet in the Pit. From this point forward, there will be absolutely no talking to anyone until after we have started the Propheet. Do you understand?"

Charlie was all gooseflesh and his brain seemed to be swimming in molasses. "Yes," he managed finally.

Toby disappeared to the other side of the room. Whispers hissed, unintelligible and unseen, behind Charlie's head followed closely by groggy protestations from Jonathan. More whispers from Toby, steady and insistent. A few hard consonants punched through Charlie's thawing ears as he strained to listen: "Propheet", "Pit". Jonathan said "Yes" with the indelicate volume of the half-asleep. Austin stirred, Shawn grunted. But, Toby had no cause to approach the other two boys, and with the flick of a thumb, the flashlight blazed again and Toby left the room as quickly as he had come.

The first breath of dawn was dissolving the night into ruddy streaks of incandescent alabaster in the mountain sky. A few puffs of clouds, mottled dark with purple on their billowy edges, floated lazily across the heavens. The air, neither warm nor cool, stirred gently. Somewhere on the slope above a woodpecker greeted the morning, hammering into a distant tree. Below and across the field, an owl hooted mournfully from within a grove of firs. Between, there was silence.

Charlie descended the dorm trail with a feeling of unreality--an enchantment that bore him forward without effort. His body seemed to weigh nothing. His thoughts seemed to be suspended in a cool, shock-absorbing jelly. As he walked, he watched the silent, ghostly figures dotting the trail before him, walking towards the lodge and through the dying shadows of the towering trees.

No one ever mentioned that the Ascent took place at dawn, he thought. No one had tipped him off that it was going to happen today. Nobody had seen it coming.

Now, he had been invited to a secret ceremony, and someday there would be new students who would wonder at the things he had seen, the things he knew. He walked with quiet dignity as if he had been called to a high-level meeting, or to war, or to the gallows.

He crossed the Microwave road. He could see the New Wing now, clinging to the slope, streaks of morning light striping its half-timbered face. The dark, lifeless eyes of the dormer windows watched him as he passed. Looking back at his feet, Charlie headed for the main door of the lodge. His resolve wavered as he laid his hand upon the cold wrought-iron handle. He paused, blew a burst of air from his lungs, and entered the building.

The lodge was dark and cool. The deserted back rooms glowed with hazy light. Picture lamps burned above the stoic faces of the Dutch portraits, the kaleidoscopic French gardens and the pastoral English landscapes that hung along the walls of the big room. Charlie passed Heywood's "Run to Earth". The portrait depicted mounted gentry halted in a misty wood. One of the hunters had dismounted and was crouching by the agitated pack of dogs which had cornered an unseen but surely doomed fox.

There were six other boys in the Pit: Aaron Golldenberg , Devon Childs, Kevin DeWilt, Kenny Bootman, Scott "Smitty" Smith and Jonathan Becker. There were five girls: Dana Abby, Vicki Brennan, Sharon Gallap, Alicia Thornton and Carolina Eversol.

Charlie sat, with hands folded in his lap, staring at the large slabs of stone of the fireplace. His eyes locked on the witch stone.

The witch stone, according to unofficial Ponderosa legend, would become illuminated at a certain time of day and during a certain solstice, but Charlie had forgotten which. Allegedly, during this time, a narrow beam of light from the sole skylight in the western corner of the lodge would strike the chimney, landing squarely on the witch stone.

Charlie studied the contours of the freeform stone embedded halfway up the wide chimney of the fireplace, and marveled again at how much it looked like a proverbial witch. The gray slab had a point for the hag's hat, a flared bottom for her billowing garments, and a narrow, dog-leg peninsula surrounded by worn mortar that evoked an outstretched arm. At the tip of the arm, a bony finger pointed directly at a heart-shaped stone on the floor of The Pit.

Supposedly, beneath this heart-shaped stone was buried the previous owner of the property: a man named Clay Meyer. The man had been a film director from Hollywood who had built the lodge as a retreat. As the story went, he was murdered by a disgruntled maid with whom he'd had an affair, and who had been shunned when Mrs. Meyer had begun to suspect the tryst.

Now, Meyer's ghost became the preferred scapegoat for any strange occurrences on the property, everything from unexplained sounds, to misplaced objects to nightmares. Charlie glanced at the heart-shaped stone below the coffee table and brushed it reverently with his foot. He felt foolish in doing so, but he focused his thoughts on the stone and appealed to Meyer's ghost for strength, protection and good luck. He hoped that the beam of light would suddenly hit the witch stone, rattle the bones of the old man, and summon his spirit to exact chaos, or at least distraction. But nothing happened. The silence and gloom persevered.

Toby Heiser, dressed in jeans and a short-sleeved polo shirt, stepped into the Pit holding a pen and a clipboard. He surveyed the gathered, made a series of marks on his paper and then spoke.

"Good morning," he said. "Welcome to your Ascent Propheet. Please follow me."

Everyone rose, their eyes darting nervously, and followed Toby in a single-file line out of The Pit and through the threshold to the staircase of the New Wing.

Charlie gripped the varnished handrail and ascended into the narrow stairwell. A landing led to another flight that terminated in a vestibule with a door ahead and a door to the left. An Empire console topped with a shaded lamp and a small open box of burl wood sat along the right wall of the small antechamber. Toby halted and the group huddled close together behind him.

"If you need to use the bathroom," said Toby, "please do so now." He indicated the door on the left. He continued, gesturing at the wooden box. "If you brought any personal effects...paper, food, jewelry of any kind or medicine...please put them in the box and they will be returned to you after you have completed the experience."

Nobody moved. Toby turned around and opened the other door, the door everyone was staring at.

"Please, come in," he said.

Chapter 18

Music flooded Charlie's ears as he entered the room. A tape was playing; a woman he didn't know was singing "There's a place for us, somewhere a place for us..." through a set of unseen speakers.

The room was square, neither particularly large nor particularly remarkable. The most notable detail of the room was along the far wall: the windows were covered in black plastic and taped along the edges to block any sunlight from entering.

There was no furniture in the room except for a circle of a dozen of the black plastic chairs, set up like a Rap, and capped at opposite sides with overstuffed wingbacks. Two signs, hand-painted on butcher paper in whimsical, childlike block letters, were hanging on the otherwise stark walls.

The first read:

THE TRUTH SHALL SET YOU FREE

The second read:

TODAY IS THE FIRST DAY
OF THE REST OF YOUR LIFE

Mary Portman sat with her hands folded in her lap in one of the wingback chairs. Her hair was bundled in an informal chignon, save for a liberated wisp that fluttered at the corner of one eye. She wore an ecru blouse that hung loosely down her frame, open at the throat to reveal a thin silver necklace. The ample denim of her jeans flared around her pear shaped hips, tapering down her crossed legs to meet her crisp white Reebok tennis shoes. A monastic solemnity dignified her face.

"Welcome," she said softly as everyone selected one of the black plastic chairs.

Toby leaned over a small table in the corner of the room, stopped the tape with the thump of a button and took his place in the remaining armchair. He surveyed the circle of students, his bottom lip protruding with contemplation.

"There is a lot of work to be done in the next 24 hours," said Toby. "First, I want you all to know that you are safe in this room. Mary and I are here to provide you with the tools you will need to leave this room a better person than you were when you came in. It is up to you to accept those tools and value them. This is YOUR experience and you will get out of it only what you put into it."

Mary nodded and added: "Toby and I are here for you. But, as he has said, only you can help you. This is a beautiful, awakening experience for most, but for others who resist their truths and fail to confront their lies, it is nothing more than a waste of time. Make the decision to not sell yourself short. Really make this experience your own."

Mary refolded her hands in her lap.

Toby continued, "Before we begin, there are some agreements. After I read these agreements we will go around the room and ask you to accept them. A simple 'I accept' will suffice."

Toby produced his clipboard from beside him and read: "Number one, I agree to complete the Propheet and participate in all experiences.   Number two, I will not engage in any side conversations. Number three, I will discuss the tools and details of this Propheet only with those who have completed the Propheet. Number four, I will use the bathroom on designated breaks only. Number five, while in this Propheet I will have contact only with others in this Propheet. Number six...I will go for broke."

Toby lowered the clipboard. Starting with Kenny and preceding clockwise, the agreements were accepted by all–although with varying degrees of enthusiasm.

After Charlie had muttered his acceptance, he fought to purge himself of the cynical but obvious conclusion that threatened to gnaw his open mind down to an unreceptive nub: What choice do we have? If we refuse and walk out, we will be thrown on indefinite Dishes or even a Full Time. Accepting the agreements was not really acceptance; it was simply a rejection of a more miserable alternative.

Charlie muttered in the affirmative and then slumped in his seat, crossing his arms.

Mary picked up a book and said: "Now, I would like to read you a passage from 'The Prophet' by Khalil Gibran."

The circle of students stared back at her, trying visibly to convert their anxiety into interest.

Mary began to read from the pages of the thin book: "Much of your pain is self-chosen. It is the bitter potion by which the physician within you heals your sick self. Therefore trust the physician, and drink his remedy in silence and tranquility. For his hand, though heavy and hard, is guided by the tender hand of the Unseen. And the cup he brings, though it burn your lips, has been fashioned of the clay which the Potter has moistened with His own sacred tears."

Mary looked at the faces around her and lowered the book.

"All of you have been hurt," she said. "The hurt you carry with you weighs upon your heart and soul. However, in order to unburden yourselves of that which keeps you down, you first need to be honest with yourselves and not be afraid to identify your lies and confront them. The first tool of this Propheet is this..."

Mary pointed above and behind where Charlie was sitting. Charlie craned his neck, swiveled in his seat and saw a third sign. He was startled that he hadn't seen it before.

You're out of it, he told himself. You have to stay on your game. No matter how tired...

The sign was made of butcher-paper, like the other two, and also like the others, hand-printed with colored markers in block letters as if by a child. It read:

TO THE DEGREE YOU FEEL YOUR SORROW
IS TO THE DEGREE YOU FEEL YOUR JOY

Mary continued: "We are going to begin this Propheet with a clean slate. I'm going to go around the room and I want you to cop out to your dirt. Any agreements you have broken should be disclosed. Any personal cracks that you have used to hide in, sell yourself short or abandon your values will be sealed. There will be no Dishes handed out for your dirt. This is a one-time only pass. The important thing is to start clean."

Mary paused. Toby was stoic.

Charlie hadn't had much experience with Mary Portman-only a couple of Raps here and there. She generally worked with the upper school. He eyed her, wondering if she could be trusted.

"We will start on my left," said Mary, turning her head to Vicki Brennan. Vicki's eyes flashed with apprehension.

Some of the weight of early morning was sloughing off of Charlie and his mind began to hone itself into razor keenness as he listened to the dirt being divulged. He was at the halfway point of the circle, directly across from Mary and three chairs away from Toby. He had a cushion of six students before it was his turn to spill his dirt.

He evaluated his options. Mary looked gentle and sincere, but that meant nothing. What about Toby? Would he keep their promise about not handing out Dishes? He wasn't sure. He didn't trust it. He supposed if the dirt was bad enough they would quickly reconsider their enticing offer of amnesty.

Vicki copped out to an extra-long shower and to mentioning an unacceptable rock band to one of her roommates. Now Carolina was copping out to drinking an extra glass of milk at lunch after her tablemates had left.

Kevin DeWilt copped out to reading the entertainment section of the paper at the Bear Creek Market during a Sunday store run and looking at ads for Van Halen, Scorpions and other unacceptable bands. Mary and Toby were not fazed by any of the new intelligence--an encouraging sign.

Charlie was next. Perhaps Mary and Toby were serious about extending a free pass on Dishes. Charlie knew that everyone had to come up with something to disclose. Having no dirt was not an option; no one would believe it, and the student without at least a minor sin would appear dishonest.

Kevin concluded his confession and hung his head in what Charlie considered to be mostly compulsory shame. All eyes turned to Charlie.

Here goes nothing, he thought. Get it over with. Do it fast. Don't drag it out and they'll move on. Do it fast.

"I stole some carob chips from the walk-in while I was on Dishes," he said.

The words tumbled from his mouth in a single breath. He fought off a wince, like the kind that might accompany a cannonball jump into a freezing pond. There was no other way to have done it, but he was still surprised that the secret had flown off his tongue like an arrow, straight and true. He felt his heart pounding. His eyes swept from Mary to Toby. They both looked at him, expressionless.

Charlie hung his head to indicate he was finished. He held his breath and prayed that Smitty, who was sitting beside him, would begin talking, effectively ending the window of opportunity for the dispensing of punishment.

Come on, thought Charlie, as he stared at his twitching shoes. Come on Smitty. Go...go...go...

After what seemed like an eternity, Smitty began mumbling a confession. The eyes of the circle shifted to the left, training on Smitty, and Charlie exhaled slowly down the front of his shirt.

Typically when a staff officially begins a Rap, there's an explosion of anger, a sudden and overwrought display of emotional showmanship from the students. Such a response had become a reflex.

But, when Toby suddenly announced at the end of the morning's disclosure circle that there was to be a Rap, the students were unprepared with their usual agenda of gripes and indictments. There were no incendiary accusations lobbed across the room with the usual lightning speed and aggression. There was no pre-Rap sizzle-the nervous shifting in the seats on a pile of barely bridled ammunition. All were stunned and silent. No one had thought there would be a Rap.

It was Dana Abby who eventually hazarded an indictment. She spoke to Sharon Gallap about slacking off on her dorm chores. The accusation didn't seem to have the weight that the occasion demanded and it fizzled like a defective firework.

Soon though, the Rap began to pick-up speed and intensity as the gathered quickly devised a battle plan and jockeyed to be the first to bring their design to bear. Voices began to rise in an attempt to direct the Rap. While strategies took shape, Kenny Bootman took the road most travelled, indicting the Genesis family's paradigm of non-compliance, Devon Childs, who calmly folded his arms and absorbed the barrage with a smirk.

"You know what, Devon?" the Boot screamed. "I saw what you carved on that tree above the dorms! That was BULLSHIT!"

The room waited for Devon to defend himself but the boy sat motionless and glared at Kenny with frosty disdain.

"What did you carve on the tree, Devon?" asked Toby.

Silence.

Kenny answered for him: "A pentagram."

The room seized the opportunity to be outraged, and the circle became a din of screaming voices.

"WHAT THE FUCK!" belted Carolina.

Screams overlapped in a fresh wave of fury. But, the group was suddenly forced to swallow their performances in deference to Toby. He had raised a silencing hand.

"Is that your message to the world?" Toby asked Devon.

Mary Portman sat forward in her seat: "You deface beauty with a symbol of evil. What are you trying to say Devon? Are you evil? Do you feel evil inside?"

Devon had been on Bans from the lower school for such a long time that Charlie had forgotten what the boy's voice sounded like. It was thin and reedy, cracking with pubescence. It was an unsettling sound, like a fuming nest of wasps.

"I am evil," said Devon.

The group chafed in their chairs, eyes darted and met, and mouths worked in silent disbelief. However, Mary still had the floor and her tone was suggesting restraint.

"What if I told you that you were special, beautiful and worthy of love?" said Mary. "How would that make you feel?"

"Love is not meant for me," said Devon.

"Why?" Mary asked.

"No one has ever loved me,"

"You hate yourself?"

"Yes."

"Do you believe me when I tell you that this Propheet could help to change that?" Mary asked.

"No."

"Will you give it a chance?"

Silence.

Toby spoke: "Devon? Will you give it a chance?"

"I don't know," Devon replied, "and I don't care."

"We care," said Mary. "Sometimes, that's enough to hold on to. Hold on to that Devon."

The boy's brow twitched and his chest heaved briefly below his folded arms. Mary leaned back in her chair.

"Let's move on," said Toby.

A loud male voice cleaved the air, "I want to say something to you, Charlie..."

Charlie froze. It was Kevin DeWilt. The boy was leaning forward, locking eyes with Charlie and rocking under the cackling fuel of his impending attack. Charlie held his breath, and to his astonishment, Jonathan–who was seated at his right–motioned across the circle so that he could move and run his own indictment. Vicki switched places and Jonathan waited for an opening while Kevin continued his assault.

"I'm getting tired of you thinking you are better than anyone else here!" said Kevin.

Thinking fast, Charlie tried to force his unruly features into a mask of acceptance, but he was failing. He knew that expressions of defiance or petulance were sure to spark fresh ire and prolong his thrashing.

Kevin continued, imitating Charlie with a whiny lilt: "I didn't do anything wrong. I don't deserve to be here. Blah blah blah! Well you know what, Charlie? Your shit stinks just as bad as mine! You DID fuck up! You ARE here! Deal with it and stop walking around like a sad sack of mistreated shit!"

This was an old indictment for Charlie. He had been accused of this in other Raps. Kevin was not digging up anything new; he was going for the quick score. Charlie took a chance and looked across at Jonathan and implored him with a subtle widening of his eyes.

For some reason, Jonathan was going to piggyback on Kevin's indictment. Why? Charlie considered Jonathan his best friend at the school and couldn't imagine having done anything to anger or disappoint him. The anticipation was crippling Charlie, his peripheral vision darkening as the blood pounded through his head. Unconsciously, his hands found the lip of his chair and he braced.

Jonathan spoke softly: "Charlie...I don't feel you've ever really accepted this program. I think you're just sliding by, doing time. You don't clear space in Raps much and you keep your story to yourself. I consider you my friend and I still don't know a lot about you."

A pause. No other students piled on, although there were a few fashionable hums that indicated that certain members of the group considered the feedback to be legitimate and profound. Others considered with pursed lips and thoughtful nods.

Not too bad, Charlie thought. Not too bad at all. Jonathan had brought Kevin's tone down to one of concern. Jonathan had actually done him a favor.

Charlie also recognized that he and Jonathan had slowly developed a friendship-sometimes a brazen one-and consequently, one in danger of being Rap bait. A student could accuse them of spending too much time together, or worse, being contracted up.

Well played, thought Charlie. Jonathan had shown publicly that he was willing to bust his friends. By demanding a better performance from Charlie, he had both addressed preemptively the inevitable suspicions that were bound to be leveled at the relationship while cleverly reiterating his commitment to the tenants of The Academy. As a result, the potency of a future charge of collusion between the two boys, at least for a while, would find no traction.

"What do you think of what they are saying, Charlie?" Toby asked.

"I think it's right on," Charlie replied thoughtfully.

Suddenly, Kevin began screaming at him again: "You've said that before but nothing changes, Charlie! My gut is flipping right now! I don't believe you! Jonathan is right, you are just doing time!"

Smitty, on Charlie's left, motioned across the room with his finger to Alicia, who got to her feat with a drowsy blink. Smitty meant to gain a seat across from Charlie; he meant to pile on. Charlie went cold. The situation could deteriorate fast.

It angered Charlie that Kevin had referenced Jonathan's comments to bolster his own indictment. It had never been Jonathan's intention to hand Kevin another loaded gun, and Charlie knew it. Across the room, Jonathan's frustrated grimace fell to a hangdog frown.

Charlie shifted and dug a stocking foot into the carpet. Little did Kevin know, Charlie had his own ammunition and it was time to use it, but he had to be quick.

Smitty and Alicia crossed in the middle of the circle. Smitty was about to sit in Alicia's vacated seat and detonate some other bomb, maybe a big one that couldn't be shaken off, although Charlie could not guess what Smitty could possibly have against him. Yet, Charlie knew well that this was a Rap, and a Rap--as much as the staff would want it to be so--was hardly ever personal; it was self-preservation through misdirection.

No matter what the kid was going to say, one thing was sure: the situation was heading out of Charlie's control and could turn into a feeding frenzy if he didn't stop the bleeding.

Kevin was still spitting accusations: "So you don't have a drug problem. Neither do I. Big deal. Do you really think that makes you a FUCKING ANGEL?"

Suddenly, everything Charlie had seen and heard in Raps flooded him with cool fluency. He knew he had to go for it and go for it now. Time was up. He narrowed his eyes and filled his lungs.

"FUCK YOU, KEVIN!" Charlie roared. "DO YOU REALLY THINK I GIVE A SHIT ABOUT A FUCKING WORD YOU SAY AFTER WHAT YOU PULLED ON WORK CREW?"

Charlie could feel his face heat with anger. The more he thought about the incident branding the center of his mind, the more his quaking rage threatened to pull him from his seat. Finally, it did. Charlie kept a flattened palm on the seat of his chair--a permitted maneuver—as he lunged suddenly towards the center of the room in a crouch. Kevin's eyes widened. The gathered held their breath in astonishment.

Charlie thrust his finger towards the stunned boy at the other side of the circle, spittle raining from his mouth: "I'M NOT GOING TO HEAR ANYTHING FROM YOU! I DON'T RESPECT YOU AT ALL AFTER WHAT YOU DID! YOU CAN SHOVE YOUR NEEDSY INDICTMENTS UP YOUR ASS, KEVIN! DID YOU THINK IT WAS FUNNY? HUH? ABUSING ANIMALS?"

Charlie stopped, clapped his back into his chair again, shut his eyes, and rode a wave of boozy adrenalin. His anger had been more than a ploy; it was the real thing, and when its heaviness left him his head swam and his breath rattled.

"Charlie," said Mary Portman, "what happened on the work crew?"

The room sat stunned and motionless. No one had seen Charlie explode before and they greeted his awakening with a reverent silence. Kevin knew what was coming. He was starchy white, his defeated glance swimming around the circle of students hoping to find an ally. Smitty had no intention of bringing his indictment now and was absently massaging the end of a shoelace between two fingers as he sat deflated and cross-legged, staring at the ground.

"What happened on the work crew," Mary repeated.

Charlie opened his eyes and spoke, quiet and even, so as to not awaken the now retreating beast within him: "He called me into the barn. He picked up a cattle prod and shocked the ram on...shocked his balls. It hurt the ram a lot, I could tell. The ram jumped. Then, Kevin laughed. I just...I don't like cruelty to animals. I just can't...I just don't"

The mood of the room changed and bristled with a new energy. Expressions tightened and twisted into masks of revulsion and anger as all eyes fell on Kevin.

"Tell him, Charlie," said Toby.

Charlie locked eyes with Kevin again: "I don't like it when animals are abused. There's nothing...not a goddamn thing, funny about it."

The Rap turned on Kevin, reduced him to tears and eventually moved on. Charlie felt no victory in this, instead, he felt sick to his stomach. He clutched his belly, trying to still the churning mess inside. The Rap continued. It continued for hours until every last one of them had been confronted, until every last one of them was raw.

Yet, the Ascent Propheet had only just begun.

Chapter 19

A horsefly was trapped in the room. It buzzed at the bottom corner of one of the taped-up windows. Its resonant bursts of frustration caused Charlie to turn his weary head and glance down at the sill where the insect wiggled upon streaks and cracked bubbles of glossy white paint, relentlessly ramming its plump body into the bottom pane of glass in an effort to escape.

Charlie had no idea what time it was now. There had been a lunch break hours ago when the participants were led into one of the two doors on the far wall. Sandwiches and juice had been set out on a long oaken table. The sandwiches were simple and dry, but Charlie had eaten them with large, grateful bites.

Three bathroom breaks had occurred, all of them silent and accompanied by the repetition of some kind of soaring easy listening song glorifying honesty, friendship, or the wonders of childhood innocence. Only one student at a time was allowed out of the door and into the short hall to the bathroom while the disinclined sat on the floor and stewed in their feelings.

At one point, a restless Aaron Golldenberg –rocking at his place on the floor, performing a pantomime of perplexed impatience, and looking like he was about to pee on himself–drew the attention of all when he got to his feet and whispered into Toby's ear.

Only one at a time could go to the bathroom, and Charlie figured that the last student to use the bathroom had not returned yet. From the corner of his eye he watched Toby leave the room, then return and whisper something into Mary Portman's upturned ear. The intelligence produced an expression of concentration that ripened into anguish, deepening the wrinkles at the corners of Mary's mouth and along her brow. She left the room for a while.

She eventually returned, concluded the break by cutting the music, retaking her seat, and instructing the group to do the same.

"I have some unfortunate news," she said. "Devon has decided he will no longer be attending this Propheet."

Charlie sat on the floor and cradled the invisible chrome ball in his hands. He was told to see how tarnished it was and how shiny it was beneath its layers of grime. He was told that it was solid and indestructible, but needed to be polished, cared for, and kept safe. Music played; something about "the pain you carry with you". There was crying, always crying, from all corners of the room. Charlie did not cry although he believed it was expected of him. Instead, he tried his best to look stricken in an attempt to avoid a charge of "running from his feelings" that was sure to be leveled later if he didn't perform. He kept his head low and caressed the invisible ball, hoping his manufactured anguish was convincing.

Someone had broken through, somewhere across the room, had broken through to a well of sorrow, but Charlie was only vaguely aware of it, desensitized to it. He knew only that it was one of the girls and that she was wailing.

Everyone was asked to find a partner. Charlie picked Jonathan. Charlie was Partner A and Jonathan was Partner B. The chairs had been put aside and the paired students faced each other, standing in the center of the room.

"Partner A," said Toby, "tell Partner B what you need as a friend, what you value about your friendship."

Charlie did so.

"Tell Partner B how you feel right now," said Toby.

Charlie told Jonathan that he was tired, sad, and lonely.

"Partner A," said Toby, "reach out to Partner B for a hug."

Toby came up behind Charlie and raised Charlie's outstretched arms high and wide and whispered: "Really reach for your friend."

Toby continued around the room and Charlie heard him urge others to do the same.

"Partner A," said Toby, "tell Partner B that you need them. Keep reaching for them and tell them."

Charlie, in a soft voice, said, "I need you."

"Now..." said Toby, "Partner B, turn your back on Partner A."

Jonathan, looking distressed, slowly turned his back on Charlie. Music began to play: "I am a rock, I am an island" voices sang.

Toby spoke above the music: "This is how you turn your back on your friends, on your fellow human beings, every day. And this is how they turn their backs on you when you need them the most."

Wet sobs percolated from the same handful of students who could bring forth their tears with little effort. Charlie felt more anger than sadness. He thought the exercise abusive. He clenched his teeth and stared at Jonathan's back.

The tears flowing from the others around him were raising the expectation for him to vocalize some inner turmoil so that it would attract Toby and Mary's favorable notice. Charlie could not feel anything but embarrassment and his interminable numbness.

He had never been quick to cry. The ride up the hill, the home call, had been the only times in recent memory. He had always tried his best to be strong; he had to be in the presence of Kurt and he had to be for his brother and his mom who...had...

Abandoned him.

An overwhelming sense of distance between his family and a feeling of utter helplessness shot through him like a bolt of lightning. A shuddering breath escaped him and then his vision swam. To his surprise, a tear was tracking his cheek.

Everyone stood in a circle. Kenny Rogers was singing "tell it all, tell it all brothers and sisters".

"Don't cheat yourself," said Toby. "Really dig deep and find the dirt that you hold on to, the one you tell nobody. It will hold you back if you don't rid yourself of its poison. The lies you tell yourself, the things you beat yourself up about, the things you have a hard time forgiving yourself for--tell them all and release yourself."

The students formed a circle, and in stocking feet and with tousled hair, began, one at a time, facing each other and laying bare one of their deepest secrets. Kevin was first to make his way around the circle. He stood first before Dana.

"Kevin," said Toby, "look her in the eye."

Charlie took a quick count. He would be fourth. He stood at his place in the circle, waiting. He was glad he hadn't gone first, but it looked like Kevin was going to set the bar high. The boy approached with his head down, shuffled his feet a couple of times, raised his head and met Charlie's eyes.

"I tried to kill myself with my father's pain pills."

Kevin lowered his head and took a step to Charlie's left, continuing his circuit. Mary was instructing the next person to make the circuit while Kevin was half-through. Pretty soon there were a total of three making their way around the circle.

Dana approached Charlie from the right, raised her head, and looked him in the eyes. "I think I'm ugly and I hate myself."

Charlie stared straight ahead until the next face filled his vision. It was Aaron. "I threw fireworks at a cat. It blew one of its ears off."

Charlie's stomach squirmed. Aaron was consumed with shame. It covered his glistening face in a feverish sheen. He stepped to the left.

Charlie stared straight ahead, his jaw tight. The top of Carolina's blonde hair came into view. She lifted her gaze to meet his. The blue within her red-rimmed eyes startled him with its brilliance. He was transfixed, and tried to convey comfort and trust without words. She smiled, ever so slightly, in recognition of his effort.

"I masturbate with my hairbrush," she said, and moved to the left.

Charlie stared straight ahead, astonished. He trembled as an effervescent concussion of titillation, embarrassment, and shock slammed into him.

That was for me, he thought. That one was just for me.

Mary tapped him on the shoulder.

"Charlie," she said, "you're next."

A new sign had been taped to the walls after the second meal of the day. It was longer than the others had been and it had only two words printed on it at opposite ends:

JOY   PAIN

A thick, horizontal line with a circle at the bottom was drawn down the middle of the page, separating the two words.

It was getting hard to concentrate. Charlie deduced from the end of the second meal that it must be evening, if not the dead of night.

Charlie heard a sound below his chair. He had almost forgotten his tiny companion. He glanced down. The horsefly was walking in agitated circles on the sill of the taped-up window. Occasionally, with an optimistic burst of strength and a deep, reedy drone, the insect would launch its fuzzy body at the corner of the glass, rebounding to the sill in a fluttering tangle of pearly wings. Then it would begin walking again, dazed and tottering, in a tight circle. A buzz like the sound of a cheap apartment doorbell would mark its mounting frustration as it paced, steeling itself for another run at the shrouded window.

Charlie turned his heavy head back to the circle of students. There was an empty chair. He looked past the circle at the closed door to the entry hall.

Devon is really not coming back, he thought drowsily. If he can go, why can't I.

Then, he shuddered at the thought of all those Dishes Devon would be doing.

What were you thinking, Devon...

He pictured himself floating straight for the exit, passing them all like a ghost, feeling the wood of the door caress his cells as he passed through it. His vision fogged. He shook his head.

Soon, Devon would walk through the door. The door handle began to turn. The next thing he would see would be the skinny frame of the dark-haired kid with the pasty face and the hard, glittering stare.

Charlie squeezed shut his eyes and opened them wide. The door handle was still. No Devon.

Leaving a Propheet? Charlie's thoughts swirled: So much trouble...it's crazy...why didn't you stay...so much worse now...so much worse...

Charlie snapped his head up. All eyes were on him. Someone had clapped, clapped loud.

He had fallen asleep in his chair.

He widened his eyes and tried to shake the heavy cotton fog from his head.

Fell asleep, he thought.

"Sorry," he mumbled.

Carolina had fallen asleep earlier and had been instructed to stand behind her chair if she couldn't stop falling asleep.

She sure did look cute when she was sleeping, Charlie thought.

He smiled to himself.

Stand up. Stand. You better...behind the chair.

Toby sounded far away. Toby pointed at the new sign and said, "Joy and Pain. Between them is a pendulum. As it swings one way, so it must swing equally the other way."

Toby pointed to the sign on the other wall.

"To the extent you feel your pain is to the extent you feel your joy."

He returned to the new sign and rapped it with a finger. "If the pendulum swings equally to both sides, then feeling your pain will enable you to feel greater joy. If the pendulum does not move at all then you are inert, motionless, and by definition, dead inside. Swinging the pendulum to pain first not only produces an equal swing to joy, BUT..."

Toby tore the sign from the wall. Beneath it was another version of the sign with a larger field of Joy and a smaller field of Pain. The pendulum had been moved to off-center. "Your Joy will increase as your Pain is identified, confronted and destroyed."

Charlie teetered on his rubbery legs, holding the back of the plastic chair. Woozily, he glanced down at the horsefly. It was still. It was dead.

"What is your lie, Charlie?" Mary whispered.

He was on the floor now, everyone was, and they were all flat on their backs looking up at the ceiling with arms spread. The strewn bodies were far enough apart that no one could touch or see one another.

Charlie felt raw, alone in the universe and tired, tired so that the ceiling rippled like a stretched piece of canvas. He was suffused with fatigue, his thoughts tumbling through his head like a kaleidoscope.

"What is the lie you tell yourself, Charlie," Mary asked again, her warm breath caressing his ear. Charlie began to breathe in punchy bursts.

"You hold it all together don't you?" Mary cooed, stroking Charlie's hair from his face as he lay on his back. A pair of cool, thin silver bracelets tinkled like distant wind chimes from her arm and grazed the side of his brow. He shuddered. They were magnets, pulling the buried wreckage in his soul from its grave. Something was surfacing, clawing through the tender tissue within him. It meant to be born without his effort, without his consent.

"While you're holding it all together," Mary continued, "who is looking out for you, Charlie?"

"Nobody," Charlie croaked.

The act of saying the word was the incantation that called his long propagating pain, his abandonment and his fear into a terrible vitality, one that hungered only for his tears.

"Say it again," Mary urged.

"Nobody! Nobody! NOBODY!" Charlie screamed.

He was sitting on the floor now in a fetal hunch. Mary was before him, sitting on her knees with a seat cushion in her lap.

"Whose face do you see?" she asked softly.

Charlie stared at the pillow, his vision refracting with stale tears.

"Tell your mother," said Mary. "Let it out. Hit it Charlie. Hit it for all those years, all that pain."

Charlie balled up his fist and struck the cushion.

"Harder!" Mary insisted. "Harder, Charlie! Let it out! She let you down, didn't she? Ask her why!"

Charlie struck the cushion again: "Why!"

"Say it again, Charlie!"

"WHY!"

"Why what? Ask her!"

"Why did..." he began and then faltered. Something was breaking within him.

"Dig deep, Charlie. Why did she what?"

The dyke was crumbling. He could feel it in his mind. First a spray, then a gush and now pieces of his construct were blowing apart as a deluge of memories flushed him into a dark and lonely sea.

"WHY DID YOU GIVE UP?" screamed Charlie, slamming his fists into the pillow. "WHAT ABOUT ME! WHAT ABOUT BRANDON? WE NEED YOU!"

"Say 'I need you'," Mary urged. "Say 'I need you, Mom.'"

"I NEED YOU, MOM!" cried Charlie. "WHY DID YOU LET HIM RUIN OUR FAMILY?"

"You mean your stepfather? You mean Kurt?" Mary asked. "Say it."

Charlie wailed and he beat the pillow, bringing his fists down hard. "YOU'RE NOT MY DAD! YOU'LL NEVER BE MY DAD!! GO AWAY! LEAVE ME ALONE! LEAVE US ALL ALONE! I HATE YOU!"

"That's right, Charlie," whispered Mary, "say it again."

"I FUCKING HATE YOU!"

His fists were a blur as they connected with the cushion. He stopped, leaning forward into the pillow, breathing in rattling gasps. He was vaguely aware of others screaming in the room: curses, sobs, and moans of anguish. His body was hot, the room was hot, a conflagration of misery and anger. He flexed his hands and stared at them uncomprehendingly.

"What is your lie?" asked Mary again, softly.

Charlie panted into the cushion as his anger died. He clenched his body, hugging himself, trying to hold in whatever was still clambering up through his hollows.

"Tell me about your father," said Mary.

Charlie's heart suddenly trembled with a spasm of sadness and loss. Mary stroked his spine from the small of his back to the base of his skull. A box of tissues appeared at his side. He knew he was supposed to pluck a few from the floral print box, but instead he just stared at them as if they were a colossal absurdity. There was nothing that those impotent sheets could help him wipe away, and for a moment, he was afraid that the mess he had become would never be cleaned up.

"Tell me about your father," repeated Mary.

Chapter 20

The man appeared to Charlie in the fall of '78. It was lunch recess and the soccer field was full of screaming kids. Over by the kindergarten classroom a handful of children were setting up the annual pumpkin patch, struggling to reposition a few decorative hay bales. Above the deep orange gourds, a green, cardboard witch presided, holding a sign that read "Adams Elementary School Pumpkin Patch".

At first Charlie thought the man was just clinging to the cyclone fence to watch the hubbub surrounding the upcoming Halloween Carnival, but the man didn't look interested in pumpkins or anything else that was happening before him on the school grounds. He seemed preoccupied, staring beyond the games of tag, hopscotch, and dodge ball as though he were looking for someone.

The man was tall and had long salt-and-pepper hair and a beard that fell to the neck of his dark green jacket. He wore amber-tinted glasses. Charlie didn't think they were sunglasses, but probably that new kind of lens that got darker when you went outside--the kind that everyone was beginning to wear lately. The man was now talking to Trey Stewart through the fence and Trey was pointing across the soccer field in Charlie's direction.

"Who was that guy at the fence earlier today?" Charlie asked Trey after catching up with the sixth-grader on the way home from school.

"Dunno," said Trey dismissively. "He said he was looking for Charlie Hoff."

"What was his name?" asked Charlie.

"Didn't say," Trey replied. Charlie slowed his pace and let the boy pull ahead. As he did so, Trey turned back, speaking over his shoulder: "He was looking for your brother too."

"Brandon? What for?"

"Why don't you ask him yourself?" Trey replied, walking backward for a moment to face Charlie. "Maybe he thinks you're pretty."

Trey's companion, a brawny kid with a gleaming retainer in his mouth, laughed and urged Trey to stop wasting his time with fifth-graders--advice that Trey promptly took.

For days there was no sign of the man, but for a few days after the sighting, Charlie made it a point during recess to glance in the direction of the long stretch of fence on his way out to the field until he lost interest and all but forgot about the man.

Charlie commanded a view of the entire playground from the top of one of the oak trees along the periphery of the sports field. He ascended his favorite tree during most recesses to survey his brethren from the private roost. His preferred limb: a wide, smooth, natural saddle, surrounded by sporadic foliage; windows of parting leaves offering birds-eye vistas from the redwood bark-padded playground to the outdoor tables of the cafeteria.

The sun was bright and cold during the morning recess of October 18th as Charlie lowered the curled fingers that served him as a telescope and began to carve his initials into the bark of the limb with the end of his drafting compass.

"Charlie..." said a voice from beneath and behind him. It was a gruff voice, a man's voice.

Charlie's legs had been dangling from the thick limb; he now tucked them under himself. He crouched, turned around and peered down at the small section of chain link fence just visible through the papery foliage.

"Charlie Hoff?" the voice called again, and this time the man stepped into view far below, sliding his white hands through the fence and gripping the links. Charlie dared to spread apart two clusters of leaves for a better look.

There he was, the Salt-and-Pepper Man, looking up at him with amber-tinted glasses.

"Don't be afraid," the man said, "I just..." The man faltered, gripped the fence tighter, dropped his head, paused, and then lifted his gaze resolutely to the top of the tree again. "I have news about your father."

Charlie released the spread branches and the tawny clusters of leaves snapped back into place, a few of them fluttering to the ground. He was still crouching on his bent sneakers and he teetered suddenly. A thin branch snapped in his left hand; he grasped wildly and grabbed a handful of young shoots that steadied him. He looked over his shoulder at the expanse of field and felt suddenly very vulnerable. Unless someone over-kicked a soccer ball, no one was likely to venture out to the dirt shoulder of the field. He was alone.

Charlie spread the branches again, and with the tone of a sentry atop a castle wall, demanded: "Who are you?"

The man smiled, "A friend of your father."

"I don't have a father."

"Sure you do."

"Okay," said Charlie, "then what's his name?"

"Gerald Charles Hoff," said the man, "but we call him Jerry."

Charlie went hollow. No one had uttered the name of his father in so long that the words seemed blasphemous, or likely to incite some natural calamity. A confusion of feelings kicked up within him: he wanted to cry, wanted to throw something at the man, wanted to run.

"Who are you?" Charlie asked again. "I mean, what is your name and how do you know my dad?"

"Can't talk here," the man replied. "You have a brother. His name is Brandon." The man stated these facts perfunctorily, not waiting for confirmation. "Bring your brother to the McDonalds on Homestead after school today. It's on your way home isn't it? You do live in the Mariposa Garden apartments?"

Charlie felt a chill crawl down his spine. Somehow the man knew where they lived, knew he had a brother. Charlie said nothing.

The man continued, "Meet me there. You'll be safe; there are lots of people around. I'll tell you everything I know then."

Charlie stared down at the man. The man nodded slowly, reassuringly.

"Just tell me your name and how you know my dad," Charlie

demanded.

"You can call me Jack," said the man. "We were in Monterey together...in the Army."

Charlie almost fell out of the tree.

❖

Brandon couldn't care less about the meeting. To him, a trip to McDonalds was incentive to endure just about anything. He fished through his Happy Meal looking for his toy. He produced a Garfield on a skateboard and began tearing it from its plastic wrapping.

The Salt-and-Pepper Man's glasses didn't turn completely clear, even in the garish light of the restaurant, and his eyes looked like two bugs trapped in an amber paperweight. The man fed a french fry into his mouth. Charlie watched it shorten and disappear into the hole in the modeled whiskers.

"Relax," said the Salt-and-Pepper Man. "I just thought you would want to know-thought you deserved to know-about what happened to your father."

"Is he alive?" asked Charlie, who was still trying to retain power by feigning disinterest.

"Yes," said the man, "and in pretty good health."

"Where is he?" asked Charlie.

"Why don't I just start from the beginning," said the man.

Brandon stopped scraping his Happy Meal toy across the table and looked soberly at the bearded man as the stranger leaned forward, rubbed the whiskers on his chin and began to speak in a confidential tone: "I'm sure you know that your mother and your father were not getting along all that well. Your father was very unhappy. Your grandfather did not approve of the marriage and your mother..."

"Leave my mom alone," said Charlie. "I don't care what he told you about her, he's wrong. He left her when she was pregnant with my brother. Hard to beat that when it comes to being a jerk and a...chicken shit."

"Okay, okay," said the man, "sorry, I don't blame you. You have every right to be upset. I was going to get to that."

Charlie channeled his agitation into pulling the pasty thick ice cream of his shake through the straw. With indented cheeks, he kept his appraising eyes on the stranger.

"It was February, 1972," continued the man. "You were almost three. Your father was drafted into the Army. He tried to get out of it but he couldn't. He applied for 'conscientious objector' status but it was denied. Do you know what that is?"

Charlie didn't answer.

"Doesn't matter, I guess," the man said under his breath. "Anyway, the Army would not let him leave. He had to show up and learn how to kill. So, with no other option, he showed up for basic training at Fort Ord in Monterey, crossing his fingers that he would not get shipped out to Vietnam. It was a terrible war. You have to understand that there were nothing but horror stories and disturbing pictures of body bags flashing through his head. For years we had heard about what happened to those who went to 'Nam. I knew a few of them from my old neighborhood, guys I had grown up with. Some of them went crazy, and some of them were missing parts of their bodies. The thought of going to Vietnam...well, it meant that you would probably come home in pieces if you were lucky enough to make it home at all."

Charlie gazed obstinately out of the window while Brandon stared at the stranger.

The man continued, "Sure enough, your father was ordered to ship out, ship out to 'Nam. We were in the same company, your father and I."

The man paused, pulled thoughtfully on his straw, and continued: "There was an underground anti-war newspaper at the base. There was lots of talk. It was a movement, y'know? Well, I guess you wouldn't. But the bottom line was, everyone knew there were options. So, your father decided to run for it."

"Chicken," Charlie spat, without looking at the man.

"Maybe so," said the man, who seemed genuinely stung by the words and unable to continue for a moment. The man took another shaky sip of cola. "Maybe so. It was a strange time, a dark time. Your father was not alone. Thousands were doing the same thing. Running away from the meat grinder, I mean. It wasn't an easy decision. The consequences were great."

"What about us?" Charlie said, eyes blazing. "What about us!"

The man looked around nervously. The booths directly beside them were empty, but a family of four was spread out two tables away and one of the young girls turned her head at Charlie's outburst.

"He didn't know that Sara was pregnant," said the man. "He had no idea. He loved you Charlie, he still does. He was a coward. He was irresponsible. He was selfish. He was too young. He has paid for his mistake for a long time. Every day he has paid..."

The man trailed off. Charlie turned his attention back to the traffic outside the window.

The man took a breath and continued: "The journey was long and frightening. We took the underground railroad to Canada."

"Really?" Brandon put in, brightening.

"Not what you're thinking, kiddo," said the man. "It wasn't really a railroad, and it wasn't really underground. They just called it that."

Brandon deflated.

The man continued: "It was more like a series of people who helped you sneak around. First, we met our contact at an old hippie flophouse on Masonic Street in the Haight-Ashbury, you know, up in San Francisco? You used to live not too far from there. You remember?"

Charlie continued staring out the window.

Realizing that his efforts at warmth were falling on deaf ears, the man continued methodically: "The guy then took us to meet a fisherman down at one of the piers along the Embarcadero. We slept in the cabin of the boat that night and sailed for Portland, Oregon the next morning. This was to throw the bloodhounds off our trail a bit. Anyway, the boat had a special hiding place beneath the cabin in case the Coast Guard pulled us over or if anyone else came snooping around. It was a secret cargo hold, but we had no problems and we never had to climb into it. Sailing away from all that we knew was the hardest thing we ever did. I mean, we threw it all away: families, friends, country, everything. You have second thoughts, but then you feel it's too late. Some decisions can never be taken back. In the end, so much and so many get thrown away by our fear. All that we love...discarded by our own hand."

The man clenched a napkin and continued: "Your father never wanted to leave you, but he thought it would be best to give you a chance with a better man, a better man than he was."

Charlie stared at the traffic outside the window. The man swallowed hard and dragged on his straw until he sucked air and rattled the shards of ice..

"Anyway," continued the man, "from Portland your father and I boarded a vegetable truck that took us to a town in the Canadian Rockies where we crossed the border on foot. Following a map provided by our driver, we met up with a contact that was waiting for us at a cabin the forest. They set us up with a brand new life."

"Isn't the war over?" asked Charlie. "Why didn't he come back?"

"You can go to prison for a long time for deserting the Army. It wasn't until last year that President Carter announced that he would no longer punish those who had fled the country. That is, if you believe him."

They sat in silence. Brandon was getting restless and held his drink with both hands, pulling the straw up and down through the aperture in the thin, plastic lid with his teeth. The straw squeaked like a rusty door hinge. Charlie admonished the boy with a quick shake of his head. Brandon put the cup down and hunched his shoulders dejectedly.

"Why doesn't he come here himself," said Charlie. "Why send you?"

"He doesn't know I'm here," said the man. "He figures you pretty much hate him, and if he were to show up you would probably blow the whistle yourself, or at least, tell your mother he was here and she would go after him."

"You're right about that," said Charlie.

"I'm in just as deep as he is. If they find me here I could be in a lot of trouble. I just thought you should know how your father feels about you. I just thought you should know that he loves you, wants you to be happy..."

"Tell him he's not my father," Charlie said. "Tell him I hope he gets caught. I have a new father now. I don't need him anyway."

"Yeah," said Brandon, "we don't need him anyway."

Charlie looked at the man, his lower lip quaking, his eyes clouding with tears, "My mother cried forever when he left. She cried forever."

The Salt and Pepper Man hung his head. After a long moment he said, "I'm sorry. I don't know what to say. I know there is nothing I can say. I'll tell him. I will tell him what you've said, Charlie. I have to go. It's not safe for me here.. Please...don't tell your mother I told you these things. It will only hurt her. It will only bring up more bad memories and turn up the heat on me. Let her alone. She always knew what happened. He wrote her years ago and explained the whole thing. She was protecting you. I think it's best that she not know I was here. Tell your brother to keep it quiet, too. I ask this favor of you in exchange for the great risk I took in coming here, coming back to the States."

Charlie looked at the man blankly for a long time. The man finally looked away, supporting his heavy head with a hand to his forehead.

"Fine," said Charlie, "I have to go. My parents will be worried. Brandon, let's go."

The two boys slid out of the booth and left the man, and their garbage, and headed for the door. Charlie hit the crash bar to the restaurant's exit and looked back at the Salt-and-Pepper Man. The stranger was motionless, his elbow still on the table, his hand still on his forehead. Charlie turned, grabbed Brandon's hand and headed down the street for home. He never saw the man again.

The Ascent Propheet sat in their circle of chairs. The black coverings and tape had been removed from the windows and a bright meridian sun beat on the panes of glass, the students blinking against its brilliance. Mary raised one of the double-hung windows. The day's cool breath, scented by the pines, entered like a whisper and blew gently on the gathered. They all looked haggard, but serene. The signs had been removed and replaced with a single piece of butcher paper stretching the length of one wall. It read:

THE NEW YOU

The young explorers took turns standing before one another with their arms outstretched and their palms open to own, loud and clear, their newfound wisdom.

Mary repeated the question she had asked in the middle of the night: "What is the lie you tell yourself?"

Charlie now had an answer. He stood, opened his palms, spread his arms, and surveyed his seated companions, his face lit with a peaceful smile.

"My lie," he said, "is that it's all my fault."

Chapter 21

The House stood, holding hands, in an elliptical formation that stretched the length of the Floor and bowed around the Pit to the far side of the lodge, forming a long horseshoe of smiling, expectant faces. The speakers rattled in the rafters, the woofers barking Kool and the Gang's "Celebration".

Charlie gathered his shoes from the floor of the vestibule of the New Wing, tied them with haste, and descended the stairs just behind Jonathan and Vicki.

He imagined that this was what being a celebrity felt like, what it felt like to be celebrated, your presence anticipated. He knew there was a horseshoe downstairs and around the corner, full of students who would congratulate him, hug him, and admire him.

He had done it. He was now part of an exclusive club, a society of those who knew at least the first of the secret rites of The Academy. He was now someone who, despite paralyzing fear, had stared down something terrible and had beaten it into submission, possibly destroying it. The smile on his face stretched from ear to ear. The fatigue that had tried to drag him under for so many hours was now a tingling euphoria that made him feel like he was floating down the staircase, the meat of his palm glancing over the varnished surface of the handrail as he began to take the steps two at a time. Then he landed in the hall at the bottom, turned the corner, crossed the threshold, and was received by the throng.

The floor within the long circle of kids was clear, save for the dancing graduates of the Ascent Propheet. The sides of the circle undulated as the snaking ring of spectators swayed to the music, the chain of clasped hands breaking only to allow a clap or a quick, lunging hug.

The beat thumped from the speakers as Charlie burst into the center of the horseshoe in a trot. He saw Austin Spencer along one side of the horseshoe, smiling big and wiggling a hand to set it free from the grasp of the girl next to him. He reached towards Charlie and enfolded him in his outstretched arm, pulling him close.

"Good job, buddy," Austin said into Charlie's ear. "Congratulations."

Charlie was aware of his rawness, as though his soul had been exfoliated. However, this intense feeling of vulnerability, as consuming as it was, did not yield the embarrassment or anxiety he would have expected. Instead, his spirit was nimble and flexing in the spaces that were once crowded with armor. He was giddy with not only the relief of leaving the Propheet, but with the relief of leaving something else in that room upstairs; something predatory that would have hungered for more of him and taken it in spite of his defenses--taken it in large, tearing bites.

"Thank you," said Charlie, wrapping his arm around Austin and laughing through his words. "It feels good!"

He looked for his "big brother", Vince Russo, but he didn't see him. All was frantic and confusing. Catcalls demanded Charlie's attention from all quarters of the lodge. The song on the stereo repeated. He saw Smitty standing on a couch, stretching his arms wide. Then, with a feral yelp, Smitty jumped off, twirling. Sharon and Alicia hopped onto the edge of the Pit for a moment and then jumped to the floor.

"Good job," said Karen Whittaker, the girl from Evolution who ran House Crew. She had come up behind Charlie. "Way to go!"

Charlie beamed and suddenly broke from the circle and headed for the rim of The Pit. He hopped up on its edge and turned to face the crowd.

"YEAH!" he screamed. He raised his clenched fists at the rafters and shook them in triumph. He jumped down, his shirttail fluttering.

Carolina ran up to him, throwing an arm around his shoulder, "Chuck! we did it!"

He turned to face her. Her eyes sparkled like moist sapphires. She was radiant.

"We did," said Charlie, "We sure did."

Kool and his Gang, were still beating their message of celebration into the eaves as the two looked around in wonder.

Carolina said: "It was big for me. It was big for you too, I think."

"We belong..." said Charlie. He said it slowly, as if solving a riddle.

Suddenly, Jonathan was beside them, throwing an arm around them both. "I think I'm going to sleep for a year,"

The music was being turned down; the circle was breaking up. Shawn came up behind the three huddled voyagers and clapped them on the back.

"Welcome back," said Shawn. "What did you think?"

The three raised their eyebrows and nodded contemplatively in reply.

"Austin and I had to do all the dorm chores this morning," Shawn said, with a pout, although his eyes smiled. "At least you had a good excuse." He laughed and clapped them all on the back again before taking his leave.

Archie Goetz, the math teacher, walked by, hugged them, and expressed the pride he had in them all. He excused himself and stepped down into the Pit and put his back to the fireplace.

"Can I have your attention?" Archie called through cupped hands, a patient, affable smile beneath the thick lenses of his glasses.

"House around the Pit!" called a voice from the other side of the room. The directive was hardly necessary since the entire House was already at the Pit. Consequently, the toady herald was promptly derided with a series of rolling eyes.

"Thank you, Jennifer," Archie teased from the floor of the Pit. "Okay, I want to congratulate the members of the Ascent Propheet for all the good work they have accomplished."

A round of applause pattered through the room.

Archie continued: "And, I would ask that we all respect their space today. After lunch they will be going to their dorms to sleep for a while, clean up, and prepare for the feast we have in store for them tonight."

More applause and a series of good-natured but affected "oohs" and "ahhs" peppered the room. Charlie laughed. He turned to Carolina, but she was gone. Jonathan was still beside him however, his palms flat on his girth and nodding with gritted teeth and comic vigor at the prospect of a feast. Charlie smiled and shook his head at Jonathan in mock disappointment.

Archie continued, "So give some hugs, and say goodbye for a while. Genesis...you have the day off! We will see you back in the lodge at 6:00 tonight!"

❖

Charlie didn't remember falling asleep and Jonathan admitted that he didn't remember what happened either. Charlie wrote in his journal until his eyes could not focus and his lines began to slant, the two talked for a while, and what seemed like a moment later, they were awakened by Shawn's alarm.

Before long, Jonathan and Charlie had shed their humid films of sleep into the shower's drain, dressed for dinner--or feast, as it were--and headed for the lodge, swinging their arms and marching with springing steps.

Entering the dining room they found that the entire Upper Level had been reserved for Genesis and was festooned with colorful signs, hand-lettered by the Upper School:

ASCEND

SUMMIT OR BUST

Bowls of fruit, plates of cheese and crackers and multiple pitchers of milk were spread plentifully about the level. Best of all, each place setting had a bowl of chocolate pudding topped with a snow-white floret of whipped cream.

The rest of the school stole envious glances at the upper level as selected older students brought Genesis burgers and fries from the kitchen, carrying them on large, colorful platters.

Kenny Bootman shared Charlie and Jonathan's table.

"You know what I don't get?" said Charlie, scraping the bottom of his pudding bowl. "I thought for sure Devon would be on the Middle Level, doing a Full Time. Have you guys seen him?"

"You haven't heard?" Kenny asked.

Jonathan bristled. The rumor mill was his territory and he had somehow fallen to the back of the line to receive what was probably going to be the gold standard of gossip.

"Taken away," Kenny said simply. "Not long after he walked out of the Ascent."

"You're KIDDING," Jonathan said, salivating, "By who? The men in white coats?"

"Provo?" asked Charlie, his elbows lighting on the table as he leaned in.

Kenny pulled a cleaned spoon from between his lips with a smack and spoke calmly into his bowl as he scraped it clean. "I heard it from my big brother, Andre Puegot, and he said that during Floor Time last night he saw some kind of white van parked up at North Walden. There were a few other vehicles too, and a couple of squad cars..."

"Cops?" Charlie asked with wonder. "No shit?"

Jonathan looked skeptical.

"Yep," Kenny confirmed. "Police cars were surrounding the van so he couldn't get a real good look. It was pretty dark up there and too far away to see much detail, but he did see that the cops didn't have their cherries lit. Anyway, Andre was going to go take a look but Michael DiFranco, who was standing at the edge of the Quad, told him to get back inside. DiFranco was patrolling the outside of the lodge, making sure no one went up the hill to the dorms."

"Holy crap," said Jonathan.

Kenny continued, "Yeah, they must have told Devon to go to the dorms and pack up. That explains the escort."

Charlie and Jonathan sat in awe, looking at each other, with their mouths hanging open.

"Yep," said Kenny, "he's out of here. I thought he would just get thrown back on Full Time too, but I guess they were done with him. How many Dishes can they make you do before it hardly matters anymore? The guy was unfixable."

After a long pause Charlie said, "What did DiFranco say? What about the other staff? Did they say if he went to Provo or not?"

"No one is talking," Kenny replied. "I asked around. It happened during Floor time last night so no one was anywhere near the dorms when it went down. Who knows what we were doing at the time in the Ascent. There was no way to tell time in that room. Who knows how long it had been since Devon walked out. Immediately? Or, was it hours later after a good talking to and plenty of chances? Who knows? Anyway, I asked Archie on the way into dinner. I figured, for sure, Archie of all people would tell me, but he didn't. It was weird. He put his arm around me and said 'This is your night. Be proud of the work you've done. We will tell everyone later.' Then he walked away. He seemed depressed."

"Who walks out of a Propheet?" asked Jonathan. "I don't think the staff even saw that one coming. No wonder Archie is depressed, I bet all the staff are. They don't like rebellion for sure and they like failure even less. I'm sure they thought they could help him and now..."

"Walking out of a Propheet?" said Kenny. "The balls on that kid."

"Well," said Charlie. "Maybe Vince Russo knows where he went. He's my big brother and Devon's dorm head. I'll ask him when I see him."

"That's another thing," said Kenny, "Vince is gone too."

Charlie and Jonathan stared blankly.

"What do you mean, gone?" asked Charlie, alarmed. He remembered looking for Vince in the horseshoe and not finding him.

"Why did he go too?" asked Jonathan. "To make sure Devon didn't flip out or something? When will he be back?"

"You said there were cops there," said Charlie. "Escorts. Probably men in white coats too. Why would they need Vince?"

"Don't know," Kenny replied. "Andre said DiFranco didn't say squat and Andre didn't want to get on his bad side. He said DiFranco looked like a wild animal or something, pacing the Quad and breathing hard. He was probably embarrassed that they let the kid run amuck. Probably pissed off too. DiFranco snapped and told Andre to get back inside, and that was enough for Andre."

"Sheesh," said Charlie. "Well, he missed some damn good pudding."

"He might be eating nothing BUT pudding where he's going," said Jonathan. "Thorazine Pudding with a plastic spoon."

Kenny looked horrified by the joke.

"Oh relax, Kenny," said Charlie. "I'll be the first to admit that I'm running off fear. The guy wasn't built for this place. Maybe not for any place. Didn't we all know it?"

No one answered, and that seemed to be answer enough.

The next morning, House Crew began shortly after First Light, and Karen once again assigned Charlie to the upstairs rooms: the library, the Gallery, and the staff offices.

Armed with his vinegar and sections of old newspaper, Charlie ascended the stairs and began work on the diamond-pane windows overlooking the foggy valley.

The floors of the canyons below looked as if they were filled with pearly batting. The morning sun beat weakly on the billowing haze, managing to burn some portions away into fleeing tendrils of mist.

"Beautiful," Charlie said to the window.

The hands of Charlie's body clock were still spinning madly from his all-nighter. He felt as if he were floating through the wood-paneled room, surveying it from some other world.

He eyed the bookcase as his newsprint squeaked across the windows beside them. There were a lot of shelves to dust and he was still so tired. The euphoria from the Propheet had worn off and it was being replaced with consuming weariness, a weariness that he had to fight. He passed the mahogany rods that held the day's newspaper in sections and as he always did when working the library, picked up the front section to see the headlines.

There was no masthead, no front page.

Confused, Charlie scanned the page. "A3" was printed at the bottom corner. He looked behind the section to see if the front page had been folded over, but it hadn't. The back page was missing as well. He shrugged and settled for the first A3 headline:

IS LOS ANGELES READY FOR THE OLYMPICS?

He replaced the rod back on the rack and looked to see if the Entertainment section had been mistakenly threaded onto one of the other rods for once. It hadn't.

Not like he needed a big piece of dirt right after a Propheet anyway. Even if the section was hanging there, he would not look at it if he knew it was going to be full of unacceptable bands announcing their concert tours. Was it dirt to have even checked? That was a Catholic thing wasn't it? He thought it might be. Then again, he hadn't paid a whole lot of attention at Sacred Heart.

He pulled the wadded-up dust rag from his back pocket and began to dust the floor to ceiling bookshelves. After completing the library he turned his attention to the hall of staff offices, careful not to disturb Jonas, or any staff, who might be having a private session with a student.

Some students needed a little extra help accepting the program, he thought, a little one-on-one time. Even he had been resistant himself once. But, the offices were empty.

He decided to start at the front of the hall, at Michael DiFranco's office. The room was of a modest size, with a view of the lawn below, a view obstructed only by the jutting bough of a coulter pine laden with a cluster of large, golden cones. A cold puddle of muddy coffee still sat in the ceramic mug on the desk. The mug was emblazoned with a bleary-eyed green monster clasping its head and screaming the word "coffee" in a spiky dialogue balloon.

Charlie moved the leather blotter that covered the top of the desk so that he could dust. A pencil rolled onto the floor. He cursed and bent to pick it up and saw part of the familiar Bear Creek Crier newspaper sticking out of the wastebasket that sat in the shadows of the knee well.

It looked like he might have solved the mystery of where the front page had gone. Out of all the times he had cleaned the library it had never been missing before. Why it had been separated from the rest he didn't know. It was odd, and he paused to stare at the crumpled page protruding from the trash.

"I guess we'll find out why," he mumbled.

He popped his head up over the desk and looked through the open door to the hall. He listened. All was quiet. His heart began to race.

There was nobody around.

Something unacceptable was on the page. Why else would it be separated from the public?

What are you thinking, his mind warned. What if Van Halen or some other band made the front page. Do you want to be dirty the day after your first Propheet?

The image of piles of dishes flashed through his mind, his weary limbs tightening with the thought.

But, he had to know. It wouldn't hurt anyone. It was probably no big deal, probably nothing at all.

He knelt in the knee well of the desk, rolled the office chair aside with one hand and reached into the wastebasket with the other. He popped his head over the desk one more time to be sure the hall was still clear. He heard nothing. Quickly, he shook the crumbs of a discarded muffin from the page and spread it open on his lap.

He froze. His mouth went dry, sinking horror filling him as he stared at the headline:

❖

BOY HANGS HIMSELF IN SCHOOL DORMITORY

A 13-year-old Ponderosa Academy student hanged himself in a dorm at the private school Monday, authorities said. The boy, who was from Boston, Massachusetts, was found by another student at the secluded Bear Creek County school. The boy's name was not released. He apparently had tied a belt to a pipe on an overhead sprinkler system and hanged himself, according to Bear Creek County Sheriff Cole Wilmington. He was found about 8:30 P.M. when he failed to show up for a regularly scheduled evening social gathering. Staff at the school for troubled teens tried to revive the boy and called for an ambulance. Wilmington said the teenager was unresponsive and pronounced dead a short time later at Bear Creek County Community Hospital. His death is still under investigation. Several reports said the boy might have been taking medication for manic depression prior to his enrollment in the school. Authorities would not comment on any details until the investigation is complete. Jonas Portman, Program Administrator at Ponderosa Academy declined to comment Tuesday.

The private school specializes in teens that have had trouble at home or are drug and alcohol abusers. About 100 students, ages 13 to 17, are enrolled at the school, which commands tuition of more than $3,500 a month. Students who have attended the school in the past include the sons and daughters of notable businessmen and...

"Vince found him," Charlie said to the stillness. The paper began to tremble in his hands. "Vince found him."

His guts were cold, writhing snakes of frozen lead. An icy hand wrapped around his heart and squeezed. A moan escaped him, the strangled sound of many words of disbelief spoken at once.

Then, a phantom voice whispered through his head like a rustling of dead leaves. It was the echo of Devon's words from the Propheet, the last words the boy had said before he had disappeared, and the last words Charlie would ever hear him say:

"I am evil. Love is not meant for me."

Charlie watched his hands as they let the newspaper fall to his lap.

PART THREE

FALLING FROM AVALON

Chapter 22

Autumn came early to Bear Creek County. The smell of the first Sunday morning fires from the surrounding cabins drifted on a lazy current of crisp air through the center of town. Charlie inhaled deeply and made his way to a patch of sun that fell in a warm triangle between oblique shadows cast by the A-frame roof of the store. He waited for Jonathan who was still inside, indecisively staring down the candy shelves.

The market door's bell tinkled and Jonathan exited with a small, brown paper sack, peering into it and rifling through its contents.

"Man," said Jonathan, approaching Charlie and producing a candy bar from his sack, "I couldn't decide, and then I saw this. Have you seen these?"

Jonathan held up the bar so Charlie could read the label.

"Never heard of it," Charlie said. "What is it?"

Jonathan inspected the label: "It looks like another version of a Heath bar, English toffee."

"I had to go for peanut butter cups," said Charlie. "Gotta have my peanut butter cups. How much you got left?"

"I'm tapped," Jonathan replied. "What about you?"

"Twenty cents," said Charlie, thrusting a hand into his jeans pocket to double-check.

"I'm going to hoard this stuff for as long as I can," said Jonathan, glancing into the bag. "A buck and a half of WAM doesn't cut it for this gut." He grabbed his stomach and shook it. The pounds had mostly melted away from constant work, but his self-image had yet to catch up. The act was such a habit that Charlie wondered if his friend noticed just how little punch line he had left to jiggle.

Jonathan tugged open the school van's sliding door. It rumbled open and revealed the content faces of the other students who had already made their purchases, some of whom had already torn into their spoils and were chewing furiously.

"About time," said Aaron, who was one of the lucky dozen to have secured a place on the Store Run sign-ups. "Where's Dave?"

Dave was a "townie", an epithet given to locals serving as peripheral staff who performed generally menial tasks. Dave always drove the Sunday Store Runs. He was a jolly, overweight man in his mid-40's who drove the Barf Van to town on Sundays; he was also taking his sweet time, somewhere in the village.

None of the waiting students really knew the true derivation of "Barf Van". According to legend, long ago during a routine Medical Run down the winding mountain roads to the city, a former student had violently and copiously puked somewhere within the vehicle. To the present day, every student who entered the nondescript passenger van would wrinkle their nose in anticipation of smelling the ancient sick. Some swore up and down that they could still smell it, others just played along. Either way, the Barf Van was unlikely to ever shake the name.

"Yuck," said Jonathan, sliding the door closed and ducking his way to the available seats in the back with Charlie in tow, "it smells like puke in here."

Dave, with a jingle of custodial keys, threw open the driver's door of the van, hopped into his seat, took a quick roll call, and pulled out of the parking lot to return to campus.

Charlie gazed through the window at the fall leaves and the bright circles of light stabbing through the canopy of trees above. A month had passed since Devon's suicide and September was approaching its end. The sadness still visited Charlie though. But, from what he had seen in Raps, he was not alone.

Things felt different now. One of them had died, alone and irredeemable, and the tenacious residue of that horrific fact tarnished them all still. The hope that their absolution was possible had been obliterated by one pathetic boy, by one kick of a chair.

As no one really knew Devon, the tears flowed primarily from abject fear. All feared their susceptibility to despair and their perceived predisposition for failure. A dream had died with Devon Childs, a dream of salvaging themselves--the discarded ones--and leaving no one behind. Hope and reality were now irreconcilable.

Charlie remembered abandoning his work in the upper rooms the morning he had discovered the headline and running straight to Archie Goetz' classroom in the annex on the hillside. Thankfully, Archie had been there, preparing papers for his late morning class.

Charlie had been inconsolable; Archie had been candid: Charlie would have to keep the details to himself until the House was told formally--a bewildering request from an officer of an institution obsessed with honesty of the most difficult sort.

Of all of them, no one had it worse than Vince Russo. The boy had returned a week after his disappearance, changed. Gone was the good-natured smile he had offered all who passed, gone was the twinkle in his eyes, and fallen was the painstakingly constructed scaffold to salvation, labored on over his 20 months at the school during countless hours of Raps, Propheets, and individual therapy.

Vince had returned to The Academy--presumably after being under observation in some other facility. He was expected to clear space for himself in Raps and it was a pathetic and uncomfortable sight to behold.

Fate had put Charlie into one of those Raps with Vince--a Sonia DiFranco Rap in the Quest Family Room--only days after the boy had returned to campus. Vince began to mechanically describe a horrific scene of a stark white Devon hanging from a pipe, his head slumped over a looped belt, his eyes popping from his skull, and his purple tongue jutting from his mouth as he hung above a desk chair that had been overturned and then drenched in the boy's post-mortem urine.

Vince could not get through his recounting of the scene without hyperventilating and eventually throwing up. Of course, witnessing the ignominious defeat of another human being, especially one so young, would have been unbearable for anyone. Yet, the hand of fate had chosen to shove that particularly bitter pill down Vince Russo's unsuspecting throat, and he was choking on it still.

"You have got to try this," Jonathan said, breaking a piece of his candy bar into his hand and tapping Charlie on the shoulder with the small chunk. "Oh, my flippin' God."

Charlie peeled his gaze from the van's window and popped the morsel into his mouth.

"No way," said Charlie, considering the chocolate with the gravity the occasion demanded. "Oh wow...good stuff."

"Crazy, huh?" said Jonathan.

Charlie nodded slowly. Aaron turned around in his seat in the front of the van and asked for a bite. The request was politely declined. Sharing your sugar limit with another was extremely rare, but asking for it to be shared was almost unconscionable. Aaron frowned and turned back around in his seat.

Charlie returned his attention back to the sun-dappled forest outside the van's window, to the quilt of fallen leaves. He felt a calm settle over him, figuring that he was about halfway back to campus.

Lately, he felt strange leaving the school, interacting with the few townspeople who crossed his path on the brief Store Runs. Did the townspeople know he was from Ponderosa? What did they know about what went on at the school? Why did the school allow Store Runs anyway?

Oddly, nobody had split during a Store Run, ever. Charlie figured it must have something to do with the way he felt now. He had felt lost in town, almost frightened. Absurd, considering that the van had parked in the all but deserted lot of the general store and no one was allowed to wander far. Still, there was a relief when it was time to head back to campus, back to safety, and back to the freedom to be a "problem child", to own it, to proclaim it aloud and often and to be accepted in spite of it.

What was happening to him? He wasn't sure. In only three months he had assimilated into someone's utopian construct that not long ago had seemed insufferable and totally absurd. It seemed inconceivable that he would not have dived behind the counter of the Bear Creek Market and frantically dialed his Mom, his friend's parents, his old teachers, anybody...

But, nobody could help. Could they? What was happening at Ponderosa Academy could not be explained. No one would understand. It would take too long to tell them, and the bearer of the news would look unstable or maybe even insane.

Making matters worse, Charlie had found out that most of the counselors of The Academy had been former students. They had themselves completed the program long ago and had ascended from graduate, to peripheral staff, to head counselors, and to administrators of the school—making their bones from a long, almost constant immersion in The Academy's brand of New Age therapy.

Eventually, Charlie had been in enough Raps to hear enough horrible stories to last him a lifetime. But, the worst of these tales did not come from students. The worst ones came from the top.

Michael DiFranco had run numbers for the mob in Las Vegas as a youth and had spent his cut on cocaine. According to his account, his work had been slipping and he was sure that either the blow was going to kill him or that his captain was going to bury him in the desert. He had also done time for grand theft and aggravated assault.

Jonas Portman, once all muscle and now all fat, had preferred heroin. He had run with the Detroit chapter of a motorcycle gang called The Highwaymen. His war stories included an incident in which he had forced a miscarriage of a woman he had knocked up by stomping on her stomach with a boot. Earlier in life, he would perch himself on a milking stool and screw the calves at his father's dairy farm in Vermont.

Then there was Charlie Hoff who had been kicked out of two private schools as a result of his inability to accept the lame replacement of his real father. Regardless, he too had been sent here to lick his conventional wounds alongside men like Jonas Portman.

Charlie was beginning to realize that The Academy did not care if your mistakes that brought you to them were bad enough, or if your pain was deep enough to need them. If the checks continued to clear, then you were not going anywhere.

So, there would be much more to come, so much more.. Of that, he was sure.

And one of them was already dead.

Charlie turned away from the window and looked to the front of the van, through the driver's window. The road narrowed ahead, like a funnel. Soon, the tires were crunching gravel. The van rocked gently, easing down the slight hill and into the parking lot of Ponderosa Academy.

Chapter 23

Much had happened in three months. Most notably, Charlie was no longer in the bottom peer group. A total of 6 kids had arrived since he had been the Nate, and the new arrivals were stumbling around campus with the same old plots and schemes. They were very easy to spot too--something Charlie could not have known in his first days. Their eyes failed to meet yours and their body language was unreceptive. They stewed observably in their own bitter juices, consumed in what they assumed was a private misery that only served to make them appear as if they were up to no good, which of course they were.

Charlie did not know if he was finally achieving the X-ray vision he had once felt boring into him, or if the Nates were just too off-balance to throw a proper curve ball. Either way, Charlie knew that Robert Babcock--a street kid from New Orleans--would not last the week before he tried to split.

Three days after the kid arrived his big brother was sent to retrieve him after Jonas Portman called the lodge from his house overlooking School Road to inform Toby that he saw Robert sneaking off into the woods.

The story came from Shawn, who had heard it from the kid's big brother--one Mark Gallagher, Shawn's peer in the Source family. Evidently, Robert had been trying to look like he was taking a stroll to the farm--which was out of agreement anyway for a Genesis kid without an older student present--when he passed the fork and at the last moment, mounted the incline to School Road and began to double-time it towards the village. All this while Jonas, bemused, chewed on an English muffin lathered in butter while gazing through the window of his breakfast nook, calmly dialing the kitchen phone with his free hand.

Shawn conceded that the last part of the story was probably an embellishment, but a damn good one and not likely to be far from the truth.

Charlie had seen the escape attempt coming though, and he shuddered when he considered how completely delusional it had been to ever have fancied himself a step ahead of them all during his first days on campus. Jonas' words, spoken that first dinner in the dining hall as Charlie sat looking up at the fat man, came back to him:

"It's a big place Charlie but we'll make sure you don't get lost."

It seemed that Jonas had extended the same courtesy to Robert Babcock, who was now on indefinite Dishes and lucky to have avoided a Full Time.

As fall approached, Charlie fought fresh pangs of homesickness. Schools throughout California were starting the new school year, and they were starting without him. He wondered if he would be missed, and if so, how long would the world notice he was gone before he was forgotten completely. His family had only moved in with Kurt a couple of years ago, but Charlie had made good friends in San Hose and he missed them. His generation would go on without him, sharing the pathos of the age. In the meantime, he was experiencing an entirely different world that he feared would make it even more difficult to relate to his peers back home when it came time to resume his place in the great suburban myth.

Aside from knitting-which he vowed he would tell no one about-he had learned many skills at great expense to his ligaments and joints. Leaving House Crew and being put on Wood Shed was supposedly a promotion, but the work was much harder. Short of felling the trees--a task reserved for the gleaming teeth of the townies' chainsaws--Charlie and the rest of Wood Shed Crew were responsible for turning the recumbent tree, from where it lay, into firewood for the lodge's coffers and for the hearths of the staff homes along School Road.

Charlie had never seen trees so tall and thick. The smell of sheep's fleece, pinesap, and sawdust were new to him. He was sure to have stories to tell and new skills to regale the city slickers back home. He was trading in his video game pallor for the rare, healthy glow of an adolescent kissed by the mountain sun and caressed by the unpolluted breezes that shook the needles of the ancient firs.

He wondered if anyone would notice the new Charlie. He wondered if anyone would care.

Jonathan climbed the Microwave Road and Charlie followed. After leaving the Barf Van, it was decided that the two should stash their purchases from the Bear Creek Market safely in the drawers beneath their beds and then kill some time with backgammon before the Sunday movie.

Sunday night was movie night, again, providing one had not received Dishes during the week, in which case the flick was forfeited. Otherwise, one was free to grab a spot on the floor of the lodge, and tonight, Charlie and Jonathan were free.

On this particular Sunday, Michael DiFranco was the staff on Floor. With the help of hand-selected acolytes, Michael rolled the projection unit from the Quest family room into place in the center of the lodge. The huge walnut cabinet had a removable panel on its front that revealed three colored guns of light that were now trained on a retractable screen that was pulled down from the ceiling of the lodge. Keeping the Pit at their right and facing towards the short wall at the end of the room, students began to mound cushions and form smush piles.

"It's Camelot again," said Jonathan.

"How do you know?" Charlie asked.

"I saw the tape on DiFranco's desk."

"What were you doing in his office?"

"Snooping."

"Gee, at least you're honest," Charlie said.

"The truth shall set you free," said Jonathan.

They lay, fashionably, in each other's arms, propped on a cushion, as Michael focused the projector. A crude shadow puppet of a spiny reptile of some kind loped across the bright white screen.

"Down in front," warned a lethargic voice from the tangle of students.

The dinosaur-thing paused, turned towards the crowd, and sprinted from the screen.

The film began. Jonathan had been right; it was "Camelot", the 1967 Lerner and Loewe musical, and the second showing of the film in 3 months. Charlie did like Richard Harris well enough but the film was hardly a replacement for Star Wars or Indiana Jones.

"Why do they like this movie so much?" Charlie whispered.

"I don't know," Jonathan whispered back as the cast sang "I Wonder What the King Is Doing Tonight."

"I know what the king is doing tonight," Charlie said glumly, "because I've seen this already."

A girl behind Charlie shushed him crisply.

Dessert was served after the movie on the Middle Level. That night the familiar stainless steel fruit bowl had retired from the brick hearth of the potbellied stove, and in its stead a selection of cookies was arranged on a sheet pan.

"One cookie apiece," implored the townie kitchen lady--a fat, bespectacled woman with hair that looked like a mousy brown helmet.

The crush of students funneled through the dining room door from The Floor.

"One cookie apiece, please," she repeated through cupped hands.

Carolina and Alicia fell in line behind Jonathan and Charlie.

"What do we got?" asked Carolina.

"Oh, hi," said Charlie, looking back over his shoulder. "Well, it looks like, maybe, chocolate chip and..."

"Peanut butter," said Jonathan.

"Peanut butter," relayed Charlie.

Charlie's hand vacillated between the two piles of cookies and finally lit upon the chocolate chip.

"What happened to 'I gotta have my peanut butter'," Jonathan gibed.

"Peanut butter cups," corrected Charlie. "Big difference. Plus, you see those huge chunks of peanuts floating around in there? I HATE that."

"I don't mind," said Carolina, selecting the peanut-riddled variety and grabbing a napkin from the adjacent stack. "I'm a Southern girl. I was raised on peanuts." She delivered the line with a smoldering Southern-belle accent that made Charlie tingle. They moved together towards a booth on the middle level.

Charlie didn't even notice that he had instinctively calculated the girl-to-boy ratio as they walked, approved the math, and dismissed the thought. As with many considerations at The Academy, this one had become simply reflexive over time, like swallowing.

At least, that was how it was supposed to work. Occasionally, he would lapse and regard his world with alarm and panic. It was as if some mental anesthetic would wear off periodically, allowing him access to his old perspective, his old self. Ignoring the relapse, forgetting it, and accepting the program afresh became a constant struggle-though it was much easier than it had been in the first days. It was, he had finally realized, a compulsory discipline, a daily exercise in extraordinary acceptance. The preservation of all he had left of his freedom was predicated on his compliance becoming second-nature. Considering the odds, he thought he was getting quite good at it.

"Oh crap!" exclaimed Charlie. "You have GOT to be kidding me."

"What?" asked Carolina with concern.

"It's oatmeal-raisin," Charlie said, dismally, chewing with his mouth open with a pained expression. "What a dirty trick."

"Sure fooled me," Jonathan said, staring at his cookie. "I can't see any oats. It's weirdly smooth...fascinating."

"Fascinating?" asked Charlie, smoldering theatrically. "This is an outrage!"

Carolina laughed and blew peanut crumbs from her mouth in a fine spray.

"Yuck," said Jonathan, shielding his face with an open palm.

"How dainty," said Alicia, giggling.

"What's wrong with oatmeal-raisin?" Carolina asked, regaining herself.

"What's wrong with it?" replied Charlie, incredulously. "It's not chocolate chip. That's what's wrong with it."

"It wouldn't have been chocolate anyway," Jonathan said. "It would have been carob chip."

Charlie bristled at the mention of carob chips.

"Do you want my peanut butter one?" asked Alicia.

"No," Charlie replied, "that's sweet, but I'll live."

"Raisins are good for you," said Carolina.

"Everything here is good for me," Charlie lamented. "Honey on my granola. Milk instead of Coke. Raisins instead of chocolate chips. These are like..." he inspected the cookie in his hand, "like little dead flies imbedded in sand."

"Oh, that's nice," said Jonathan, "now I'm going to puke."

"I bet they just plucked them off that fly strip in the Veggie Prep," Charlie continued.

Jonathan mimed regurgitating over the side of the booth.

"Did you know that Sandra Carberry got her hair stuck in the fly strip?" Alicia asked brightly.

Everyone moaned a condolence.

"Yep," Alicia continued, "she was scraping her plate and backed into it to go around me and it sucked right onto her hair. She screamed. I felt bad."

"She is pretty tall," Carolina conceded, straining to contain a laugh.

It was of no use. The four began to cackle with laughter, but the giggles fizzled quickly. Laughing at another's misfortune was very bad form, no matter how funny it was, and being within earshot of two other booths made it particularly dangerous to continue. Making the "environment unsafe" was a stalwart armament for the Raps. It could be defined as anything that would make another student feel self-conscious, withdrawn, or compelled to alter themselves for acceptance. Undoubtedly, everyone benefited from this mutual caution, but as usual, the names of the temporarily careless were sure to be destined for the Rap request Box. Hurtful intentions were hardly required for someone to at least try for the easy points in the next Rap. Mostly because the charge was much harder to shake than it was to level. Barring an obviously malicious intent, "making the environment unsafe" was highly subjective, and therefore, a particularly potent charge.

"So," Jonathan said, changing the subject and leaning across to Alicia, "what did you think of the movie?"

"It was okay," she said. "I liked some of the songs."

"You'll know them by heart pretty soon," said Charlie.

Alicia looked confused.

"They play the movie a lot," offered Jonathan.

"Why?" asked Alicia.

Carolina replied: "The staff like it. It's got a good message, you know? King Arthur dreamed of a place where things were perfect. Everyone got along. Everything was how it should be. And then, one day, the round table cracked. I think the movie is sad really...to watch such a dream exist for awhile and then just die."

"It was an unrealistic dream," said Jonathan.

"All dreams are unrealistic," said Carolina, "that's why they're dreams."

"A perfect world and a perfect society is a pretty tall order," Jonathan mused. "No one will ever have the same idea of what that kind of world should be. Sometimes I think that chaos only exists because everything and everyone is struggling so hard for their own brand of perfection."

Turning in the booth to hide what he was sure was his pale face, Charlie watched the students around him finish their snacks and file to the Veggie Prep to throw away their napkins, stack their glasses and head to the Pit for Last Light.

Vince Russo glided by, paused to look at the four sitting in the booth, caught Charlie's eye and smiled joylessly before moving on. Charlie realized he was sitting in the booth that Devon Childs had called home for most of his final days on Full Time.

Suddenly, a strange thing happened. Charlie could see him. He could see the boy in his white t-shirt sitting beside him, dead eyes below his shock of dark hair, lips pulling back into a terrible grin. Ice ran down Charlie's spine as the Devon-thing turned and stared at him. Then, it spoke, its voice rattling with grave dirt: "You're in my seat, Charlieee..."

Charlie snapped shut his eyes and looked again. There was nothing there.

Meyer's ghost, he thought to himself and laughed dully..

He glanced at the others. They hadn't noticed. They were busy gossiping about something. Charlie caught his breath.

Carefully, he stole another glance at the empty spot in the booth beside him.

Nothing, or nothing yet...

Maybe his imagination was running wild, but Devon had always been a presence on the Middle Level, sitting here alone and Charlie wondered if the imprint of the boy could ever be effaced. Devon had surely stained this place forever. Eventually, Devon would be resurrected. It was only a matter of time. Generations would fill his lifeless lungs with whispers of the legend that he had become.

Glassy-eyed, Charlie scanned the wood tabletop for carvings, for initials, for pentagrams, for evidence that the boy had ever existed.

"Lose something, Charlie?" Carolina asked.

"No," Charlie muttered, "At least, I don't think so. We should go. We're going to be late for Last Light."

Chapter 24

Austin made no attempt to hide that he was masturbating when Charlie and Jonathan entered the dorm.

"For the love of God," muttered Jonathan, heading for his own bed with his head down. Charlie groaned.

"You could've waited until lights out," said Charlie, grabbing his journal to log the daily entry, which he began to do in haste, relieved that he didn't have to flounder in devising some other activity for his eyes.

"All done," said Austin, breezing by and heading for the bathroom.

Dorm life at Ponderosa was not for the squeamish, especially when it came to such carnal realities. A living situation in which scores of adolescent boys were packed into small rooms on a hilltop and prohibited from even thinking of forging sexual relationships made for a startling lack of shame. Compounding the problem was the constant physical contact on the Floor. Although the contact was supposed to be considered pure, beautiful, and therapeutic, it was little consolation to the hormone-soaked nerves in North Walden.

As a result, masturbation was rampant, and Austin was not the first guy Charlie had seen pulling his pud--though certainly the most prolific. In fact, the masturbatory culture at Ponderosa had taken on a life of its own. Spanking the monkey was not only fashionable, but all the trappings that went along with it were sought after, improved upon, and brazenly displayed.

Austin had been a trendsetter in this regard, being the first student to screw a "jack caddy" to the wall beside his bed-a term that he coined. The name caught on and the device became a must-have item among the discerning of North Walden. Austin maintained a quiet pride in having contributed something important to society, as if he were a young Edison.

Some of the examples were rather well-executed. Austin's prototype debut had been crafted with the care of a Venetian gondolier. It featured scrollwork in crude arabesque with a whittled indentation to secure the lotion bottle. On its heels, Andrew Hall, a Vision student from North 3, had drawn a crowd and gasps of wonder when he unveiled the Regency fluting on his own version: The Duke. With its sleek cantilever and space-saving design, it was destined to become the paradigm of masturbation accessories.

Austin pooh-poohed The Duke publicly as "impractical", but was secretly overheard confiding to Shawn one morning during chores that Andrew's talent was undeniable and that he had "a gift".

At first, Charlie had been mortified by the shameless self-gratification. Then, he understood. After all, jerking off was the only unregulated activity of pure pleasure, the only joy and the only freedom that could not be taken away.

Austin emerged from the bathroom: "Boy, I needed that. Only two weeks left before we leave and Michael is cracking the whip to get us in shape. We had to run the School Road and do calisthenics. I've had a boner all day."

"Is there anything that DOESN'T make you horny?" asked Jonathan.

"YOU don't," Austin replied and stretched out on his bed, his grin devilish.

Jonathan rolled his eyes.

"But Charlie does," Austin continued, wiggling his eyebrows at Charlie.

"Shut up," said Charlie, closing his journal.

In truth, both his roommates knew to what Austin alluded, but talking about it would have been out of agreement. Watching the girls do calisthenics was plenty of motivation to want some dorm time to toss one off--squat thrusts and deep knee bends being a standard part of the repertoire of exercises. They had witnessed the stretching and flexing of flesh and the effect of sweat on fabric enough times themselves to know what Austin was going through, but it was an indelicate subject and a potentially hazardous one.

The girls on campus were to be treated with platonic affection, almost as siblings. The crude gossip so prevalent in adolescent boys of who wanted to sleep with whom, who looked good in a pair of jeans, and whose bra-less nipples had been poking through their blouse at lunch was quashed by the constant threat of indictment in a Rap.

Additionally, Austin's comment about leaving in two weeks was well understood to be referring to his upcoming departure date for Wilderness Trek whereby all Quest students in good stead were dropped into the wilderness for two weeks to test their newly-acquired survival skills. As of late, Austin had become increasingly jittery, for the day was approaching fast.

"Aren't you nervous about going?" Charlie asked. "I mean, it IS the desert. All I know about the desert is that you crawl through the sand and start seeing things."

"A little bit, I guess," Austin admitted, "but it sure would be nice to get off the mountain for a while. Plus, I hear it's beautiful. I talked to Tony Martin before he graduated--his W.T. was in Death Valley too--and he said it was awesome. I guess there's this place called the Devil's Racetrack where these huge boulders crawl across the desert. The boulders are so huge that they couldn't possibly move, but you can see the trails they leave behind as they somehow--I guess, through the shifting of sand and stuff--move across the valley."

A crescendo of chirping crickets and a blast of cool air announced Shawn as the door opened and the dorm head lumbered into the room, unbuttoning his collared evening shirt as though he couldn't wait to rid himself of its hold.

"Hey Shawn, where was your W.T.?" asked Austin. "I forget."

"Golden Trout," Shawn replied, as he pitched his wadded-up shirt into the hamper at the corner of the room. He flopped, supine, onto his bed and stared slackly at the ceiling.

"Where's Golden Trout?" Charlie asked. "Was it fun?"

"In the high Sierras," Shawn replied, "and yeah, it was fun...except there were some tough times."

"Like what?" asked Austin, starved for information.

"Well," Shawn began, sitting up under the power of his reminiscence, "we split up into hiking groups one day and our group got pretty lost. That's not something you want to do when you're humping an eighty-pound frame pack on your back through a box canyon called Devil's Hole. Learn your map skills. That's all I can tell you. I think that was the worst. Solo was tough too, but in a totally different way."

"What's Solo?" asked Charlie, realizing that he was taking full advantage of Shawn's rare chattiness, hoping to ingratiate himself to the dispenser of dorm chores.

"Solo is the hardest part of W.T.,' Shawn replied. "You are left alone for three days in the woods without contact with anyone. They put us along a river; I don't know what they do in Death Valley. Anyway, all you have is your journal, some required reading, some iodine to make the water drinkable and 1 pound of gorp for the three days."

"What's gorp?" asked Charlie.

"Oh yeah," Austin interjected, "we're supposed to make and pack our gorp later in the week. Do you remember what's in it, Shawn?"

"It's basically granola," Shawn answered, "with some nuts, coconut flakes, and carob chips. You have to ration it out. I ate way too much on the first day and I wish I hadn't by the end. I was out of food"

"I'll remember that," said Austin.

"Why are the packs so heavy?" Jonathan asked. "What's all in them?"

"Everything you need," Shawn replied, "your bed roll, your clothes, and your food. Twice during the trip you come across a cache of supplies. That's good and bad. You have a fresh supply of food, but your pack is at its heaviest."

They all fell into silence.

After a moment, Shawn continued, "All in all it's an amazing experience. I'd go again in a second." He looked at Austin who looked grave. "Don't worry. So far, everyone has come back alive."

Chapter 25

Pat Conner was running Charlie's Rap today. He pushed his thick-rimmed glasses up the bridge of his nose and waited for the last black plastic chair in the circle to click into place beside its neighbors. He sat with authoritative calm, his curly hair unruly as ever, his burly frame hugged by his tobacco-brown wingback like he was a cork in a bottle.

The world beyond the windows of the Vision family room was awash with broad swatches of murky grime. A forest fire was burning somewhere far away in the canyon below. The firefighters had informed the school that the campus was in no immediate danger, but the soiled sky offered no solace. Through the room's pine-framed windows, clots of sickly light billowed into the cataract eye of the sun. The dim table lamps of the Vision family room did little to cleave the funereal gloom.

"We're all here?" Pat asked the slack faces. "Okay, there has got to be a more interesting way to begin a Rap."

He reached for one of the tissue boxes that sat beneath each alternate chair, plucked out the exposed sheet and held it up with a sly smile. "When this hits the ground we begin."

Anxious glances were exchanged before all eyes turned to the tissue suspended between thumb and forefinger. They watched as the tissue rose into the air and then fluttered to the ground. It lurched sideways and lit on the toe of Charlie's sneaker.

Then, with sudden force, screaming pierced the silence. "YOU KNOW WHAT, ROBERT?" a girl from Quest yelled, leaning forward and hugging her body as she emptied her rage onto the boy. "IT'S NOT FUCKING OKAY TO TREAT PEOPLE WITH DISRESPECT! THIS IS MY HOME AND I DON'T WANT IT SHIT ON!"

The sun burned through its gauze, and a ray of light, the color of rotten apricots, splashed across the piqued faces of the room.

Robert Babcock, the boy who had tried to walk off campus, looked sick with fear. His ill-conceived stunt had occurred in the first week of his enrollment and the staff had been lenient. He had dodged both Bans and Full Time, being saddled only with Indefinite Dishes as a shot across his wayward bow, but he had not yet grasped his good fortune, continuing to behave like a typical public school brat. Weaning him from snide comments, negativity, and constant testing of agreements was proving difficult. His belligerent behavior--a logical and often effective defense in a public school--was too ingrained in the boy. Consequently, he was becoming the preferred chew toy for the conformists of The Academy.

"What did he say to you, Lisa?" asked Pat.

"I told him to stop threatening violence and he said..." Lisa paused and gulped, "...blow me, you fat ass."

The Rap erupted with indignant fury as all voices came to the defense of Lisa. Charlie did not join the fray, instead, he sat and watched, disturbed, as the boy wilted under the attack. He could see that Robert was different than Devon Childs had been. He looked scared, he looked shocked and remorseful, and hardest to witness of all--he looked utterly alone.

Robert was a small kid, a fact that undoubtedly accounted for his preemptive hurtfulness; he had probably survived on that ability alone. He seemed to value his Napoleonic gall and he wore it like spit-polished armor. He did not seem to believe that he would be safe if he were to lower his defenses, for it wasn't intuitive to do so and it required a level of trust that the school had not yet earned. In the meantime, Charlie would witness the emotional drawing and quartering of the kid with the darting eyes and the spray of freckles across his nose, as the boy clung to his mistrust with the diligence of the forever hunted.

Tremors of empathy stirred Charlie's heart and he turned his eyes to the floor as Lisa piled it on, crying hard. With no feel yet for the program, all Robert could do was   slump in his chair; the breakthroughs that could alleviate his torment, far beyond his grasp today.

"Let's move on," said Pat.

No one filled the silence and all eyes darted.

"How are you doing, Charlie?"

It was Pat who had spoken.

Charlie started and looked up.

The Rap waited for a reply.

"Me?" Charlie asked.

"You've been quiet," said Pat. "Where are you at?"

Charlie knew at once that this was pre-arranged. Flying under the radar only worked for a while. Then, your emotional excavation would simply be scheduled.

"Clearing space" (volunteering to be analyzed) was the preferred way to dump your feelings all over your shoes as it demonstrated initiative, an enthusiasm to heal. In this case, however, there had hardly been enough time since the start of the Rap to do so. Charlie's nature was not inclined to clear space anyway, though it sure would have looked better. But, being confronted preemptively by whomever was running the Rap was alright with Charlie for it always meant that his peers had missed the opportunity. Still, it never failed to stop his heart.

Charlie's mind clenched like a shocked muscle. He had to come up with something, some issue to confront, work through, and resolve. He hated being put on the spot. He had always marveled at how easy it was for some to appear afflicted, to cry rivers of tears, and to seem grateful for the opportunity to do so. After more than three months and only one of the eight Propheets under his belt, he still had to suffer the indignity of faking it because he still found garish displays of emotion completely unnatural.

"I'm feeling good about myself," Charlie offered.

This would not suffice, but it bought time. He was not free of sadness, anger, or hurt, he simply could not call them forth with the required speed. He still considered his pain private and raising it on a flagpole to take the breezes of countless opinions and theories was not only contrary to his nature, he was just not very good at it.

He was sure that Pat's intentions were good. But, as cool as the man was, Pat was hired as a wrecking ball to knock down walls and remodel the little haunted houses that surrounded him in the black plastic chairs. Pat probably thought himself a healer so Charlie didn't resent Pat for picking on him. Still, he had been put in the crosshairs and once you were under the gun you never squirmed away.

Resigned, Charlie looked on the bright side: at least when a facilitator cleared space for you there would be no surprise grenade lobbed at you in the coming hours. And, if there had been a bomb meant for you somewhere in the room, it would now be diffused. It was the ol' get-out-of-jail-free card, provided you manage to do some emotional work to the satisfaction of all present.

He had to perform. After all, there were only so many Raps that one could skate through, no matter who you were, without being screamed at. There were only so many bullets in the loaded guns around you that had a name other than your own engraved on their obsessively-polished shells. In a strange way, Pat had given him a gift.

"How have you been living with your Ascent?" asked Pat.

Charlie's mind spun like tumblers in a slot machine trying to line up profitable fruit. Sure, he missed his family and worried about them. Sure, he was angry that he was chosen to pay the price for his mother's mistake, his father's mistake. But, the paradox was that he was only able to tolerate his predicament by ignoring these gnawing preoccupations. Yet, he was expected to live with them on his sleeve; the theory being that this would eventually cause them to dissolve, thus freeing him to reach a greater potential. Charlie did not believe this. Instead, he believed that they lived and breathed with the independence they had earned. He believed they would die naturally someday as they were suffocated by new experiences, better times.

Charlie swallowed hard and said: "It's tough sometimes."

Ambiguity gained him time; now he had to pick a topic. He could cry forever about the loss of Papa Pete. He could cry tears of rage about his betrayal, his coward father somewhere in Canada who had sent his buddy, the Salt-and-Pepper Man, to appease his conscience. And, of course, there was always the coward's abusive replacement: Kurt.

Someday, as he had finally done in the Propheet, he might suddenly break down and let his "issues" have their way with him again. But since the Propheet had worn off, since Devon...

It was different now. Now, he often felt numb, fearing that he could not keep up the façade forever. The Academy might work for some, but he didn't think it was working for him. He would concede that he didn't know half of what was in store for him, but he was convinced--no matter what they said--that he wasn't defective. Being mistreated by others was not a defect, it was a deficiency. To cure it, he would need an infusion, not a bloodletting.

"Tell me something, Charlie," said Pat, "are you still trying to save your mother?"

Charlie knew this was the time to slowly assume the position. It was as common a sight as any at the school: the histrionic Rodin's Thinker, the famous sculpture's contemplative burden personified. Charlie leaned forward, planted an elbow on his knee and shielded his face with his hand. He was now "getting into his feelings" as expected. At least, that's what it would look like. He was really just staring at the pink light between the fingers of the palm that covered his eyes.

An absurdity filled his mind: If he failed to achieve an emotional breakthrough, Pat would be disappointed and would appear an ineffectual counselor. Charlie liked Pat and did not want to see him fail. Charlie closed his eyes and rummaged through his battened hollows, searching for a drop of moisture to wring from his phlegmatic eyes.

"You can't save your mother, Charlie," Pat continued. "It's not your job. You have to save yourself."

Charlie leaned further over his legs and spread his palm wide across his face. He knew he was supposed to accept what Pat was saying and confirm its validity with a groan, a gasp, something.

But, only one thought filled his mind: "Of course I will save my mother. I WILL save my mother. Who else is going to?"

He rocked slowly in his seat, with his face hidden, hoping the tears would come.

Nothing.

Charlie licked the middle of the palm that covered his face, and with the pretense of rubbing his eyes in agitation, smeared the spit across his cheeks. He bucked in his seat with a fraudulent sob.

Pat had asked to see him after the Rap and Charlie was a bundle of nerves. His performance had been gleaned from the successes of his predecessors and he had no reason to believe everybody had not swallowed it whole. The only thing more distasteful than faking progress was questioning if someone had faked progress. One would have to be damn sure.

Still, what business had Pat with him? Granted, he had not

scored the slam-dunk of a snot rope, the kind that wended its way to the carpet--there was no real way to fake such a thing. Although expectorating gallons of inner pain onto a pile of tissues had become almost fashionable, he doubted that it was yet compulsory. He hoped to God he would never have to live up to that standard.

No, he thought. It must be something else.

The group disassembled, taking their chairs with them to stack beneath the staircase by the coat closets. Some, were visibly relieved that they had not been annihilated this afternoon, and some were a tangle of emotion with their puffy eyes and tousled hair. They milled briefly, congratulating and condoling each other before eventually filing out of the room.

A thought occurred to Charlie: maybe he was moving up to Vision Family. Since graduation there had been a lot of advancement. That would mean working on the farm, finally off of Wood Shed. He dismissed the idea as quickly as it had come. He had only been on Wood Shed for a few weeks, hardly long enough. Realistically, he figured he had another month before he joined Vision. He continued speculating, his stomach fluttering.

He was alone in the room now and he kept to the corner, gazing out the window at the weird and alien sky. The sun had continued to win the battle against the encroaching pall from below. Charlie could not see flames in the canyon, and it seemed the smoke had thinned some. A bronze film lay over the horizon as the October sun slipped away, the trees in the deep shadowy valleys below nothing more than patches of black cut only by the thin, beige tendrils of distant access roads.

"Charlie," said Pat, "come on in."

Pat, whose head had been poking out of the office on the side of the Vision family room, waved a beckoning hand and tucked his head out of sight. Charlie crossed, and with a pounding heart peeked into the little room.

"Have a seat," Pat said.

There seemed to be nothing to fear in the man's voice and Charlie's nerves began to slowly unwind. If he had learned anything, he had learned that if a confrontation was impending with an adult they would always make you sweat before they hit you with the bombshell. They would never squander their power with charity. They would make it clear as crystal that you were in trouble, or that they were disappointed in you, long before they opened their mouths.

The office was a narrow room, with a window on one side and a built-in desk on the other. Pat fumbled with the guest chair, its legs entangled with his own, in a hospitable haste. Charlie was convinced that this was not about his Rap. If it had been, he would have been required to perform the clumsy task of untangling the legs of the chair himself.

Pat spoke: "Toby is down the hill this afternoon for a dental exam and he asked me to give you this."

Pat reached to the corner of the desk and grabbed a package. It was a cardboard box, a large cube, and one of its flaps had sprung up, loose from the clear packing tape. The box had clearly been previously opened and the flaps unsuccessfully pressed back into place with the original tape.

There was hardly a need to conceal the fact that the package had been opened; any package coming to a student at Ponderosa was pre-screened for contraband. Still, when Charlie saw his mother's scrawl on the packing label his smile was tugged down by the feeling of violation.

A crumpled piece of the San Jose Mercury News obscured the contents. A color circular for Pacific Stereo proclaimed a sale on cassette decks, and beneath that, a black-and-white picture of Ronald Reagan shaking some man's hand amidst blocks of news print proved to be the final sentry between Charlie and his surprise.

Charlie laughed.

He pulled out the object and held it up for Pat to see. It was a plush toy, a stuffed Tasmanian devil from the Loony Tunes cartoons.

"Taz!" Charlie exclaimed. "Cool."

The creature, burly in the middle and tapering to little legs, had a wide-open mouth and a lolling red tongue, its wild eyes fixed with a feral glaze. The tags still hung from the creatures' tiny ears and Charlie could see that his family had gotten the gift at Great America--the amusement park not far from their home. The park's star-spangled insignia on the tag evoked such a flood of sensation that Charlie's mouth actually dropped open as he pined for the roar of the coasters.

He turned the stuffed toy over in his hand, defending against a wash of brilliant memories that threatened to carry him off: red, white and blue ice cream cones; the smell of corn dogs; the carousel, flanked by a reflecting pool, belting out a calliope tune as the brightly painted horses undulated beneath its Victorian dome; the always-wet seats of the log ride and the turquoise fiberglass of its flumes; the necklaces sold by the barkers at night, that with one crack of their plastic tubing, glowed firefly green; running with his friends from ride to ride through that whooshing night, consumed in its electric fantasy.

He clutched the stuffed character to his chest and shot Pat a distant look.

"You okay?" asked Pat.

"Yeah," replied Charlie, softly. "It was always my favorite character. My mom and I used to watch Loony Tunes on Saturday mornings when I was a kid. I used to imitate him."

Charlie held up the toy."You know? Slobbering and growling and spinning in circles and stuff." His voice trailed off.

Pat did a brief and respectable imitation of the rabid beast, wiggling his fingers at his sides. Charlie laughed in spite of himself, but his smile soon slid from his face, leaving a bittersweet stain where it had been.

"I think there's a note," said Pat, sensing the mix of feelings and trying to save the moment.

Charlie fished into the box and produced a note in his mother's handwriting:

Dear Charlie,

I hope you like this. We're thinking of you and we're proud of you. Keep up the good work. Can't wait to see you next month for your visit!

Lots of Love,
Mom, Kurt, Brandon and Bowser

P.S. Bowser actually ate Brandon's homework because it had cinnamon roll icing on it! Haha! Can you believe that dog?

Charlie was now late for art class and still conflicted from the receipt of the package. The Tasmanian Devil hung from his limp arm as he walked through the lodge with his head down, still walking the tightrope. He could feel himself wobbling--threatening to fall into an abyss that would take far too much energy to climb out of. A package from home was an emotional earthquake and there was nothing left to do but to clean up his once organized feelings and hope they would fit back into their tombs.

Of all these emotions, the shattered denial was the hardest to mend. He had been graced with periods of acceptance and he had been grateful for them. Now, however, he had been reminded of his distance from home, from all he championed and loved. There was no denying that the world outside still existed without him. His family had gone to Great America and had bought him a stuffed animal.

Out of guilt, he thought.

He fought the cynicism, and instead, held on to gratitude for the toy that linked him, if only briefly, to home. He figured if he could just get to art class he would make something out of his mixed-up feelings. He glanced up as he walked through the lodge.

The lodge was deserted. Students had already headed for their afternoon class. It was rare to be in the lodge during classes and it was strange to see the Floor so empty, dark and lifeless.

Then, he heard a sound, a quiet moan. His stride broke. Someone was on the Floor after all. He looked around. The moan came again.

He spotted Jonas Portman on a darkened section of floor on the far side of The Pit, supine on a couch cushion. There was someone lying beside him, almost atop him. The other had blonde hair.

It was Carolina Eversol.

The two were smushing, alone, in the quiet gloom. Charlie averted his eyes and kept walking. He figured Carolina must have had a tough Rap. It was not uncommon to see staff conducting one-on-one therapy sessions whenever and wherever they needed to take place. In fact, someone was always being pulled aside to dump in private, or to work through something that could not be put to rest in the day's Rap.

Poor Carolina, thought Charlie, and he wished he could help her, soothe her pain. He wondered what had gotten to her, why she had broken down and why Jonas Portman had seen to her personally. Charlie hadn't seen Jonas on campus all day.

It must be important, Charlie thought.

He stole another glance at the pair as he walked. Jonas was kissing the side of her face. She had her eyes closed. One of Jonas' legs--like sausages ready to burst from their casings--was entwined with one of hers. He nuzzled her neck. Charlie could hear a slurping sound as Jonas kissed her ear.

Charlie looked away. He banished the scene from his mind, dismissing it as another misunderstanding. After all, public affection was a daily occurrence; it was required to show openness and support the ideal of a society that literally embraced one another.

Yet, he knew what he had seen was different, very different. The insistent questions posed themselves over and over as if the clear answers could somehow be altered by desperate repetition: What's going on? What were they doing? What's going on?

Charlie lowered his head, quickened his pace, and threw his body into the wooden door. The warmth of the late afternoon sun hit his face. He gulped for air. He didn't realize he had been holding his breath.

Chapter 26

Late October was unexpectedly fierce. The wind blew the piled leaves that lined the path, scattering them in a thick mosaic before the rakes of the Wood Shed crew. Each fist-sized stone that bordered the trail to the ropes course had to be moved and replaced to rid the way of leaves. Once their rakes had finally striped the path with decorative lines, the students watched more leaves shower before them and the process was repeated.

Before they had graduated, Evolution had built a ropes course at the far edge of the Leach Fields, and a new trail, just above the intersection of the Microwave Road and the Dorm Trail, had been cleared to access the new feature of the campus. At first, Genesis had been excited about their project of blazing the access trail. That was, of course, before the winds had kicked up. The Ropes Course Trail was to debut tomorrow, but currently, it was looking nothing like a footpath.

"Oh, come on," pleaded Jonathan as a gust of wind obscured his rake with a wad of crunchy leaves. "This looks terrible."

Charlie, working on a rise just above Jonathan, was cursing into the sky. "AHHH! Go to hell, wind! You're NOT HELPING!"

Sharon, working further down the trail, her section of path flanked by sheltering boulders, only laughed.

"Hey, Charlie," she yelled up the hill, "you tell the wind who's boss!"

"You try working up here," Charlie shouted back. "It's like a freakin' tornado! It's like COLD HELL!" He raked with exaggerated fury, gritting his teeth.

It was only after Genesis had been honored with the task of blazing the Ropes Course Trail were they informed that only Quest students and above would be allowed to use it. As a result, the labor was now tinged with bitterness and remorse. It would be a long time before Genesis could ride on the zip line or walk the suspended rope bridges. The ropes course was to be a training ground for Quest, preparing them for Wilderness Trek. Knowledge of how to tie webbing, sit-harnesses, and knots was required to safely use the course, and that knowledge would not be imparted until they had lived to fight another six months.

Morale had suffered with the news, but most of Genesis was just happy to be away from the monotony of producing stores of firewood. All would agree, however, that the work--no matter what it was to be--was to always be backbreaking, repetitive, and fraught with challenge. Not only a physical challenge, but one of attitude; how long could one maintain a positive outlook? How long could one ignore the rebellious voice within that demanded justice, demanded respect as they ached without reward?

"What's going on, Charlie?" Toby Heiser asked, walking into view from between two coulter pines. He looked up the trail at the kid whose blonde fringe of bangs tossed wildly on his forehead with the gusts like a dancing pile of hay.

Charlie continued to rake and said nothing,

"Knock off the screaming," said Toby, "and knock off the negativity. No one needs that. Suck it up. If you think this is bad, wait until it snows."

Then, Toby turned to the rest of the crew, who being spread far along the route and deafened by wind, had to relay any message. They were to put away their tools. Due to bad weather, they were being allowed to quit early--fifteen minutes early.

Charlie was in a bad mood as he loped into the Lodge. He was looking forward to his home call, but the work crew had drained him of an ability to appreciate anything. All he could feel was his numb bones and his hot ears. His lips were chapped. He went up the library stairs and knocked on the door of the Medical Office. He told the townie nurse of his problems and she gave him a jar of lip balm. He descended the stairs, flopped on a couch in the Genesis family room, jabbed a finger into the jar of waxy gel, and coated his lips.

Toby soon arrived, unlocking the office door. The man seemed to have forgotten about his admonition on the work crew; he seemed to not notice any tension between them and even deigned to whistle a tune as he took his seat.

Charlie had admittedly lost his cool on the trail, but being pulled up by Toby in front of the crew had humiliated him, only compounding the vexation that was still clinging to him with a steal grip. And of course, he had his next Rap to look forward to. He had all but offered everyone his head on a platter.

Toby produced the tabletop timer from the drawer of the desk and fumbled with an address book. Charlie knew he needed to thaw from his pout, but it felt like swimming against a current. He was about to talk to his family and he was in a dangerous mood. He was not the green and broken kid with the darting eyes that had sat in this very office before, ready to embrace whatever conditions were set forth if it meant a few precious words from his family. Today he felt that his caution had been blown into the hills with the unforgiving wind, leaving his heart pounding the prelude to an insurrection. He breathed deeply. Toby dialed the phone.

Home, Charlie thought. I'm calling home. Easy now. Just relax. Make the most of this. It doesn't happen often.

Toby leaned back in his office chair with the receiver, waiting for an answer.

"Sara?" said Toby. "Toby Heiser, Ponderosa Academy. I have Charlie here."

Toby handed Charlie the phone and twisted the dial on the plastic timer.

"Mom," said Charlie.

"Hi, honey," she said. "How you doing?"

"Okay, I guess."

"What's wrong?"

"I had a hard work crew. It kinda sucked. Well...it sucked a lot."

"What kind of work crew?"

"It doesn't matter," said Charlie.

"They're not working you too hard, are they?" his mother asked.

"Yes. Of course," replied Charlie. His eyes grazed over Toby and it seemed the family head was none the wiser. He was only hearing once side of the conversation. There was an uncomfortable silence on the phone.

"I'm sorry, honey," came his mother's voice. "Are you learning anything? Are you having some fun?"

"Not exactly," replied Charlie. "Doesn't matter, does it?"

He was laying it on thick. He was being cruel. It wasn't in him to keep it up for long though; he just wasn't that ruthless. His mother was starting to sound sad. If his time ran out, and she was left that way, Charlie knew he would be a useless puddle of regret.

He fought the pang of indignation that was rising from his depths like lava: Why was it okay for him to be miserable but horrifying for her to be? Why did he feel compelled to coddle her when it was her duty to sacrifice for him? Was she sacrificing anything? As much as he felt he was?

Her denial seemed to protect her, giving her an odd innocence. She could never truly stare down the impurities that had befouled their little family and Charlie could not bring himself to make her do so. He could not shatter her because he feared she might be nothing beneath but a fragile husk.

He thought of the Ascent Propheet and Mary Portman's words: Who is looking out for you?

He feared he might start to hate her, hate her for her weaknesses. The idea was unfathomable, but he knew it was possible and that was the real horror of it all.

His mother laughed faintly and nervously into the phone, "Well, I'm sure it will get easier. Things are always hard at first, but you're strong Charlie. You always have been."

Thank God for that, Charlie thought, but he didn't know the limits of his strength and he didn't feel much like testing them anymore.

His mother's voice was melting his layers of calluses. He knew it would. He could not decide whether this was a mercy or not. Often, her soothing served no purpose other than to defer his concerns, pushing them into recesses where they would eventually fester and grow even more confusing. Either way, her voice was his sustenance, and he closed his eyes to savor its familiar sweetness.

She was a victim too. Being angry with her for being a victim seemed inhumane. Blaming her for her weaknesses would only make her suffer the tortures of facing her unwitting dereliction. Charlie doubted she was powerful enough to withstand such unforgiving reality, the way he was now made to. It was the absence of intention that had always exempted her from ever really being hated by him.

Contrary to the advice of the counselors at The Academy, he was about to save her again, to again pull her from the wreckage of the plane that she had clumsily flown into a mountain- and a very remote mountain at that.

"So, what's going on around there?" asked Charlie, casually. His mother seemed grateful for the change of tone.

"Well," she replied, "where do I start? Let's see...work is getting really crazy."

"How so?" asked Charlie. His memories flashed to the Knight Ridder building in San Jose where his mother worked. He had gone to her office after school a few times. It was a news organization, that was all he knew, and the last he had heard, his mother had become the assistant to one of the Vice Presidents.

"Do you remember me telling you about Viewtron?" she asked.

"Yeah, kinda."

"We were working on it at the end of '82 and we're going to launch it at the end of the month. Users will be able to share and access information from special terminals with graphic interfaces. The Miami Herald and the Associated Press are on board, sharing news that will be accessible to anyone who has a Viewtron terminal. You will also be able to get airline schedules and do your banking from the computer terminal. Neat huh? Wouldn't it be cool to have information come to your computer from other places? If Viewtron catches on, it could be a big deal."

"Sounds cool," said Charlie.

"What else," his mother clicked her tongue. "Kurt is foreman on a new high-rise project in downtown San Jose. It's only a skeleton right now, but it's going to be a mixed-use building with storefronts on the bottom and condos on the higher floors. He's happy to have the work. Oh! And we also wrapped up Papa Pete's estate. And guess what? We are working with a real estate agent to find a house, a big house, Charlie."

"Really? Where?"

"We don't know, but we're thinking of somewhere on the Peninsula...maybe Palo Alto or Menlo Park or something. I always wanted to live there."

"Not the City?"

"Do you want to live in the City again?"

Charlie thought for a moment, "Not really, I guess."

"No swimming pools up there," said his mother. "Plus, it's getting so expensive."

"So when do you think we'll move?" asked Charlie

"As soon as we fall in love with something," she said.

Charlie's feeling of separation and loss had always ached dully behind whatever flimsy comportment he had devised. It was like a young scab covering some festering wound that he had to avoid picking at, with preoccupying forbearance, so that it could heal. Now, it began to throb. First they were traipsing off to Great America without him, now they were house shopping, uprooting his life again before he had even returned. He was losing his grip on his mood. He breathed deep, steeling himself.

"Thanks for Taz," said Charlie. "I love it."

"I thought you would get a kick out of that," said his mother. "I'll always remember my little Tasmanian Devil."

Charlie blushed and blew a laugh through his nose.

"He sleeps on my bed," said Charlie. They laughed softly, sighed contemplatively and fell into silence.

Charlie said, "Mom, I don't have tons of time. I guess I better talk to Brando before the bell goes off."

His mother said nothing.

"Mom?" Charlie repeated. "I better talk to Brandon. I'm afraid I'll run out of time."

"He's...um..." she trailed off, cleared her throat and started again. "He's not feeling good."

"Is he sleeping?" asked Charlie. "He's faking it; he just doesn't want to go to school. Just wake him up. He's just laying there with his eyes closed anyway, I betcha."

"He's...he can't," said his mother. "He's not here."

"What do you mean he's not there?" asked Charlie, suspiciously. "You just said he was sick."

"He's not sick," said his mother. "He hurt himself. He got hurt. It's not a big deal."

"What? Where is he?" Charlie asked with blooming alarm. "I want to talk to him."

"He had to go to the hospital," she said.

"The hospital!" Charlie cried. "What happened?"

Toby began to watch Charlie and Charlie hunched over and away from Toby, cradling the receiver possessively.

Charlie spoke quietly: "What's going on, mom? Tell me, please. What happened?"

"He's fine Charlie, really. Just a bump on the head."

"How did it happen?"

"Well..." his mother began. Her voice was faint. "You

know...just...an accident."

Charlie's stomach flooded with acid. His limbs went cold as sudden realization grabbed hold of his lungs and squeezed. Brandon had not fallen from his bike. He hadn't been hit by a car, or by a baseball or by a bully at school. No, none of that.

She was faltering. She had no story, and if she had one prepared, it had stuck in her throat. He knew his mother better than anyone. She was lying.

The spit glands in his mouth constricted and a pasty, electrical bitterness coated his mouth. It was the taste of hate. His trembling and cracked lips worked to form the word.

"Kurt..." he hissed.

"Charlie, "his mother's voice shook, "Charlie, now just listen..."

"What did he do to him?"

"Brandon is going to be just fine," said his mother, but her voice still shook and the consolation sounded more like a desperate prayer.

"What did he do to him, mom?" Charlie cried. The pulse of the timer on Toby's desk weakened and the bell clanged. Toby's hand landed softly on Charlie's hunched shoulders.

"Charlie," said Toby, "take it easy."

Charlie was now hyperventilating, the phone pressed to his ear with both hands.

"Try and wrap it up," said Toby. He gingerly placed a hand on the receiver. Charlie twisted in his chair and wrenched it away.

"WHAT DID HE DO TO HIM MOM?"

"Just...a mild concussion," Sara replied, her voice small, "and his arm...it...wasn't on purpose. Please, Charlie...it was an accident."

"IT WASN'T A FUCKING ACCIDENT, MOM!" Charlie screamed, "AND YOU KNOW IT!"

Toby tried for the receiver again. Charlie absently jerked away.

"THAT PIECE OF SHIT!" Charlie screamed. The line went dead. "FUCK!"

Charlie spun around. Toby stood at the edge of his desk, his finger pressing down on the phone's cradle.

Chapter 27

Mary Portman, sat on the other side of Charlie, opposite Toby, on the couch overlooking the Quad. They rubbed Charlie's back, they offered assurances and promises to gather details for him. They vowed he would be kept up to date with any new information on his brother's condition. Charlie sat hunched and stared at the floor with unblinking eyes, the condolences sounding like white noise.

He didn't know how long he sat, unresponsive and rigid, as they continued to talk soothingly at each ear. They said they understood how he must be feeling. They said they knew it must be hard. Charlie figured they were waiting for some confirmation, a sign that he was all right and moving past the news to some resolution. He was not all right, however, not all right at all.

He finally determined that he would be free to go far more quickly if he simply nodded in acknowledgement of their words, whatever they might have been, and hope that he would begin to appear healed. He had to be rid of their platitudes. He had to get out of this room.

They asked again if he was all right. He croaked an affirmation. They asked if he was sure. He had not cried, nor had he broken down, and he knew they were suspicious. He reassured them. They asked if he was ready to join the rest of Genesis in the Muir Hut for Experientials, and stated that they were of the opinion doing so would help him take his mind off of what he could not control. He told them that it sounded like a good idea. They promised again to provide him with more details about his brother. He thanked them tightly, and then with excruciating effort he lit his face with what felt like his last smile. They were satisfied and they demanded a hug. He gave them one.

❖

The Muir Hut was in uncharacteristic disarray. The preparations for the impending Wilderness Trek overran the far side of the craft room with an overflow of random supplies. Coils of candy-striped climbing rope and a large cardboard box of tin mess equipment and Coleman stoves had been shoved into the far corner of the room. A bulky North Face frame pack leaned against the section of wall and beside the door to the back room. The door was ajar and the lion's share of supplies was littered within, beneath a fluorescent panel light.

"Sorry about the mess," said Jenny Curtis, the townie craft teacher, tucking a strand of long brunette hair behind her ear and staring irresolutely at the clutter. "Michael DiFranco is working in here today with some members of Quest," she continued, a fingertip in her mouth.

She was clearly flustered by having to share her craft room with the encroaching mess. She looked up and saw Charlie at the door with Toby Heiser.

Charlie entered the room and integrated warily into his peers beside one of the craft tables, being careful to not betray how he felt. He didn't want any more sympathy and he certainly didn't want to be put under any extra observation, not now.

Jenny Curtis talked privately at the threshold with Toby, both of them occasionally regarding Charlie with solemn, circumspect glances and barely perceptible nods while feigning nonchalance. Charlie figured they were talking about his need for special attention, about how his behavior might be unstable. Jenny, in spite of her attempts at discretion, seemed uneasy with her added responsibility. Toby left the doorway, walked past the windows of the Muir Hut and passed out of sight.

"Okay," said Jenny, repairing to the comfort of her station at the head of one of the craft tables, "today we are going to collect supplies for our annual Christmas wreaths. Every year we make wreaths for the town of Bear Creek. Now, I know it's only October and we haven't even had Halloween yet, but the wreaths are delivered just before Thanksgiving, which will be here before you know it."

Jonathan sidled up to Charlie: "You look like shit. Are you alright?"

Charlie looked at Jonathan, his chapped lips pressed into a thin line. He couldn't find the words at first. Then, he said: "Not really,"

Jonathan recoiled at the sight of his friend, and the perpetual twinkle in his eyes extinguished. After heaving a sigh, he whispered: "Whatever it is, I'm here for you. Just know that okay?" and he squeezed Charlie's arm.

For the first time since the call, Charlie felt on the verge of tears. Jonathan's touch had thrown a light on a great irony: that he was surrounded by people that meant well, but alone in the world. No one could help him. He was beginning to realize that they never could. What he needed he had to give himself.

He began to mourn the loss of hope, not from weakness, but as if out of respect for the passing of an invaluable friend, a friend he had leaned on many times. Hope was not going to be good enough this time.

He blew a bracing puff of air from his mouth. Tears did not come. He swallowed hard and set his jaw. He thought he hadn't been listening, but the echo of something Mary Portman had cooed into his ear in the Genesis family room earlier came back to him: "Everything will work itself out," she had said.

She was right, but not in the way she thought. Things would indeed "work out". They would work out just fine. He knew it because he would see that it did.

Soon.

Jenny Curtis went on: "The wreaths are going to hang on the light posts in the town square, and the biggest one will be the backdrop to the Christmas Pageant at the town hall. This year, we are going to try something new and something that we can start earlier than the wreaths--a pinecone tree."

She held up a sketch: "We have so many different kinds of beautiful pinecones up here. As you can see, the bottom of the tree will be the larger coulter pinecones and then ponderosas and sugar pinecones closer to the top. Today we need to collect as many pinecones of all kinds as we can find and put them in these trash cans."

She tossed a gesture at a pair of rubber bins in the corner of the room. "So, everyone take one of the burlap bags and fill them up. Choose only the cones with the best shapes, the ones that are undamaged. We will meet back here in an hour,"

❖

Charlie wandered aimlessly with his empty burlap bag dragging the ground. Just as he had suspected, Jenny Curtis had pulled him aside to see if he was okay. Her nervous concerns were quashed with a few appeasing words from Charlie. Jenny, with the disappointment of a nurturer deprived of intervening, had finally set him free.

Jonathan too had offered his help again, suggesting that they hunt for pinecones together, but Charlie declined. He told his friend he needed some time and that he wouldn't be much company. Jonathan had reluctantly peeled away, ducking into a copse of trees beside the parking lot where a cluster of pinecones sat on a downy bed of needles, reinstating his offer over his shoulder in case Charlie were to change his mind.

Charlie walked up the Microwave Road and was just at the Dorm Trail intersection when Carolina Eversole came up behind him. "Charlie! Wait up!"

He turned.

"I'll hunt with you," she said. "You look like you need some company."

"I need to think," he replied tersely. "Thanks, anyway."

"What do you need to think about?"

"It's a long story."

"Any story worth hearing is long."

"I'm not in a very good space right now."

"You were late to the Muir Hut," she said. "Did you get chewed out about something?"

It was clear that she was not going to leave him alone. He stopped trudging up the hill and shot her a glance that he intended to load with inflexibility, but he had a feeling it came off as just huffy. She smiled sweetly at him, grabbed his forearm and tugged on it gently before releasing it and going on ahead.

"Let's go," she said. "You can tell me later. Follow me. I know where the good pinecone stashes are."

Carolina passed the dorm trail and continued up the Microwave Road where it became much steeper as it led up to the ridge. As Carolina leaned into the grade her well-toned buttocks flexed and pumped like pistons through her jeans. Charlie was entranced. He had no intention of following, but his legs began to move and soon he was climbing the hill as her silent shadow.

She gestured at the head of the Ropes Course Trail, not bothering to look behind her to see if Charlie was following.

"I think we're sick of that trail for a while," she said, and then she pointed to the other side of the road. "Let's go this way. Oh, look! There's a widow maker."

She stooped, panting, and grabbed a golden cone that had been shed by the coulter pine towering above them. The cone was nestled at the bottom of the hillock leading into the dark woods. Carolina held it aloft; it was as big as her head. She eased it into her sack.

Soon the two of them reached the top of the Microwave Road. The ridge stretched before them. Far to the right and above them on a rise was the County's microwave tower. Several large boulders were scattered along the cliff. A short field of rocky soil separated the two hunters and the drop to the valley below. Carolina approached one of the shorter, granite boulders and scaled its slight incline with two quick pumps of her legs and stood looking over the valley. She looked down at the boulder known as The Couch. The rock had been etched by time into a natural sofa-shaped promontory jutting from the cliff six feet below.

"There's a monster pinecone right there," she pointed down towards the area of The Couch. "Grab it."

Charlie walked to the foot of the boulder, rounded it, and descended three natural steps to where The Couch jutted out into thin air. Then, he sat on the wide rock with a doleful sigh. Carolina soon quit her lookout, rounded the boulder and joined him.

"What happened?" she asked. "You let the pinecone get away."

The comment tickled Charlie and he cracked a smile, surprised that he still could. He looked at her and her face was patient and kind, her eyes the color of the sky. He was grateful that she was here. Her proximity seemed to be slowly refueling him. They leaned their backs against the cool, rough granite, their legs dangling from the stone seat. They were silent for a while. Then he told her about the call, about Brandon and about what Kurt had done.

"I want to kill him," he said simply.

She grabbed his hand. He was happy she had not cautioned him for his rage, and instead, chose to simply understand it. They looked across the valley. The sun had shed the veil of smoke from yesterday's canyon fire and its mild warmth bathed their upturned faces. Stratus clouds stretched like batting across the sky. The windstorm was a memory and only a slight breeze sent tremors through the leaves of the scrub oak on the slope below them.

"The sun looked so sick yesterday," said Carolina. "It looked like it was going to blink out, like a candle flame or something. It was all that smoke. I guess the fire is out."

"Sometimes I have nightmares," said Charlie distantly. "I had a nightmare that my brother was...that he was...hurt."

"I'm sorry..." Carolina said softly and squeezed his hand.

Charlie went on, "If the fire had swallowed up the sun yesterday I wouldn't have been surprised. It's chaos. Everything feels like chaos sometimes. My grandfather used to tell me that the sun is a ball of chaos. I mean, if you saw it up close you would see that. He spent his whole life thinking about the sun, figuring out ways to...control that chaos. He thought that its power wasn't being used like it should. It is right there in front of us, the most awesome force we could imagine, and all we do is take it for granted or ignore it. For some reason, we never use the power that was given to us."

"He was the inventor, right?" asked Carolina. "Your grandfather? You were close, I remember. He was like your father."

"Yeah," Charlie trailed off. He clenched his jaw against his welling eyes.

"You look so sad," said Carolina, and with a fingertip, wiped a single tear from his cheek. Charlie turned to her.

"I feel like the sun was swallowed up anyway," he said softly. "My brother is hurt. He's in danger. It feels dark. It feels dark inside."

She met his look and consoled him with a whisper. She brushed his hair back from his forehead. Another tear escaped from his leaking eyes. Carolina hushed him and grabbed his face in her hands, wiping away the tear.

"I feel powerless," he said, "like the way the sun looked yesterday--like it couldn't burn through the darkness."

Carolina, with her hands still at the sides of his head, pulled him close and rocked him. "You love him, I know...it's okay."

She pulled back from their embrace. They looked into each other's eyes. Charlie mumbled softly, something about satellites falling from the sky. She kissed his mouth.

His breath caught in his throat. It was his first kiss and his eyes widened with the new sensation, the enfolding and healing warmth. He seemed to levitate for a moment, the cold stone disappearing from beneath him, drawing closer to heaven. Their lips parted. He looked at her with amazement, with gratitude. He smiled.

"UNACCEPTABLE!"   a   voice   shouted   from   above. "UNACCEPTABLE!"

Charlie whipped his head around and then up the granite wall at his back.

Smitty stood above them at the top of the boulder, an accusatory finger stabbing the air.

"That's unacceptable!" cried the boy. He dropped his finger to his side, turned and disappeared from view.

Chapter 28

"Smitty!" Charlie cried, springing to his feet. "Wait!"

Rounding the boulder he saw Smitty's head vanish as the boy descended the Microwave Road. Charlie ran across the clearing to where the road began and saw the boy, framed by tall pines, walking determinedly down the center of the road, a bulging bag of pinecones at his hip.

Charlie was going to call after him again, but his mouth only opened in a silent gape. His heart was pounding like a jackhammer.

"Shit," he hissed through his teeth. "Shit!"

He turned and looked back across the clearing. Carolina was scrambling up from The Couch. They met in the barren, rocky field and stared at one another with wide eyes.

"I'm sorry," she said miserably. "I..."

"Don't," he said, catching his breath. "Don't be sorry about anything. Please. Look, we have to split up, okay?"

"Yes," she said. She hung her head. Charlie looked around them at the empty forest.

"Carolina," said Charlie. She looked up and he kissed her. They stared into each other's eyes for a long moment and then Charlie turned and ran down the hill.

His mind raced as he came to a halt at the confluence of paths. To his left the dorms, to his right the Quad and the lodge, and ahead the parking lot and the path to the Administration building and the Muir Hut. In twenty minutes he would be expected back in the craft room with pinecones. He had left his empty bag at The Couch.

From his vantage, he spotted Smitty and watched him with narrowed eyes. The oversized lout of a boy was walking across the Quad to the lodge.

The Rap Request Box, Charlie thought, son of a bitch. He's wasting no time.

It was Tuesday, the next rap was tomorrow at 3:00 P.M. and it was 3:30 now. That meant that in less than twenty-four hours he would be neck deep in shit. He could bet on it. A pervasive buzz would drone through the logs of the lodge and through the clapboards of the dorms. This time, the whisper of the pines would be polluted with murmurings of crime and punishment, sex and the disgrace of two of their own. The talk would spread like a wildfire, fueled by the unimpeachable testimony of Smitty who, it would be agreed, had no reason to lie, his allegiance to The Academy considered to be nothing short of devout, exasperatingly so.

Soon after, the two dirty ones would be stripped of all remaining freedoms and privileges; they would be given the mandatory sentence: Full Time.

Charlie doubted that Smitty would talk before tomorrow's Rap. After all, the offense hadn't been a violent episode or an act that threatened property or the safety of others. It would be considered a witnessed "sex contract" and it was one of the rare bombshells that could be kept in the accuser's back pocket for a short time without facing charges of collusion or negligence through silence.

Even Smitty, as slow as he was, understood the advantage of busting someone else's dirt with a flourish and this one would be a jaw dropper. No, Smitty would save it and, with the unctuousness of an exorcist, would dominate the next Rap with the details of Charlie and Carolina's forbidden lust. He would go on, at full scream, about how the actions he had witnessed had so shocked him and profaned the environment they had all worked so hard to create.

It was a grand slam of an indictment and an extremely rare one. So called "sex contracts" were almost never witnessed because they were almost always premeditated with extreme steps taken to ensure secrecy. Usually, once suspicion had grown to a fever pitch, one of the two would-be lovers would crack under pressure in a Propheet or during a particularly arduous Rap and sell out the other if enticed with the promise of leniency. But, an eyewitness account from a "look-good"? That was a sturdy nail in his coffin lid that no amount of wiggling was going to pry out.

In 24 hours Charlie knew he would be forced into a solitary existence at a table on the middle level, his every move watched, worked until his limbs were numb and put on Bans from his peers. No one would be allowed to acknowledge his existence.

He would sit in Devon Child's space.

He knew now that he'd wallowed in his fear and misery for too long. It had been a luxury. Soon he would know what powerlessness was really like. Soon, he would be even more useless to his brother, and probably deprived of   information about his condition. His plans to petition for a follow-up phone call to the hospital would be denied on the grounds that calling home was a privilege he had now forfeited.

He was in deep. He didn't think it was possible to be cut off from his old life any more than he had been. How wrong he was. It was going to get much worse.

His mind reeled as he walked. What could he do? How would he do it? If he could get home, well, then what? Could he kill Kurt? Could he beat him with his own beer bottle while he was passed out? Could he do such a thing? Is that what it was going to take?

Suddenly, his mind sputtered curses at his mother for designing such a horrible situation. Would he be able to forgive her someday? He didn't know. What he did know was that being tethered to this mountain was enraging him and the cruelty of being spoon-fed information on his family while he struggled to avoid hair-triggered reprimands was insufferable now. He had to leave. He had to do what his heart insisted, what every nerve in his body, frothing and chafing like wild horses, demanded.

His feet carried him across the access road below the dorm trail, avoiding the Quad where a few of his peers milled with their bulging sacks. His mind whirred like a turbine and beat on the inside of his skull. His vision tunneled. He yanked open the door to the lodge and marched into the main room.

He halted at the threshold to The Floor. The lodge was empty. Smitty wasn't there. Nobody was in sight. He glanced up at the library balcony. No one was there either. He knew that the staff offices off of the main room were probably teeming with counselors and that they could appear at any moment. He didn't know why he had come into the lodge; it was stifling and dark and the last thing he wanted was to be questioned. With haste, he crossed the room to the scale replica of the lodge.

The Rap Request Box was locked as always. He stared at the slit across its peaked slate roof. He could hear nothing but his breath chugging from his nose. He turned around to leave.

A ray of sun was streaming through the lodge's only skylight and its light splashed on the stone chimney in The Pit, directly on the witch stone. Charlie's eyes fixed on the crooked finger that protruded from the witch's rocky sleeve. He followed it to the floor of The Pit. His mouth fell open.

"Meyer's ghost," he whispered with a thick tongue.

The heart-shaped stone on the floor of The Pit was just visible beneath the heavy coffee table. He looked back up at the glowing witch. Her garments seemed to billow as the light rippled with the passing clouds through the skylight.

His eyes widened. A girl from the Upper School was crossing the Floor. She mounted the library stairs. Charlie crouched, his palm falling flatly on the cool heart stone. The girl had either not seen him or had not cared.

Get going, he thought.

He left The Pit, passed the stack of chairs beneath the staircase to the New Wing, and slammed against the door to the outside. The Quad was filling with Genesis students comparing their finds.

Smitty was there. The boy had his back to Charlie and he was holding up a pinecone, like the skull from that Shakespeare play, to Kenny Bootman who nodded with an impressed smile.

Charlie couldn't face them yet, he needed to think. He wished he could talk to Jonathan, but he couldn't. It would be too much to put on anyone, especially since just mentioning his intention to leave would force Jonathan to either betray him or become implicated in a split contract.

Perhaps Carolina would leave with him. If anyone could be trusted it was her. After all, her head was going to roll tomorrow as well. There was a big problem though: she didn't want to leave. Charlie had never forgotten what she had said that night, when they had told their stories, because it had seemed so alien a concept: "I don't want to go home.".

He flashed on Jonas and Carolina in the dark. Rage blew through him like hot wind. Jonas would have her. She was lost to him. He could not force her to choose between leaving the school and a home life she considered worse, a life that she feared more than anything. He would lose that decision and that would wound his heart, and wound hers as well.

Being careful to not be spotted, he quickly skirted the front of the lodge and went to the back of the building where the great log edifice leaned out over the rim of the canyon, supported by large pillars. He needed a few minutes to calm down before rejoining the group. He could let nothing betray his intentions. He had to remind himself that if Smitty kept his mouth shut like he thought he would, he would have enough time to figure out what he was going to do. But, he was confused, his mind choking as if it was slipping out of gear, unable to fire its cylinders.

How to leave? When to leave? Maybe tonight. No, not in the dark. Maybe tomorrow? No, the schedule was tight and the roll calls frequent; there would be no time to put distance between him and his pursuers.

He looked down at the thickets of manzanita bushes that stretched across the ridge like barbed wire. The bare branches, bleached by the relentless sun of the recent summer, intertwined like skeletal fingers. He scooted down the hill a few yards on the side of his shoes and grabbed at one of the bush's bone-white branches. It snapped loose with a loud crack leaving a jagged edge. He hurled the branch into the canyon and it disappeared from sight.

Not that way, he thought with a shudder. I'm definitely not going that way.

He would think about how later. Now, he had to figure out when. He wanted to march away now, but he knew that would be useless. There had to be a gap in the schedule long enough to allow him a head start.

He calculated quickly: After Experientials there was dorm time and then an hour allotted for chow. The clocks had already fallen back an hour and darkness would come early, around dinner. Then, Floor Time would officially begin around 7:00. House Around The Pit would be called for Last Light at 9:00. He would be expected in the dorm no later than 9:30 before Shawn started asking questions, and shortly after that the alert would go out. That gave him three-and-a-half hours from the start of dinner, by far the longest stretch in the schedule where he could slip away.

He considered the middle of the night, but dismissed the idea immediately; it was too risky. He couldn't walk around anywhere in the middle of the night without being stopped, nothing would be open and there would be fewer opportunities for hitchhiking. It had to be after dinner.

He would have to miss dinner. He would not get away with sitting alone in the dining room without being intercepted.

Although he was sure that no one except Smitty knew about the kiss, everyone would know about his concern for his brother by now and he would be watched by staff. Worse, his fellow students would find it irresistible to exploit his condition, exercising their amateur psychology skills. His responses would have to be forthcoming and convincing and it would go on all night. If he entered the dining room at all, he would lose time, a lot of it.

Somewhere beneath the sour swill in his stomach he knew the stress and emotion were consuming his energy and that he was probably very hungry. He had to bring something just in case. He thought briefly of sneaking into the kitchen.

No, not when the kitchen staff was in the throes of prepping dinner. The place would be crawling with townies. Maybe he could slip into the walk-in refrigerator unnoticed if he used the delivery entrance and grab some carob chips or some other ready-to-eat food. That would give him energy if he had to survive in the woods.

Surviving in the woods?

His mouth fell open, an idea flaring through his mind.

"The gorp," he whispered.

The Wilderness Trek food was somewhere on campus. Austin had said they were packing the trail mix this week. Maybe it was already packed and locked away, but maybe it wasn't. Most of the WT gear was in the Muir Hut right now. He hadn't seen gorp, but it could be in there, maybe already in the packs or stacked on a shelf in the back room. In fact, he could take a lot of the supplies and maybe...

He had to get back.

He had been gone too long. He stood and wiped the dirt from the seat of his pants. Appearing casual seemed impossible, but it had to be done if he was going to have a shot at his plan. He walked around to the front of the lodge, crossed the lawn, and entered the Muir Hut.

There was playful commotion in the craft room. Everyone was unloading their pinecones and gasping at the biggest examples. His entrance was hardly noticed. That is, except for Smitty. The boy glowered at Charlie, his bottom lip protruding like a moist slug. If there was ever the slightest doubt that Smitty was going to sing in tomorrow's Rap, it was now erased.

"Charlie."

He jumped. It was Jenny Curtis' hand that landed on his shoulder.

"You didn't find anything?" she asked.

"I have a lot on my mind," Charlie said flatly, he looked at Smitty again, but the boy had turned his back.

"I know," she said. "It's okay. I'll see you on Thursday. I hope you feel better."

"Thanks," said Charlie as he locked eyes with Carolina who stood at the edge of one of the two craft tables. Her eyes were those of the condemned, accepting of her fate. They were sorrowful and resolved, frightened, but dignified. They peeled their gaze apart before others noticed.

Charlie's eyes darted. The door to the Wilderness Trek supplies was still ajar and an unclasped padlock hung from the hinged bracket on the door jam. Jenny had mentioned earlier that Michael DiFranco was coming back to clean up after her class was concluded. Did that mean in minutes or an hour? Charlie didn't know.

Jenny dismissed the class. Genesis began heading for the door.

"You want to walk up?" asked Jonathan, threading towards Charlie.

"I would," said Charlie, thinking quickly, "but I have to see Toby about something first."

"Oh," said Jonathan, unfazed. "Okay."

He turned and left. All of Genesis had left, except for Aaron Golldenberg , the final straggler, who was making his way to the door. Jenny Curtis had her back to the room, gathering her sketches from a shelf in the corner. Charlie silently followed Aaron outside. Aaron went left; Charlie broke right and disappeared behind the building.

Charlie stood, pressed against the back of the Muir Hut in the shade of the little alley that was shared with the administration building next door. The terraced stone walls, four feet away, rose before him to the Quad above. Vince Russo had taken him out of the back door of the administration building, onto this very walkway, the day Kurt had dropped him off and after he had been processed. It seemed like a thousand years ago.

He glanced at the backdoor of the admin building no more than twenty feet away. He walked the length of the Muir Hut wall and peered around the corner between the two buildings where a few feet of soil supported some healthy ferns, thriving in the narrow shade. A window in both buildings looked onto the small garden. The admin building's window was frosted. Charlie figured it was a bathroom window, maybe the very bathroom where he had been told to hand over his Raiders jersey and his wallet.

He shook the leaden memories from his head and walked back down the Muir Hut wall. He had to concentrate on his plan. He didn't know if it would work, but at least he had one. Now, all he need do was wait for his cue.

As he pressed his back against the wall, waiting, time began to stretch like hot taffy. He stood motionless, his breathing shallow, his ears pricked.

Then he heard it, the clop of Jenny Curtis' wood soles on the paved pathway that lead across the lawn to the parking lot. They were receding rapidly. He took off his windbreaker, wadded it up, and laid it against the building in a spray of tall grass. Next, he would go right into the Muir Hut, do what he had to do, and get out quick.

This was where it could all fall apart. If anyone were on the path between the lodge and the parking lot he would be detained. If anyone were looking out the window of the library, DiFranco's office, or the Source family room that overlooked the lawn, he might be seen, but that risk was minimal. The goal was to avoid anyone who would want to chat, he just couldn't risk being stopped or questioned. He had to beat Michael DiFranco--wherever he was--into the Muir Hut and get out in time. He hoped he would only need a minute or two inside, and if detained once he emerged, he would only have to say that he thought he had left his jacket, snap his fingers, feign a recollection of leaving it somewhere else, and make some comment about "always losing things."

He fortified himself with a deep breath and rounded the Muir Hut to the front, walking briskly. He kept his head down. Surely, Jenny Curtis wouldn't have locked the door if she knew DiFranco was coming after class to finish arranging the back room.

He hoped.

His eyes flicked left and then right. The path was clear. There were voices above from the Quad, cigarette smoke on the wind. He gained the path, and without hesitation, made for the Muir Hut door.

Chapter 29

The door was closed, but unlocked. He shouldered the door open and entered. Jenny had turned off the lights, even the fluorescent panels in the back room. He hesitated, unsure if he should leave the door open or closed. Neither choice seemed right. He closed it.

The late afternoon October sun was falling down the other side of the mountain. The Muir Hut's windows afforded nothing but feeble ambient light. Charlie stood in the thick shadows listening to his pounding heart and his panting breath. He let his eyes adjust and moved towards the back room. The door was still ajar. He turned sideways and slipped inside.

It was very dark. He hadn't wanted to risk turning on the bright fluorescents, but he found it too hard to see. He held his breath, his ears searching for the slightest sound from the walk outside. He had no excuse ready as to why he was in the Quest storage room. His story about losing his coat would not make any sense if he were caught in here, but he decided that standing in the dark looked even worse. He pawed at the wall, found the light switch and flicked it on. The florescent panel above ticked and sputtered into life.

Harsh light splashed onto Quest's gear. The room was bigger than he thought, a lot bigger than the closet he assumed it was. More than a dozen frame packs lined the walls. Climbing helmets, rope, sleeping bags, and mess equipment overflowed from boxes along the walls. He could benefit from all of this stuff, but he only had come for the basics.

His eyes swept the room. He didn't know where to start. He shook a backpack and it weighed nothing; it was empty. He leaned it back against the wall, turned, dropped to his knees, and opened the flaps of a cardboard box.

He heard a hiss behind him and then a loud clang. He jumped

and wheeled around. The vinyl backpack had slid down the wall and the aluminum frame had hit the linoleum floor.

"Shit," he hissed, and then held his breath to listen.

He peeked into the craft room and looked across at the windows to the lawn.

All was quiet.

He breathed again, righted the backpack and returned to the cardboard box. Nothing but stacks of journals just like the ones he had filled with his thoughts all of these months, along with pencils bundled with rubber bands.

He scanned the room again. He saw a yellow flashlight. He picked it up, flicked the switch. It worked. He put it aside. Then his eyes lit on a plastic bin in the corner. He dashed across the room, crouched before the bin, and tried to open the lid. It was stuck. He saw that the lid was designed to grip the bin and lock into place. He found the protrusions on the side of the lid, pulled the wings out and upward, and broke the vacuum seal. The lid peeled back with the popping sound of a string of firecrackers.

Inside was...

Dozens of bags of trail mix were stacked to the brim of the bin in neat piles. He grabbed one of the pouches of food and held it up. Golden oats, flecked with coconut, carob chips, and raisins bulged at the plastic.

"Yes," Charlie whispered.

With his other hand he grabbed another of the packets. Was it Shawn that had said they weighed a pound? One was supposed to last for three days during the Solo portion of the Wilderness Trek? He hefted the bags in each hand. It felt like plenty of food. If luck were on his side, he would only need food for a few days.

He replaced the lid of the bin, pounded it down, picked up the two bags and the flashlight, and crossed the room. He killed the light with his wrist.

Footsteps on the path outside.

DiFranco's voice.

Charlie froze. His heart pounded harder, his mouth went dry. Then he heard another voice, a girl's voice. The girl and Michael were talking on the path outside, but Charlie couldn't see them from the two windows at either side of the front door. They were somewhere in a blind spot. Charlie eased out of the back room, keeping his hands and their incriminating contents at his sides. He slowly crossed the room and leaned forward to peer out of the left front window.

Nothing.

Now he could tell that the voices were coming from the right. He peered out of the right front window. DiFranco's back was to the Muir Hut, about twelve feet up the path towards the lodge. He had been stopped on his way here for a late afternoon ass-polishing by some girl from the Upper School. It was all the delay Charlie needed. He gulped a lungful of air.

As fast as he could, he crossed back to the left side of the room to where the double-hung window looked out at the Admin Building and over the patch of ferns. He laid the bags of gorp and the flashlight down on the closest craft table and grabbed the window's latch. He tugged. It was painted shut. He cursed through his teeth. Di Franco and the girl laughed on the pathway.

He used his thumb and pushed at the latch. It moved a little, and then with another grunt it wrenched open. He shoved up on the frame of the bottom window.

He only needed a few inches, just a few inches.

The muscles in his neck strained. He squeezed his eyes shut and lifted. The window cracked open with a shriek. Charlie picked up the two bags and the flashlight from the table and shoved them through the opening in the window and into the ferns below. He heard the soft thuds as they landed. He pushed down on the window frame, closed the latch and turned to the front door.

Michael DiFranco passed the window on the right of the front door. He was coming in. Without thinking, Charlie dropped and launched himself under one of the craft tables. The front door knob began to turn.

"Okay, Melissa," Michael DiFranco shouted at the closed door, "you got a deal."

The girl, now far away, yelled something back at DiFranco whose hand must have been resting on the knob of the front door, arrested by the last volley of conversation. Soon he would push open the door. Charlie realized he needed better cover. The craft tables were too high and the cavity beneath them too big. He padded across the room on his hands and knees beneath the tables to the furthest, darkest corner of the room where rubber garbage cans full of pinecones sat in the shadows. He crouched behind one and huddled into a ball. The front door creaked open.

The lights popped on. Through the spindly forest of table legs, Charlie watched Michael DiFranco's topsiders squeak across the floor. The man's breathy, atonal whistle filled the room. Charlie did not dare to breathe.

He had panicked and now he was stuck in the room. The supplies were already safely out of the window and he could have confidently leaned on his lost jacket story, but he had panicked. Then again, there was every reason to think that DiFranco would see through him, like they all did. A bead of sweat, a twitching brow, or a pulsing iris could have given him away.

As he huddled in the shadows, trembling and on the verge of making his stand, he hoped he would hold together. He hoped his instincts would be good enough. A sickening heat sizzled through his head like a live wire.

Michael walked into the back room and flipped on the light. Charlie's stomach turned violently. He had forgotten to close the flaps of the box full of journals. He cursed himself and closed his eyes in a silent prayer.

With a deep breath, he peered around the garbage can. His eyes widened. The front door was open; Michael had left it open. He stood up slowly, wincing as a cramp shot through his leg, and looked over the tables. DiFranco's tuneless whistle filled the back room. Charlie stopped dead. The door to the back room was also wide open.

He had to go for it though. There was a good chance that DiFranco's back was to the door. Even if he was spotted he could claim he had just walked in. At this point, he had no choice. Silently, and with long strides, he headed for the open front door. DiFranco, somewhere behind Charlie, cleared his throat. Charlie stiffened. It could have been just a cough or the classic call to attention. Charlie didn't break his stride to find out. Two more paces. Michael coughed again. One more step...

Charlie passed through the open door and onto the path. The cool air hit him and he gulped in a deep breath. He was covered in sweat. Without slowing, he walked stiffly with his head down towards the lodge. After a few paces he dared to look up. He gasped.

Archie Goetz, in hound's-tooth coat and crisp white shirt, smiled: "Hello, Charlie."

"Oh," Charlie yelped, "you scared me."

"I'm sorry," said Archie. "I'm trying out my new Halloween costume. Guess it worked."

"What...?" Charlie was confused. Then, he smiled weakly. "Oh...yeah."

It had been a joke. He usually loved Archie's jokes, but his reaction had been painfully abnormal. He felt like he had been knocked off his rails. Seeing his favorite staff during his scheming filled him with a guilt and uncertainty that probably showed clearly. Archie was going to know something was up.

"Are you okay?" asked Archie. "You look like death warmed over."

"On my way to the Medical Office, actually," replied Charlie, seizing on the suggestion. "I might have a fever."

Archie pouted sympathetically, "Aw. That's too bad. You drink plenty of water and get some rest."

"Thanks, Archie. I will."

Charlie continued towards the lodge. After a few yards he spun and followed Archie back towards the Muir Hut. Archie was well ahead, and walking briskly to his car in the lot. Charlie cut left and walked around the back of the Muir Hut. He followed the narrow path along the wall to the little garden between the buildings.

The flashlight and one of the bags of gorp had fallen deep into the cover of ferns, but the other bag of granola was still visible, buoyed on a frond. He glanced up at the frosted window of the Admin Building to see if it was lit and occupied.

It was dark.

Stepping through the plants, he tucked the exposed bag under the wig of ferns. He retraced his steps, grabbed his wadded-up jacket from the side of the building, and headed for the dorms.

Shawn, Austin and Jonathan were dressing for dinner when Charlie walked in.

"There you are," said Jonathan, over his shoulder as he crouched by his bed, rifling through the drawers beneath for a shirt. "Shawn was just telling us that we just invaded Grenada. Wherever that is. He saw it in the paper in the library."

"So, anyway..." Shawn said to Jonathan, picking up the conversation. He began talking about some foreign leader and military stuff.

Charlie was thankful that the two were engrossed in a topic and were paying him little attention.

"You doing alright?" asked Austin, coming from the bathroom, toweling his hair. "I heard your brother was sick or something."

"Or something," Charlie mumbled.

"Huh?" Austin looked confused.

Charlie offered a smile. It was forced, but he thought it was convincing. "He's going to be fine. Thank you."

"You don't look so good," said Austin. "You feel all right?"

"Not really," Charlie replied, "I think I might have a fever."

"Take a cold shower and see if you feel any better," Austin suggested. "It could just be feelings. You're dealing with a lot. If you want to talk about it, I'm here for you. Don't forget." He shot Charlie a warm smile.

Shawn and Jonathan ceased their conversation at the mention of illness, looked over and then resumed talking politics.

"Thanks, Austin," said Charlie. "You're a good friend."

Austin's towel stopped scrubbing his wet hair and he looked as if he were seeing Charlie for the first time. Charlie locked eyes with him and then turned, entered the bathroom and closed the door. Austin would tell counselors later that he had known at that moment that something had changed in his roommate, but he didn't know exactly what. It had only been a flash of recognition, like he was looking at a different kid than the one he had known.

As he stripped from his sweat-soaked clothes in the bathroom, Charlie's nerves yearned for the five-minute shower where he would be able to think in silence and refine his plan. He marveled still at how news traveled so quickly and efficiently around campus. Everyone must know by now that his drunken stepfather had roughed up his brother. He would be watched, but if he appeared sick to everyone he would also be afforded some respectful space to maneuver.

He twisted the timer on the wall and entered the stall. The warm water began to fortify him and wash some of the clinging fear into the gurgling drain.

He was still in disbelief of what he was compelled to do. He was leaving the singular idealism of The Academy and its strange solutions to disorder. He wished that he could belligerently repeat their catch phrases and change his world. His reality, however, now demanded nothing short of a steal will, free of wishful thinking.

Why the task had fallen upon him he did not know, nor did he know what he could really do to save all that he loved. But, he had to try and he had to try now. As a wave of apprehension plunged him into an insulating state of survival he let the water beat on his body and he began to work out the final details. He blew his breath out onto the tiled wall of the shower.

The next step was to shake off his roommates once he emerged from the bathroom. He knew from experience, going down to dinner was sporadic, much different than breakfast where all gathered to be dismissed after morning chores to head down together. Some would go down to dinner early, some a little later. However, no one was allowed in the dorm past 7:00 and the staff on Floor was known to walk the halls of North and South Walden, knocking on doors to flush out stragglers. Therefore, he had to somehow appear to be going down to the lodge for dinner before 7:00 and without company. Luckily, his peaked appearance was going to solve that problem for him.

Next decision was which route to take off campus. School Road was out of the question; too many had tried and too many had failed. It was by far the easiest terrain, but as he had noticed on Experientials when Genesis had run the length of School Road for exercise, even keeping deep into the shoulder of the road would require trespassing through private property that may or may not be occupied by people or dogs. This would flush him onto the road for brief periods of time where he could be spotted. Even if he were to duck each and every headlight on School Road, there would still be a long stretch of two-lane highway into town lined with cabins set far back from wide shoulders providing no cover at all.

Going straight into the canyon was out. Not only was it insane to try, but the manzanita and jumping cholla bushes that choked the slopes would cut him to ribbons even before he inevitably got lost. He had no provisions for a water supply. He didn't plan on being a mountain man, nor did he know how to be one. There was only one way left to go, and that was through the Leech Fields.

No matter how one was to spell it, Charlie figured that if he were to angle correctly through the unknown beyond the Leach Fields, he would eventually hit the town of Bear Creek from behind. If School Road and the highway formed a long "L" shape, with Ponderosa at one point and civilization at the other, then hiking the hypotenuse would surely lead to the center of town and the highway junction, with optimal cover. The terrain seemed flat enough from what he could see on work crews, but he would be hiking for an unknown period of time in darkness. Even with a flashlight, it would be tough. There was no way to know if there were major obstacles between him and an anonymous ride off the mountain.

The lights in the bathroom shut off with a click of the wall timer. The air was instantly colder on his wet body and the darkness seemed to thicken on his skin. Panic, rippled the tiled walls around him and he thrust his hand out of the stall and clawed for the timer and gave it a rough twist. The lights popped on and the timer began to tick like the admonishing tongue of a schoolmaster.

As he stepped from the stall he heard laughing in the bedroom. That was good, that was normal. He faced the mirror above the sink. His eyes looked like those of the condemned, just as Carolina's had, but with a fierce resolve that made his own reflection almost unrecognizable. He wished she could come along, wished she was with him now. The muffled laughter from the other room came again, and this time it seemed like a response to his absurd ambitions.

He spoke softly to the strange boy in the mirror: "This is crazy, but everything out there is crazy. I don't know if I will win and it doesn't really matter. I'm going to fight until I can't. What good are you Charlie? What are you for?"

He took a last look at himself in the mirror, slicked his hair back with his comb, and entered the bedroom. The others were dressed. He looked across the room at the clock radio on Shawn's nightstand.

6:46

Everyone had 14 minutes to get to dinner. All he had to do was make sure no one waited to go down with him.

Austin had joined the conversation about the invasion of Grenada that had degenerated during his time in the shower into unflattering impressions of Ronald Reagan. Charlie pulled on his clothes and hoped one of the guys would soon lead the rest towards the door, through it, and into the night.

Finally, Shawn said he was heading down.

"I'll wait for Charlie," said Jonathan.

"Me too," said Austin.

"No," said Charlie, a little too quickly, "I mean, that's okay. I'm going to ask whoever is on Floor to open the Medical Office and get me some aspirin or something and skip dinner. I don't think I can eat. You guys go ahead."

There was a pause. The two looked at him. Charlie turned and went to the closet and crouched to pick up his hiking boots. He froze.

He could not explain away hiking boots for Floor Time. He had almost made a mistake--a minor one, but a mistake nonetheless. His hands lit on his loafers. He remained crouched with his back to them. He tensed. He waited.

"Okay," said Jonathan, "we'll see you on Floor."

"See ya," said Austin.

The two left the room. Charlie spun around and looked at the clock again.

6:50

He dropped his loafers, picked up the hiking boots and shoved his feet into them, lacing them tight. He plucked his wool-lined jeans jacket from the closet, sending the hanger tinkling to the floor. He opened the drawer beneath his bed, moved his journals, and grabbed the sixty cents in errant change left over from his WAM, enough to make a long distance call on a payphone.

He cracked the front door. The outdoor lights had come on. The hall was clear. He listened. No voices. He had to be extra careful now. He could explain away the heavy coat to fever and chills, but the hiking boots had no good explanation. He left the room and walked to the end of the covered hall. He turned the corner and looked ahead at the dorm trail. There was a cluster of girls just past the Microwave Road, otherwise it was clear.

With his head down and with a brisk gait he headed for the Microwave crossing. The air was cool, but not cold--at least not yet. He cut left down to the Quad and took the stone stairs down to the Muir Hut two at a time, the building's carriage lamps throwing amber pools of light onto the path by the lawn. He paused.

No one was around.

Doubling back, he went behind the building, and followed the wall to the ferns. It was much darker now below the looming terrace and the Quad above was as silent as a graveyard. He pawed through the ferns and found the flashlight and the two bags of food, which he shoved deep into the pockets of his jacket.

He retraced his steps up to the Quad. Everyone was in the dining room. There was no one outside anywhere. He walked up the Microwave, cut right onto the new Ropes Course Trail and followed it through the woods to the ropes course. Only then did he dare to flick on the flashlight.

It didn't work.

He cursed and swore through his teeth as he shook the light. It flickered once.

"Come on," he panted. "Come on!"

He felt the top where the lamp unscrewed to reveal the battery compartment. It had loosened in its threads, probably from falling from the window. He tightened it, his fingers slick with nervous sweat. A beam of steady light splashed on the trail. He exhaled.

He crossed the Leech Fields, stopped, and clicked off the flashlight. He turned, peering through the night from where he had come, and listened.

All was quiet. The summer's crickets had gone; the animals in the barn across the field were silent. The world seemed to hold its breath with him. He stood for a while, feeling the thickness of the cloaking shadows that covered his body. He stared up at the clear sky and sliver of moon. Then, he felt the weight of the lamp in his hand.

A smile began to play on his lips. He flicked the flashlight back on, and with a deep breath, he turned his back to the school and walked off campus, into the darkness.

Epilogue

Two hours after my brother left campus, he was intercepted in the town of Bear Creek. He had called the hospital where I was spending the night under observation, assuming correctly that it was Good Samaritan-the one closest to our apartment. After a few minutes of transfers, his call was routed to the correct building and floor of the hospital and eventually a nurse put him through to my room.

I was on the phone with our mother, who had just arrived home after spending the evening with me. As a result, Charlie received a busy signal and he was transferred back to the nurse's station. As he implored the nurse for another attempt, a robotic voice demanded that he deposit more change into the payphone, change he did not have.

Shortly after slamming the receiver down in that far away phone booth, Charlie realized he was running out of time. It was 9:15 P.M. and he had fifteen minutes to get out of town before anyone back at the school realized that he was gone.

Desperate, he stuck his thumb out for a ride as a small truck approached the highway junction where he was lying in wait. The truck pulled onto the gravel shoulder and the driver reached across the cab to unlock the door. As the man straightened up, Charlie saw that it was Dave, the townie that drove the Barf Van on Sunday store runs. Charlie hadn't recognized the truck; he had never seen Dave drive anything but school vehicles.

Later, Charlie would laugh and tell anyone who would listen how he had almost pissed himself, and how Dave had probably almost done the same.

Charlie also told me later that he thought about running for it, but then figured an all-points bulletin would go out and he would just be delaying the inevitable. As depressing as it was for him, he climbed into Dave's truck and cursed his luck, cursed the odds, as he was shuttled straight back to campus. He was put on Full Time immediately. He was also informed that Carolina Eversol had been transferred to one of Ponderosa's sister schools in the mountains of Bend, Oregon.

Then, a mere three days into his solitary punishment, he had looked up to see Toby Heiser sitting at his cordoned off table on the Middle Level. Toby looked stricken and apologized for the grim news that he was obliged to impart. Charlie told me later that he had never been so scared in his life. He thought I had died.

Toby told Charlie that it was not about me and that it was news about Kurt, terrible news. Toby reiterated what Charlie already knew, that his stepfather had been working as a foreman on a high-rise project that hoped to revitalize the barren downtown area of San Jose.

A freak accident had occurred. A metal rod called a snap tie-- about twenty inches long and one-eighth of an inch thick, used to hold forms together while cement was poured--had broken loose and had fallen thirty-two stories and hit Kurt who was working at ground level. The rod pierced Kurt's skull, killing him instantly.

Charlie told me that he cried harder than he ever had. Toby expected this, consoled him, and even reduced his punishment to Indefinite Dishes. Toby never realized that my brother was crying tears of relief.

Our mother pulled Charlie from the school to attend the funeral. He never returned. He made it a point to thank Meyer's ghost. I guess the chaos that Papa Pete used to tell us was a part of the universe, and that Charlie feared would always plague him with its random acts of cruelty, came to his aid--at least that time.

Three months later as he watched in his recovered jersey, his favorite football team, the Los Angeles Raiders, beat the Washington Redskins to win their third Super Bowl. Life was good.

As for me, I left the hospital the day after I was admitted. I sustained a fractured ulna and a nasty concussion. But, that was a long time ago. I teach English now. I am married and have two beautiful girls who adore my mother. She is a good grandmother. I think she is trying to make up for her past mistakes. She did not remarry.

Deep in a closet, I found a cardboard box; a stuffed Tasmanian Devil lay atop a stack of journals from Charlie's time at Ponderosa. His journals were amazingly detailed. I sat for hours on the floor of the closet, flipping through them. I was mesmerized. I became fascinated with Charlie's tales of the strange school in the mountains. I told him he should write a book. He laughed. He said he was more of a science guy and not much of a writer. I asked if I could give it a try. He said it would mean a lot to him.

So, using his journals as a backbone, I began work on this book. I also had some help from Jonathan and Austin. After many years of being unable to reach each other, Charlie found them on the internet. They are all still friends. Oddly, there has been no sign of Carolina. Perhaps she married, changed her last name. Charlie still searches for her.

The Academy has been shut down. But somehow, a few of these schools still survive; some may be right under our noses. Searching the internet, I was surprised at what I found. Especially when I searched for one particular word:

PROPHEET

After Ponderosa Academy, Charlie finished high school in Palo Alto where our mother bought a home. Then, the Gulf War started and neither my mother nor I could seem to peel Charlie away from the cable news shows that followed the battles in Iraq and Kuwait. Charlie spoke of his need to finish what our father could not. He was determined to restore our name. He felt incomplete somehow. He felt disgraced and he was out to prove that he was a better man than his father. I begged him to drop it and that he had nothing to prove, but he would hear none of it. Putting off his plans to follow Papa Pete with a science degree, he heeded the call of duty.

He joined the U.S. Marine Corps. He disappeared to Twentynine Palms, California for basic training and graduated a Marine. When he showed up for Christmas in full dress uniform we all beamed with pride. There was nothing skinny about him anymore. His hair was buzzed and his eyes glittered with a fierce confidence that held us all in awe. We were all so proud and we showed him off to everyone we could. My mother gushed about how handsome he was and I felt important just being seen with him.

A few years back, Charlie won the Bronze Star. He had recently returned from Iraq. It was Veteran's Day, and the medal ceremony was being held at Crissy Field in San Francisco. I drove my mother and my family.

I remember it was gusting wind. We left the car, turning our collars up against the cold, and made out way towards the crowd gathered on the parade grounds. The band played. Speeches were made. Medals were handed out.

After the ceremony, my mother headed towards the stage. She wanted to be the first to hug Charlie. I watched her and smiled.

Then, I noticed a man standing beside me. I could swear he had not been there before. He was watching the stage, the wind whipping the long hair at his shoulders.

It was the Salt-and-Pepper Man.

Even from the corner of my eye, I knew it was him. Although his hair and beard were all salt now and no pepper, and although I had not seen him since that long ago day at the McDonald's near my elementary school, I knew it was him. There was something about his posture, as if a great weight was crushing him from above. He was wearing glasses. They were not amber-tinted now, they were grey aviators, but the shape of his indelible face behind them was unmistakable.

We stood shoulder to shoulder without speaking and without looking at each other. I stared straight ahead at the band shell. I don't know how long the Salt-and-Pepper Man and I stood there silent, with nothing but the sound of the wind tossing our jackets and rippling the nearby bay into whitecaps.

When he finally spoke, his voice was measured and soft, as if he were speaking in a dream.

"Your brother is a hero, Brandon," said the man.

"He always was to me, Dad," I said, and I turned and walked back to the car.

AUTHOR'S NOTE: ON PONDEROSA ACADEMY

The school that was the inspiration for Ponderosa Academy closed its doors in the summer of 2006 amidst allegations of sexual and psychological abuse. The school had also been losing money. The philosophy of the school, born from the hippie culture of the 1960's, did not work so well with newer generations. It seemed that the indulgence of one's inner pain and the mourning of one's lost innocence were now being dismissed as merely the pursuit of idealism, luxuries of the white and privileged.

Over a dozen facilities across the U.S. also closed their doors as the charges gained validity, or at least spawned enough trepidation to make parents think twice about sending their kids away to these questionable schools.

Then, there was the talk of brainwashing. The internet age brought together so-called "survivors" of residential treatment facilities for troubled teens in corners of the World Wide Web to expound on their resentments and theories.

Two distinct camps emerged: The first was populated by the brainwash theorists. They labeled Ponderosa a cult and maintained that the school fit the definition as such, citing sleep deprivation, verbal and emotional abuse, thought control, and intimidation as irrefutable proof. The other camp maintained that Ponderosa Academy had saved them and that the relationships that they forged at the school were the most meaningful and fruitful of their lives.

The investigation of the death of the boy who inspired Devon Childs was only the beginning of the unprecedented scrutiny that was to be visited upon youth treatment facilities throughout the nation. It was determined that some of the staff members at Ponderosa Academy were not even licensed psychologists, even though they had been acting as such. It was also concluded that the academic curriculum at the school failed to meet the requirements of accreditation at the time of its closing, and although the school scrambled to restructure, the unfavorable momentum was insurmountable.

Weathering the storm for years longer than anyone thought possible, the coup de grace to the posthumous reputation of The Academy came in 2009 in the form of legislation approved by the U.S. House of Representatives. The Stop Child Abuse in Residential Programs for Teens Act of 2009 won strong bipartisan support.

Investigations conducted by the U.S. Government uncovered thousands of cases and allegations of child abuse and neglect at teen residential programs, including therapeutic boarding schools, boot camps, wilderness programs and behavior modification facilities.

Although names have been changed to protect the innocent and extend some mercy to the presumably guilty, the story of The Academy is true. And, although the characters are purely of my creation, embellishing The Academy was not necessary. Given this, the novel as a piece of historical fiction based on the accuracy of the information, at least as it applies to the strange machinations of The Ponderosa Academy a quarter of a century ago.

I should know; in some other incarnation, the place you just visited had yours truly as a student once upon a time.

James Tipper
West Hollywood, California
November, 2011